PENTAGON PRESS

COMMITTED TO SERVE THE ARMED FORCES

DELHI DIALOGUE VIII

ASEAN-INDIA RELATIONS

A New Paradigm

DELHI DIALOGUE VIII

ASEAN-INDIA RELATIONS

A New Paradigm

Editors

Rumel Dahiya

Udai Bhanu Singh

INSTITUTE FOR DEFENCE STUDIES & ANALYSES
NEW DELHI

PENTAGON PRESS

Delhi Dialogue VIII: ASEAN-India Relations: A New Paradigm

Rumel Dahiya and Udai Bhanu Singh (Eds)

First Published in 2018

ISBN 978-93-86618-54-2

Disclaimer: The views expressed in this book are those of the authors and do not necessarily reflect those of the Institute for Defence Studies and Analyses, or the Government of India.

Published by
PENTAGON PRESS
206, Peacock Lane, Shahpur Jat
New Delhi-110049
Phones: 011-64706243, 26491568
Telefax: 011-26490600
email: rajan@pentagonpress.in
website: www.pentagonpress.in

In association with
Institute for Defence Studies and Analyses
No. 1, Development Enclave,
New Delhi-110010
Phone: +91-11-26717983
Website: www.idsa.in

Printed at Avantika Printers Private Limited.

Contents

Delhi Dialogue Partners and Associates

The Delhi Dialogue process, which first began in 2009, has evolved over the years with new organisations and institutions joining it. As a result, the latest edition of the Delhi Dialogue was organised by the Ministry of External Affairs, Government of India, in partnership with the Institute for Defence Studies and Analyses (IDSA), the Federation of Indian Chambers of Commerce and Industry (FICCI), the ASEAN-India Centre at RIS, the Indian Council of World Affairs (ICWA), Institute of South Asian Studies (ISAS), SAEA Group Research, Singapore, Economic Research Institute of ASEAN and East Asia (ERIA), Jakarta, ISIS, Malaysia; and ISIS Thailand.

Ministry of External Affairs, Government of India

Recognising the need for greater engagement with the ASEAN region, India's Ministry of External Affairs (MEA) has been supporting the Delhi Dialogue since 2009. Today the summit is in its seventh edition and is now globally recognised as the premier India-ASEAN Track 1.5 platform for discussion on politico-security and economic issues of mutual importance. The Ministry's participation in the form of Track I meetings extends the purpose of greater cooperation between India and ASEAN.

Institute for Defence Studies and Analyses, New Delhi

A non-partisan, autonomous body dedicated to objective research and policy relevant studies on all aspects of defence and security, IDSA serves as a forum to debate important aspects of national and international security. IDSA has been associated with Delhi Dialogue as the facilitator of the Academic session of the Dialogue since 2014. The Track II session, being hosted by IDSA, is meant to facilitate exchange of ideas and policy analyses on imperatives, challenges and solutions for enhancing ASEAN-India relationship, among scholars and bureaucrats of India and ASEAN member nations.

Federation of Indian Chambers of Commerce and Industries, New Delhi

A non-government, not-for-profit organisation, FICCI is the voice of over 2,50,000 public and private sector companies, including small and medium enterprises and multinational corporations. The federation has been part of the Delhi Dialogue since its inception in 2009. In its run-up activities to the main event, FICCI's North East Advisory Council organised the North East Connectivity Summit on 27-28 November 2014 in Guwahati. The summit highlighted the need for development of inland waterways to provide North East India effective connectivity with the outside world and also to increase inland waterways transport cargo trade between India and ASEAN nations.

ASEAN-India Centre at RIS, New Delhi

Established at the Research and Information System for Developing Countries, the ASEAN India Centre has been working to strengthen India's strategic partnership with the Association of Southeast Asian Nations. In its run-up activities, the AIC organised 'Seminar on Joining Global Production Networks: India's Opportunities and ASEAN-India Cooperation' on 11 December 2014 and 'India-ASEAN Conference on Cyber Security' on 19-20 January 2015. The Centre has published 'ASEAN-India Development and Cooperation Report 2015' which provides a comparative analysis of the global and regional economies; examines the impact and implications of India-ASEAN integration, assesses policy imperatives and challenges, and discusses themes central to the economic sustainability of the region.

Economic Research Institute for ASEAN and East Asia (ERIA), Jakarta

Based in Jakarta, ERIA's main task has been to provide the policy analyses and recommendations to Leaders/Ministers in strong partnership with the ASEAN Secretariat and existing research institutes. In its run-up activities up to Delhi Dialogue VII, the institute organised a one day National Symposium on 3 September 2014 in New Delhi. The theme of the Symposium was 'Enhancing India's Competitiveness and India-East Asia Linkages: Improving Institutional and Physical Connectivity, Harnessing India's Demographic Dividend, and Raising India's Comparative Advantage in Manufacturing.' The conference focused on bridging the gaps between Indian and East Asian economies by focusing on the issues of building enabling infrastructure, increasing connectivity, and leveraging the manufacturing potential of the Indian Subcontinent and ASEAN region to boost socio-economic growth.

Indian Council of World Affairs, New Delhi

Established in 1943 by a group of Indian intellectuals as a think tank, ICWA is recognised as an institute of national importance by the Parliament of India and is devoted exclusively for the study of international relations and foreign affairs. In its run up activities, ICWA hosted a seminar on 'Integrating Northeast in India's Act East Policy' on 23 February 2015. It included speakers from the eight North East states, eminent academicians, bureaucrats and diplomats in the deliberations. The discussion focussed on issues of trade, connectivity and tourism as well as cooperation in social, cultural and academic fields with an objective to provide policy recommendations to the Ministry of External Affairs on the subject. It centred on the Look East Policy and the Act East Policy.

Institute of South Asian Studies, Singapore

Dedicated to research on contemporary South Asia, ISAS has developed research outputs and conducted high-level consultations to understand the dynamics of India's bilateral and multilateral diplomatic relations with Southeast Asian countries. In its run up activities to Delhi Dialogue VII, ISAS conducted a roundtable workshop with the Institute of Strategic and International Studies in Kuala Lumpur on 21 January 2015 focusing on radicalisation in South Asia and Southeast Asia. The institute also hosted a dialogue with HRH Princess of Thailand, Maha Chakri Sirindhorn on India-Southeast Asian engagements on 18 January 2015.

Institute of Strategic and International Studies, Malaysia

As an autonomous, not-for-profit research organisation, ISIS Malaysia has a diverse research focus, which includes economics, foreign policy, security studies, nation-building, social policy, technology, innovation and environmental studies. It also undertakes research collaboration with national and international organisations in important areas such as national development and international affairs. ISIS Malaysia is also a continuous contributor towards improvement of ASEAN-India relations and a partner of Delhi Dialogue VII.

Institute of Security and International Studies, Thailand

The Institute of Security and International Studies, Thailand carries out research on traditional and non-traditional security issues affecting the security of Thailand, Southeast and the Asia Pacific region. Past research on security included Thai counter-insurgency policies, ethnic conflicts, the environment and competition for natural resources, as well as decision-making on Thai arms procurement.

SAEA Group Research, Singapore

Set up in 2006, SAEA Group Research provides incisive research and financial analysis services on Asian markets and Asian issues. The group specialises in the areas of infrastructure, off-shore financing and airport management. SAEA Group also has partnerships with various think-tanks on the latest economic, political and security issues in Asia. SAEA Group is the founding partner of Delhi Dialogue, which was established in 2009, and is now recognised as one of the premier India-ASEAN-centric Track 1.5 platform for discussions on regional and international issues of mutual importance.

Diplomatic Academy of Vietnam, Vietnam

The Diplomatic Academy of Vietnam was established in accordance with a decision in 2008 by the Prime Minister of the Socialist Republic of Vietnam on the basis of upgrading the Institute for International Relations (successor of the College for Foreign Affairs established in 1959). The Academy carries out strategic research in international relations and foreign policies; undergraduate and graduate training and retraining of Foreign Service personnel; serves as "think tank" in foreign policy for the Ministry of Foreign Affairs, the Party and the State.

All India Association of Industries, Mumbai

The All India Association of Industries has over 1,500 members and through its affiliates it represents over 50,000 industries. Nearly 70 per cent of its members are from the SME sector.

AIAI acts as a catalyst for industrial growth and investment promotion. It represents its members effectively on various international, national and regional level panels and also with financial institutions on economic, trade and fiscal issues.

Associated Chambers of Commerce and Industry of India, New Delhi

The Associated Chambers of Commerce and Industry of India has more than 400 Chambers and Trade Associations in its fold and serves more than 4,50,000 members from all over India.

Today, ASSOCHAM has emerged as the fountainhead of knowledge for Indian industry. The Chambers is seen as a forceful, proactive, forward looking institution equipping itself to meet the aspirations of corporate India in the new world of business. It is working towards creating a conducive environment of Indian business to compete globally.

Confederation of Indian Industry, New Delhi

As a non-government, not-for-profit, industry-led and industry-managed organisation, CII plays a proactive role in India's development process.

CII has been actively engaging with the South East Asia region for the last two decades. Recently, CII organised the 2nd India-CLMV Business Conclave on the theme 'ASEAN-India Economic Engagement: The Way Forward' in New Delhi on 11-12 December 2014. The purpose of the conclave was to create a platform for the business enterprises and government officials from the two regions to establish linkages and seek opportunities for cooperation in trade and investments.

Indian Chamber of Commerce, Kolkata

The Indian Chamber of Commerce represents some of the most prominent and major industrial groups in India. ICC has played a key role in building synergies between India and its Asian neighbours like Singapore, Indonesia, Bangladesh, and Bhutan through trade and business delegation exchanges, and large investment summits. In its run-up activities to Delhi Dialogue VII, ICC organised the North East India-ASEAN Trade Show 2014 on 22-27 February, 2014 in Assam and held 'Kolkata Dialogue' on 'Look East' to 'Act East': New

Frontiers in Trade, Investment & Business Cooperation on 9 January 2015 in Kolkata.

Indian Council for Research and International Economic Relations, New Delhi

As an autonomous, policy-oriented, not-for-profit, economic policy think tank, ICRIER's main focus is to enhance the knowledge content of policy making by undertaking analytical research that is targeted at informing India's policy makers and also at improving the interface with the global economy. ICRIER's Board of Governors include leading academicians, policymakers and representatives from the private sector. In its run up activities for Delhi Dialogue VII, it organised a discussion on 5 March 2015 on 'India and the Regional Comprehensive Economic Partnership.

About the Contributors

H.E. MRS. SUSHMA SWARAJ

External Affairs Minister, Government of India

A seven times Member of Parliament and three times Member of the Legislative Assembly, Mrs. Sushma Swaraj is an advocate by profession. In April 1990, she was elected as a Member of the Rajya Sabha and remained there until she was elected to the 11th Lok Sabha from South Delhi constituency in 1996. She was the Union Cabinet Minister for Information and Broadcasting in the first Atal Bihari Vajpayee Government in 1996. She was re-elected to 12th Lok Sabha from South Delhi Parliamentary constituency for a 2nd term in 1998. In the second Vajpayee Government, she was sworn in as the Cabinet Minister for Information and Broadcasting with additional charge of the Ministry of Telecommunications from 19 March to 12 October 1998. She resigned from the Union Cabinet to take over as the first woman Chief Minister of Delhi in October 1998. Mrs. Swaraj resigned her Assembly seat to return to national politics and was the Minister for Information & Broadcasting from September 30, 2000 to January 29, 2003 and the Minister of Health & Family Welfare and Parliamentary Affairs from January 2003 until May 2004.

Mrs. Swaraj won the 2009 election to the 15th Lok Sabha from the Vidisha Lok Sabha constituency in Madhya Pradesh and became Leader of Opposition in the 15th Lok Sabha on 21 December 2009 and retained this position till May 2014. She has been re-elected to 16th Lok Sabha from Vidisha in 2014.

H.E. SOMCHITH INTHAMITH

Vice Minister of Industry and Commerce, Laos

H.E. Mr. Somchith Inthamith is the Vice Minister of Industry and Commerce, Laos since October 2014. Prior to that, he was the Vice Minister of Planning and Investment, Laos. He has held various important positions in the Laos Government. He was the Deputy Chief of Lao Negotiator for WTO Accession. He has worked extensively in the economic sphere as the Deputy Director-General, Department of Economic Cooperation; Deputy Director-General for Bilateral Economic Cooperation; Director- General, ASEAN Economic Cooperation

Department and as the Lao Senior Economic official Leader to ASEAN among others.

H.E. DR. AKP MOCHTAN

Deputy Secretary General (DSG), Community and Corporate Affairs ASEAN 2013-2016.

H.E. Dr. AKP Mochtan is the H.E. Mochtan assists the ASEAN Secretary-General in strengthening effective support systems, procedures and resources within the Secretariat to achieve its mission. They include core corporate functions such as human resources, finance, legal issues, public affairs and outreach programmes.

As a seasoned management and international relations expert, DSG Mochtan has held top positions in various international organizations. Immediately before joining ASEAN, he directed the Japan ASEAN Integration Fund (JAIF) Management Team, which managed over US$500 million grants from the Government of Japan to support ASEAN integration and community building processes. Prior to his stint with JAIF, DSG Mochtan served for 13 years with the intergovernmental Asian Productivity Organization (APO) based in Tokyo Japan including as its Administration and Finance Director.

Within the United Nations system, Dr. Mochtan worked on human rights issues with the United Nations Transitional Authority in Cambodia (UNTAC) and Peace and Security programme with the United Nations University (UNU).

H.E. KAN PHARID

Under-Secretary of State, Ministry of Foreign Affairs and International Cooperation, Cambodia

Mr. Kan Pharid is an Under-Secretary of State, Ministry of Foreign Affairs and International Cooperation, Cambodia since July 2015. Prior to that, he was permanent representative of Cambodia to ASEAN. He has held various important positions in the ASEAN-Cambodia General Department, Ministry of Foreign Affairs and International Cooperation, Cambodia. During 1989 -1992, he was Second Secretary to the Embassy of Cambodia to India. He has received prestigious national awards such as Royal Order of Monisaraphon, Commander in 2007 and Medal of Labor, Gold in 2002.

H.E. U TIN OO LWIN

Deputy Minister, Ministry of Foreign Affairs, Republic of the Union of Myanmar

U Tin OoLwin served in the Defence Services in various capacities up to the rank of Brigadier-General (1974 to 2005). He was then transferred to the Ministry of Foreign Affairs as Ambassador (5-8-2005 to 16-9-2005). He was the Ambassador Extraordinary and Plenipotentiary to the Democratic Socialist

Republic of Sri Lanka (17-9-2005 to 10-4-2009); Ambassador Extraordinary and Plenipotentiary to the Republic of South Africa (10-4-2009 to 4-2-2011); Ambassador Extraordinary and Plenipotentiary to the Republic of Singapore (4-2-2011 to 13-8-2013).

H.E. DATUK NAIMUN ASHAKLI MOHAMMAD

High Commissioner of Malaysia to India

Datuk Naimun Ashakli Mohammad has been a career diplomat, served as Ambassador of Malaysia to Spain and Kingdom of Bahrain before his present responsibility as the High Commissioner of Malaysia to India. He was Deputy Director General in the ASEAN Department of Malaysia's Ministry of Foreign Affairs, Principal Assistant Secretary (Political- Southeast Asia) and served in the Ministry for several years. He joined the Ministry of Foreign Affairs in 1982. He is an alumnus of University of Sussex, Brighton, United Kingdom.

H.E. CLARO S. CRISTOBAL

Director-General Foreign Service Institute, Department of Foreign Affairs, Philippines

Ambassador Claro Suarez Cristobal is a career diplomat with the rank of Chief of Mission. He was designated Director-General of the Foreign Service Institute (FSI) by President Benigno S. Aquino III on 2 July 2015.

Before serving as the Head of the Institute, he was the Philippine Ambassador to the Arab Republic of Egypt from December 2011 to June 2015. He was also Consul General of the Philippines in Hong Kong from April 2009 to December 2011. He also served as Minister and Consul General at the Philippine Embassy in Tokyo from September 2002 to January 2007.

Before joining the Philippine foreign service, Ambassador Cristobal was Professorial Lecturer in Economics at the De la Salle University Manila.

Ambassador Cristobal was a Presidential Citation Awardee in 2009 and 2010 and a Gawad Mabini Awardee in 2007 and 2012.

He graduated from the University of the Philippines with a Bachelor of Arts in Philosophy (cum laude) in 1974 and a Master of Arts in Economics in 1979.

H.E. LE HOAI TRUNG

Deputy Minister of the Ministry of Foreign Affairs, Vietnam

H.E. Le Hoai Trung took over as the Deputy Minister of the Ministry of Foreign Affairs in 2014. Prior to that, he served as the Permanent Representative of Vietnam to the United Nations among many other responsibilities. As a foreign service officer, he started his career in 1982.

DR. SOFYAN A. DJALIL

Minister for National Development Planning, Head of National Development Planning Agency (BAPPENAS), Indonesia

Sofyan A. Djalil, PhD, currently serves as Minister for National Development Planning, Head of National Development Planning Agency (BAPPENAS) under "Kabiner Kerja" 2014-2019, since August 2015. Previously he was Coordinating Minister for Economic affairs under the same Cabiner since October 2014. Before joining the Cabinet, Dr. Sofyan Djalil was advisor to the Vice President of the Republic of Indonesia particularly to help facilitating and debottlenecking infrastructure development, education, bureaucracy reform, poverty alleviation and other strategic issues.

H.E. VIRASAKDI FUTRAKUL

Vice Minister of Foreign Affairs of the Kingdom of Thailand

H.E. Mr. Virasakdi Futrakul is the Member of the National Legislative Assembly, Advisor to the Prime Minister on Foreign Affairs, and Vice Minister of Foreign Affairs of the Kingdom of Thailand. Prior to that, he was Secretary General, the Asian Peace and Reconciliation Council. In the past, he has been Ambassador Extraordinary and Plenipotentiary of the Kingdom of Thailand to Japan, United States of America, France, Canada and Myanmar. In addition to this, he has served as Permanent Representative of Thailand to the United Nations Office and other International Organizations in Geneva.

H.E. DATO PADUKA SIDEK ALI

High Commissioner of Brunei Darussalam

H.E. (MS) MARIA TERESITA C. DAZA

Ambassador of Republic of the Philippines.

H.E. VIKRAM NAIR

Chairperson of the Government Parliamentary Committee for Defence and Foreign Affairs, Singapore

Vikram is Member of Parliament for Sembawang GRC. He is Chairman of the Government Parliamentary Committee for Defence and Foreign Affairs and Chairman of the Parliamentary Friendship Group for India. He has spoken on a wide range of issues in Parliament, including most recently, the importance of multi-lateral ties and the opportunities for trade, capital and labour flows with the new ASEAN Economic Community. He is also concerned about growing security threats, particularly from non-state actors, and believes regional and international cooperation are vital to address these threats.

Vikram is also a Partner at Singapore Law Firm Rajah & Tann LLP, where he is Head of the India Desk. He is qualified in both Singapore and English law and specializes in international arbitration and commercial and corporate litigation with particular experience in handling complex, multi-jurisdictional disputes in sectors such as banking, finance, oil & gas, manufacturing, mining, construction and property development. He has previously worked as a management consultant in McKinsey, in the dispute resolution team of an international law firm and the litigation team of another major Singapore firm. His work experience has focused on the South East Asian region, especially in Singapore, Malaysia, Indonesia and Thailand.

H.E. T. R. ZELIANG

Chief Minister, Nagaland, India

T. R. Zeliang is the 10th and current Chief Minister of Nagaland. He contested the Nagaland Assembly elections from Tening and won four times in a row beginning with the elections of 1989 and then in 1993, 1998 and 2003. He has served as a Minister of State for Information and Tourism, Minister of State for Relief & Rehabilitation, Minister for Environment, Forests, Geology and Mining during his long political career. He represented Nagaland in the Rajya Sabha, the upper house of the Indian Parliament from 2004-2008. After returning to state politics in 2008, he was appointed Minister for Planning, Animal Husbandry and Parliamentary Affairs under Chief Minister Neiphiu Rio. He won the assembly elections of 2008 and 2013 from Peren.

H.E. LAL THANHAWLA

Chief Minister, Mizoram, India

This is Lal Thanhawla's fifth term as a Chief Minister, which is a record in Mizoram. Lal Thanhawla belongs to the Indian National Congress. His electoral constituencies are Serchhip and Hrangturzo. He has successfully contested in the general elections nine times, in 1978, 1979, 1984, 1987, 1989, 1993, 2003, 2008, and 2013. He is founder President of Mizoram Hockey Association and Mizoram Olympic Association. He is the Chairman of North East Olympic Commission and Ex-officio Vice President of Indian Olympic Association.

MR. ANIL WADHWA

Secretary (East), Ministry of External Affairs, Government of India

Mr. Anil Wadhwa has been a member of the Indian Foreign Service since July 1, 1979. His previous diplomatic assignments include serving as Third Secretary in the Commission of India, Hong Kong (Sep. 1981 to Sep. 1983); Second Secretary/ First Secretary in Embassy of India, Beijing (Nov. 1983 to Feb. 1987); Under

Secretary/Deputy Secretary in Ministry of External Affairs, New Delhi (Feb. 1987-May 1989); UN Disarmament Fellow in Geneva (July-Nov. 1989); First Secretary (Disarmament) at the Permanent Mission of India in Geneva (Dec. 1989-Dec. 1992); Counsellor in Embassy of India, Beijing (Jan. 1993 - Jul. 1993); Director/ Joint Secretary on deputation to the Provisional Technical Secretariat and later the Technical Secretariat for the Organization for the Prohibition of Chemical Weapons (OPCW) in The Hague (July 1993-July 2000; Chief Adviser, Ministry of External Affairs (Earthquake Relief) in Gujarat State, (Dec. 2000 to Jan. 2001); and Joint Secretary, Central and Eastern Europe, Ministry of External Affairs, New Delhi (Mar. 2001 to Feb. 2004). Mr. Anil Wadhwa has served as the Indian Ambassador to Poland (March 2004 to August 2007), to the Sultanate of Oman (August 2007 to September 2011), and to the Kingdom of Thailand (Nov 2011 to Jan 2014). He holds a Masters Degree in History with specialization in Chinese history and Medieval Indian history and architecture.

MS. POOJA KAPUR

Joint Secretary, ASEAN Multilateral Division, Ministry of External Affairs, Government of India

Ms. Pooja Kapur is an Indian Foreign Service officer of the 1996 batch who is currently posted as Joint Secretary (ASEAN -Multilateral) in the Ministry of External Affairs, New Delhi.

Ms. Kapur was a Chevening scholar at Oxford University.

Ms. Kapur has previously served as Minister/ Counsellor in charge of the European Union, Environment, Education, Culture and Consular affairs at the Indian Embassy to the EU, Belgium and Luxembourg; as Counsellor (Press, Information, Culture and Community Affairs) at the Indian High Commission in Kuala Lumpur, as the Economic and Political Counsellor/ First Secretary at the Indian High Commission in London and as Second Secretary (Political) at the Indian Embassy in Paris.

Ms. Kapur maintains a keen interest in international politics.

She has co-authored the book, "Comparative Government and Politics: Concepts and Emerging Trends," Abhinav Publishing Industries, 1991.

MR. JAYANT PRASAD

Director General, Institute for Defence Studies and Analyses, New Delhi

Mr. Jayant Prasad is Director General, Institute for Defence Studies and Analyses, New Delhi. He was India's Ambassador to Afghanistan, Algeria, Nepal, and the UN Conference on Disarmament, Geneva. At headquarters, in the Ministry of External Affairs, he served as Special Secretary (Public Diplomacy), and Head of the Americas and the Multilateral Economic Relations Divisions. He was Rapporteur of the U.N. Commission on Human Rights, Geneva (1986-87), Fellow at the Weatherhead Center for International Affairs, Harvard University (1998-99), member of U.N. Secretary-General's Advisory Board on Disarmament Matters (2005-07), and Visiting Scholar, Center for the Advanced Study of India, University of Pennsylvania (2014-15). Before his 37-year public service career, he was lecturer in history, St. Stephen's College, University of Delhi, after completing his studies at Modern School, St. Stephen's College, and Jawarharlal Nehru University.

MR. NALIN SURIE

Director General, Indian Council of World Affairs, New Delhi

Nalin Surie is trained as an economist. He joined the Indian Foreign Service in July 1973. He has served in Indian missions in Hong Kong, Brussels, Dar-us-Salaam, Thimphu, New York (as Deputy Permanent Representative to the UN), as Ambassador in both Warsaw and Beijing and High Commissioner to the United Kingdom. At the headquarters, he has served both in the Department of Economic Affairs (Ministry of Finance) and the Ministry of External Affairs. Nalin Surie is a seasoned diplomat who has extensive cross- sectoral experience on issues ranging across India's northern neighbourhood, China, Eastern Europe, The European Union, Africa, Latin America, Canada, IBSA and the UN. He was appointed as Director General of The Indian Council of World Affairs on 24, July 2015.

PROF. HIDETOSHI NISHIMURA

Founding President of Economic Research Institute for ASEAN and East Asia (ERIA), Jakarta

Mr. Nishimura has a long and distinguished career of nearly 30 years in the Ministry of International Trade and Industry (MITI, which is now known as METI), Japan. During his long career, he has held important positions in the Policy Division pertaining to environment protection, territorial trade policy pertaining to Europe, Africa and Middle East. He has held numerous positions, including Representative of the Asia-Pacific Region of the Japan Overseas Development Corporation, Director of the Southeast Asia and Pacific Division of the Trade Policy Bureau, Vice Governor for International Affairs of Ehime Prefecture, Director-General of the Business Support Department of the Small and Medium Enterprise Agency, Executive Managing Director of the Japan-China Economic Association, and President of the Japan -China Northeast Development Association. He is also a visiting Professor of Miyazaki Sangyo-Keiei University and Fellow of Meiji Institute for Global Affairs, Meiji University.

His other achievements lie in the compilation of Bogor Declaration of APEC which paved the way for liberalization of trade in the region. He is a strong advocate of ASEAN-India Connectivity and has steered two major ERIA research on this theme named Comprehensive Asia Development Plan-Phase I and II.

MR. SHYAM SARAN

Chairman, Research and Information System for Developing Countries (RIS), New Delhi.

Mr. Shyam Saran is Chairman of Research and Information System for Developing Countries (RIS), New Delhi. Since joining the Indian Foreign Service in 1970, he has served in several capitals of the world including Beijing, Tokyo and Geneva. He has been India's Ambassador to Myanmar, Indonesia and Nepal and High Commissioner to Mauritius. In the Ministry of External Affairs, New Delhi, he headed the Economic Division and the Multilateral Economic Division and also headed the East Asia Division which handles relations with China and Japan. As a Joint Secretary in the Prime Minister's Office (1991-1992), he advised the Prime Minister on foreign policy, nuclear and defence related issues. He was appointed India's Foreign Secretary in 2004. Subsequent to his retirement, he was appointed Prime Minister's Special Envoy for Indo-US civil nuclear issues and later as Special Envoy and Chief Negotiator on Climate Change. During his last two assignments, Ambassador Saran served as Prime Minister's personal representative or "Sherpa" at the Gleneagles and St. Petersburg G8+G5 summits and was present at the Tokyo and L'Aquila Summits as an advisor on Climate Change issues. Currently, Ambassador Saran is Chairman of the National Security Advisory Board under the National Security Council. He is Co-Chair on the Indian side on the India-ASEAN Eminent Persons' Group. Ambassador Saran was awarded the Padma Bhushan in 2011 for his contribution to Civil Service.

MR. GOPINATH PILLAI

Ambassador-at-large for the Government of Singapore and chairman of Management Board of the Institute of South Asian Studies, Singapore.

Mr. Gopinath Pillai holds several key public appointments simultaneously. He is Chairman of the Management Board of the Institute of South Asian Studies. He is Ambassador-at-Large in the Ministry of Foreign Affairs since August 2008. He is also Executive Chairman of Savant Infocomm Pte Ltd. Mr. Pillai was Singapore's Non-Resident Ambassador to Iran between 1990 and 2008 and also served as Singapore's High Commissioner to Pakistan. The Indian government conferred Ambassador Pillai with the Padma Shri award at the 2012 Republic Day. Ambassador Pillai has received several awards, including the Friend of Labour (NTUC 1987); Meritorious Award (NTUC 1990); Friend of MCD from the Ministry of Community Development (1998); and Friend of IT from Singapore

Computer Society (2001). The Singapore government has awarded Ambassador Pillai the Public Service Star Award (BBM) in 1999 and BBM (BAR) in the 2009 National Day Awards.

DR. JYOTSNA SURI

Past President, Federation of Indian Chamber of Commerce and Industry (FICCI)

Dr. Jyotsna Suri has been associated with Bharat Hotels since its inception. In the year 1987, she became the Group's Joint Managing Director. She took on the mantle of Chairperson & Managing Director of Bharat Hotels in the year 2006 and since has been the driving force of the Group's operations across India. A multifaceted personality, she is a patron of art, culture, sports and education. Her social initiative Project Disha, being implemented under the overall CSR policy of Bharat Hotels, seeks to assist school students and local youth, to have access to quality "education leading to employment".

MR. SUMIT MAZUMDER

President, Confederation of Indian Industry (CII) & Chairman & Managing Director, TIL Limited

Mr. Sumit Mazumder is presently the Chairman & Managing Director of TIL Ltd. which is the manufacturer of India's largest range of material handling equipment in technical collaborations with world leaders - Manitowoc Crane Group, USA; Hyster; Astec Industries, USA; Paceco Corp, USA and Mitsui Miike Machinery Co., Japan. He is the Executive Chairman of TIPL (Tractors India Pvt. Ltd.). Mr. Mazumder is also the President of the Confederation of Indian Industry (CII). He has been an active member of CII and has Chaired its various Committees and Councils in the past years.

SUNIL KANORIA

President, ASSOCHAM, Vice Chairman, Srei Infrastructure Finance Limited

From humble beginnings to being at the helm of one of India's leading integrated infrastructure institutions with global reach, Sunil Kanoria has traversed this journey with integrity and determination as his core values. A follower of the teachings of Swami Vivekananda and the Vedanta philosophy, spirituality has defined Sunil's personal and work life from the very outset. With foresight and knack for taking calculated risks, Sunil has an enviable proven track record of reshaping India's infrastructure landscape. As the Vice Chairman of Srei Infrastructure Finance Limited, a Kanoria Foundation entity, Sunil has been instrumental in bringing over Rs 36,000 crore (around US$ 5.5 billion) of consolidated assets under the company's management. Sunil is a visionary who understood the latent needs of the Indian economy and successfully converted several potential ideas into business reality. Several of them were first of its kind and created new business sectors.

Today Sunil is one of the most respected business thought leaders, especially in the area of infrastructure development and financing. He has been entrusted with the honour of leading ASSOCHAM. India's oldest and leading chamber of commerce, as President. Sunil is a qualified chartered accountant with a strong academic track record.

MR. VIJAY KALANTRI

President, All India Association of Industries (AIAI)

Mr. Vijay Kalantri is a much admired industrialist and first generation entrepreneur. His business acumen and far sightedness has propelled him to take on the challenging venture of Dighi Port, a mega project, Maharashtra's first Greenfield Port at Dighi, Raigad. Besides being an industrialist and heading the Balaji Group as Chairman and Managing Director, Mr. Kalantri is the President of All India Association of Industries, Vice Chairman of World Trade Centre, Mumbai and is Director International of World Trade Centre, New York. As President of the AIAI, Mr. Kalantri is actively involved in bringing to fore the AIAI as the representative body of large, medium and small-scale industries involved in all major industrial sectors.

MR. CHANDRAJIT BANERJEE

Director General, Confederation of Indian Industry (CII)

Mr. Chandrajit Banerjee is the Director General of Confederation of Indian Industry (CII). He has been with the CII for over 28 years. He has been responsible for important areas of work including the Sectoral Verticals - Manufacturing, Services, Agriculture and Life Sciences Sectors and the SMEs. He has led key policy work of CII in the areas of Economic Policy, Financial Services and Corporate Governance. Mr Banerjee has been honoured with the China-India Friendship Award by the then Chinese Premier Wen Jiabao for his contributions towards the development of India-China bilateral ties. He has also been conferred with the decoration of Knight Commander of the Order of Queen Isabellaby from His Majesty the King of Spain in recognition of his most meritorious achievements and exceptional contributions towards promoting relations between India and Spain.

DR. A DIDAR SINGH

Secretary General, Federation of Indian Chamber of Commerce and Industry (FICCI)

Dr. Singh is a former civil servant who retired as Secretary to Government of India. He is Secretary General of International Chamber of Commerce, India

Chapter; Director General, Indian Council of Arbitration and Director on Board of Invest India (a JV of FICCI and Govt. of India). Dr Singh functions as Independent Director on the Boards of NTPC (National Thermal Power Corporation - a State owned Enterprise) and of J&K State Overseas Employment Corporation (a State Enterprise). He is a Member on the Ad-Hoc Task Forces of Department of Performance Management as also of Department of Public Enterprises, Government of India.

MR. SHIV SIDDHANT NARAYAN KAUL

President, Indian Chamber of Commerce (ICC)

Mr. Kaul is the Managing Director of Nicco Engineering Services Limited and a Director of Nicco Corporation Limited, part of the Nicco group of companies which has activities in cable manufacturing, theme parks and specialty industrial maintenance services.

He grew up in Kolkata and went to St. Xaviers School. After completing school he left for the United States where he received his Bachelor of Arts, Summa Cum Laude, from the College of Wooster with majors in Economics and Computer Science and a minor in Mathematics. Following that he attended Princeton University where he received his MSE in Operations Research & Financial Engineering. Based on his academic record he has been inducted into Phi Beta Kappa, America's oldest academic honor society and into Omicron Delta Epsillon, the International Economics Honour Society. While at Princeton he also taught as a graduate instructor and did research which has been published in The Journal of Alternative Investments. Mr. Kaul worked for over 4 years in New York at Bank of America's, Capital Markets Group, rising to be a Vice President of Fixed-Income trading before leaving to join the Nicco Group in Kolkata. He is the President of Indian Chamber of Commerce for the year 2015-16. Outside of work he is an avid lover of Indian Classical Music.

DR. RAJEEV SINGH

Director General, Indian Chamber of Commerce (ICC)

Dr. Rajeev Singh has been appointed as the Director General, Indian Chamber of Commerce, Kolkata with effect from 1st September, 2006.

Prior to his appointment as Director General, Dr. Singh was actively involved with CII for more than 5 years as Regional Director, posted in Chandigarh & Ahmedabad and subsequently in Kolkata. He has done extensive work in the fields of Central & State Policy Advocacy, Service Sector, Agro Business, Taxation and Bio-Technology.

In a period spanning over 17 years, Dr. Singh began his career with Rajasthan

Oil Federation as Deputy Manager. He was later associated with corporate houses like Arvind Mills Limited, etc.

Dr. Singh has done his PhD in Management and has also been associated with academics as Professor in Management with Specialization in Marketing.

Dr. Singh is a sports enthusiast and enjoys getting involved with social developmental activities. He is married with two children.

MR. O.P. LOHIA

Chairman and Managing Director, Indo Rama Synthetics (India) Ltd

Mr. O.P. Lohia is the Chairman and Managing Director of Indo Rama Synthetics (India) Ltd and the Chairman of the FICCI Task Force on Textiles. In his latter capacity, he has steered the textile industry to a more competitive and organized level.

Indo Rama Synthetics (India) Limited has been a leading manufacturer and supplier in India's fast growing polyester sector since the last two decades of its operations and is today India's second largest dedicated polyester manufacturer having carved a niche in the market place for its unmatched quality offerings.

MR. YADUVENDRA MATHUR

Chairman & Managing Director, Export-Import Bank of India (Exim Bank)

Mr. Mathur is an Indian Administrative Service Officer of the 1986 batch. He has had long stints in various positions in the Finance Department including Principal Secretary Finance, Government of Rajasthan. During his postings under the Department of Economic Affairs (2001-2003) at Cote d'Ivoire and Tunisia, Mr. Mathur worked as Assistant to the Executive Director of African Development Bank. He was then actively engaged with the Export-Import Bank of India in enhancing and promoting business opportunities for Indian companies in the African continent through Technical Cooperation Agreements. As an Energy Secretary of Rajasthan for over three years, Mr. Mathur contributed in the setting up of three greenfield power plants in the state.

DATO' RAMESH KODAMMAL

Chairman, Goldtex Group of Companies

Dato'Ramesh Kodammal is Co-Chairman of ASEAN Indian Business Council (AIBC), ASEAN Business Advisory Council (Council Member - ABAC), MSME ASEAN Business Advisory Council Working Group (Malaysia) and honorary member of The Kuala Lumpur Malay Chamber of Commerce. He is former Deputy President of Kuala Lumpur Selangor Indian Chambers of Commerce

(KLSCCI), Vice President of Malaysia Associate Indian Chambers and Industries and Treasurer of National Chambers of Commerce and Industries of Malaysia (NCCIM). He has actively participated in various international forums and seminars representing Malaysia as a moderator and speaker.

DATO' MUTHUKUMAR AYARPADDE

Founder and Executive Chairman of MK Tron group

Dato'Muthukumar Ayarpadde (referred to as DMK) is founder and Executive Chairman of MK Tron group. DMK, a young and dynamic corporate leader in Malaysia, embraced business entrepreneurship in his twenties by setting up a ferrous and non-ferrous commodity trading company. From this humble beginning, spurred by his dynamism and hard work, the group has grown through expansion, diversification and acquisitions. Today, the group has manufacturing facilities in Malaysia, India and South Korea. The operations of the group include manufacture of aluminium alloys, brass rods, automotive components; large metal stamped parts and welded assemblies.

DR. JAYANT DASGUPTA

Former Indian Ambassador to the WTO and Executive Partner, Lakshmikumaran & Sridharan, Attorneys

Dr. Jayant Dasgupta is an Executive Partner at Lakshmikumaran & Sridharan, New Delhi. He heads the Environmental Law Practice and also advises on Trade Remedy measures, WTO Dispute Settlement Foreign Trade Policy, Food Law and other Regulatory areas. Before joining legal practice in 2014, Dr. Dasgupta had served as Ambassador/PR of India to the WTO; Secretary, Economic Advisory Council to the Prime Minister; Chief Advisor, Bihar Planning Board; Joint Secretary, Department of Commerce and Director (Exports), Ministry of Textiles. During his long career in government, he has also presided as a quasi-judicial authority for the implementation of various national and state Acts.

MR. T S VISHWANATH

Principal Adviser, APJ-SLG Law Offices, India

Mr. Vishwanath is Principal Adviser with ASL (APJ-SLG Law Offices), New Delhi. In ASL, he works closely with different departments of the Indian government on issues related to bilateral, regional and multilateral trade and investment agreements and manages the Firm's work on policy issues related to trade and competitiveness. ASL has been retained by the Department of Commerce, Government of India to assist in matters related to the Agreement on Sanitary and Phytosanitary Measures (SPS) and Technical Barriers to Trade (TBT).

MR. O P HISARIA

Senior Vice-President, Reliance Industries (RIL), India

Mr. O P Hisaria has been working with Reliance Industries Limited for the last five and a half years as Senior Vice President looking after regulatory affairs relating to international trade. Prior to joining RIL, Mr. Hisaria has worked with the Government of India for 18 years. He joined Indian Trade Service in 1991 and worked in Directorate General of Foreign Trade in various capacities and in Ministry of Agriculture as a Director. His work experience in Government included areas such as Foreign Trade Policy - formulation as well as implementation and WTO related issues, especially WTO negotiations on agriculture. He has represented India at various multi-lateral and bi-lateral trade Forums. He has worked on negotiations for SAFTA, Sri Lanka and Singapore FTAs during the tenure with Agriculture Ministry.

DR. SIDDHARTHA ROY

Economic Advisor, Tata Group, India

Dr. Siddhartha Roy is Economic Advisor to the Tata Group. He closely monitors the developments in sectors like Auto, Chemicals, Steel, Power, Telecom, International Trade, and IT among others. He is involved in a number of projects intended to develop firm level competitiveness. He is also engaged in advising the Tata companies and trade bodies/chambers of commerce on the developments relating to macro-economic issues, regional trade agreements and WTO among others. He is on the expert committees of the leading Chambers of Commerce. He has a number of publications in professional journals in India and abroad as well as in financial dailies. He is a visiting faculty member in leading management institutes.

MR. ANDY SCHROETER

CEO, Sunlabob Renewable Energy Ltd

Mr. Andy Schroeter is co-founder and CEO of Sunlabob Renewable Energy Ltd., a Hong Kong-based company with branches in Laos, Myanmar and Singapore which specializes in renewable energy and clean water projects in developing regions of the world. Mr. Schroeter is also a consultant to USAID, the Asian Development Bank, the EU Energy Initiative and other rural development agencies. He has more than 20 years of experience undertaking sustainable development initiatives in remote, off- grid areas. Sunlabob's pioneering approaches to enabling and sustaining rural energy and water access have helped the company expand its work throughout Asia, Africa, India and the Pacific islands as well as receive recognition by organizations such as the World Economic Forum, The World Bank, the Ashden Awards and the BBC.

EDGARE KERKWIJK

Managing Director, Asia Green Capital Partners (AGC)

Edgare Kerkwijk is the Managing Director of Asia Green Capital Partners and is based in Singapore. Prior to joining AGC, Edgare was Partner and CFO for BioX Group, an integrated renewable energy firm. He has worked as a Director Institutional Sales at State Street Global Advisors (SSGA) in Brussels and was responsible for the Benelux Sales Team. Before that, Edgare held several senior positions within Rabobank International in Europe and Asia. In his last role at Rabobank, Edgare was an Associate Director for the bank's merger and acquisition team in Southeast Asia and has advised on a wide range of Corporate Finance and M&A transactions within Europe and Asia.

MR. S. KUPPUSWAMY

Advisor, Shapoorji Pallonji & Co. Ltd

Mr. S. Kuppuswamy is an Engineering Graduate from IIT Kharagpur with First Class Honours, MBA from Madras University, and Diploma in Bank Management, the Highest Banking Qualification in India, from Indian Institute of Bankers. Before joining Shapoorji Pallonji Group in 1998, he held various senior positions in Bank of India, Shipping Credit and Investment Corporation of India, and ICICI. Presently he is with Shapoorji Pallonji & Co. Pvt. Ltd. as an Advisor - Group Finance & Special Projects and Director in various Companies of Shapoorji Pallonji Group, besides heading the Group's Africa Business Centre (ABC). He also heads the working Group on Finance & Infrastructure for the Confederation of Indian Industry's Africa Committee.

MR. DANG QUOC TOAN

President & CEO of Asia Petroleum Energy Corporation, Vietnam

Mr. Dang Quoc Toan is President and CEO of Asia Petroleum Energy Corporation. He has worked for Petrovietnam Corporation from 1998-2006. He was senior consultant for Pyramid Oracle ERP software in Vietnam. He is one of the founding members of Asia Petroleum Energy Corporation and of Vietnam Bio-fuels and Renewable Energy Association. He is board member of Vietnam Industrial and Environment Association. He has contributed several recommendations and proposals to the Government of Vietnam related to renewable energy in Vietnam, and initiated the 'One million Green Homes for Vietnam' project.

DR. ASHVINI KUMAR

Managing Director, Solar Energy Corporation of India

Dr. Ashvini Kumar is the Managing Director of the Solar Energy Corporation of India (SECI), which is a Government of India Enterprise, set up in 2011 for implementation of National Solar Mission. At SECI, he has been steering to develop and implement wide ranging solar programmes. As MD, he is credited to turn around the Company into a positive net worth company during 2014-15. Prior to his being in SECI, he worked at the Ministry of New and Renewable Energy in various capacities for over 26 years. He has been very closely associated with establishment of solar radiation monitoring project at National Institute of Wind Energy, Indo-German Energy Forum and various other bilateral programmes with USA, Germany, Spain and EU.

MR. RAJAT M. NAG

Distinguished Fellow, National Council of Applied Economic Research, Delhi

Mr. Rajat M. Nag is concurrently a Distinguished Fellow at India's National Council of Applied Economic Research, Delhi and a Senior Fellow at the Emerging Markets Forum, a think tank based in Washington DC. He also serves as Chair, Look East Council of the Indian Chamber of Commerce and is a Visiting Professor at the Stephen Zuellig Graduate School of Development Management, Asian Institute of Management in Manila and the Emerging Markets Institute at the Beijing Normal University, China. Mr. Nag was till December 2013 the Managing Director General of the Asian Development Bank (ADB).

MR. SWARUP ROY

Founder & Chairman: ASEAN Affairs Media, Asean Affairs Business Council (AABC), India Business Bridge (IBB)

Mr. Roy was the President & CEO, Business Day newspaper, Thailand's only English business daily. He has launched ASEAN AFFAIRS global media - The voice of Southeast Asia in 2006. In 2008, he launched ASEAN AFFAIRS Business Council (AABC) - The business platform for C.I.A. (China India ASEAN). In 2013, he also launched India Business Bridge (IBB).

DR. RAJARAM PANDA

Former Senior Fellow, IDSA

Rajaram Panda (Ph.D., JNU), was formerly Senior Fellow at the Institute for Defence Studies & Analyses. He is the author of two books and has co-edited five books, besides contributing chapters to 18 books. He has contributed over 100 research papers, including many in peer-reviewed journals such as IFANS Review, Asia-Pacific Review, Strategic Analyses, Journal of Defence Studies, India Quarterly, Journal of Comparative Asian Development, Asian Survey, Indian Foreign Affairs Journal, Man and Development, The Korean Journal of Defense Studies, and others. His two sole authored books are Pacific Partnership: Japan and Australia Resource Diplomacy (1982) and Japan and the Third World (1994). He has also a strong presence on the websites of leading think tanks and in print media. His research interests have been focused on security/strategic issues of Northeast Asia, with focus on Japan and the Koreas. He is widely traveled and has presented papers in Japan, Australia, New Zealand, Paris, Manila, Brunei, Sri Lanka, Vietnam, Seoul, India, etc.

PROF. MAHENDRA P LAMA

School of International Studies, Jawaharlal Nehru University, New Delhi

Prof. Mahendra P Lama (b 1961), a noted development economist, has been a Professor of South Asian Economies in the School of International Studies in Jawaharlal Nehru University, New Delhi. Prof Lama was also the Founding Vice Chancellor of the newly established Central University of Sikkim in India. He also served as the Chief Economic Adviser in the Government of Sikkim with a Cabinet Minister Rank for seven years (2000-2007). Till recently he was the Pro Vice Chancellor of Indira Gandhi National Open University (IGNOU), New Delhi and Member of the prestigious National Security Advisory Board of Government of India. He is presently nominated by the Government of India as a member of the Steering Committee of the coveted South Asian Forum set up by the Heads of the States and Governments in the 16th SAARC Summit in Thimphu in 2010.

His most recent work is a book entitled "Human Security in India: Discourse, Practices and Policy Implications" (UPL, Dhaka, 2010).

MR. SRIDHAR VENKITESWARAN

Executive Director, Avalon Consulting and OC& C Strategy Consultants, India

Mr. Sridhar is an entrepreneur and a key founding member and Director of the India based, Avalon Group, consisting of multiple entities along the Information Services Value Chain ranging from Strategy and Performance Improvement Consulting, Business Research and Marketing Analytics serving global clients with Group revenues of $37mn in 2015 and employing more than 1900 people. In a career spanning 25 plus years, Sridhar has been working with clients in the Indian, Chinese, Middle East and European geographies on strategy and performance related engagements across a wide spectrum of manufacturing and service businesses.

DR. CASSEY HONG KIM LEE

Senior Fellow, Institute of Southeast Asian Studies, Singapore

Cassey Hong Kim Lee is a Senior Fellow at the Institute of Southeast Asian Studies. His research interests are ASEAN Economic Community; Competition Policy in ASEAN; Political Economy of Single Party Dominance in Southeast Asia and Political Economy of ASEAN Economic Integration.

MR. AMAN NEIL DOKANIA

Vice President & GM, HP Helion, Hewlett-Packard, Asia Pacific and Japan

Aman Neil Dokania is Vice President & GM HP Helion for HP Asia Pacific and Japan (APJ). In his current role, Aman is responsible for HP cloud across APJ, for private, public and hybrid solutions. He is driving HP's regional leadership in cloud and digital ecosystem development through partnering with leading ISVs, SIs, Service Providers, Governments and channel communities delivering customer centric solutions for both build and consume services for cloud. He plays a key role in driving HP's strategic direction on HP Helion (HP Cloud) with Open Source technologies to enable an open ecosystem for accelerating innovation across Asia Pacific and Japan. Aman is Vice Chairman of Asia Cloud Computing Association and Board member of US ASEAN Business Council.

Before moving to Asia, Aman was responsible for driving future specifications for the HP Blade System c-Class in the United States. He also led the development and introduction of HP's first management software and introduced the concept of lights-out management, for which he holds a patent for related technology.

MR. ANIRUDH SURI

Founding Partner & Managing Director, India Internet Fund

Anirudh Suri is Founding Partner of the India Internet Fund, and heads the Delhi and Mumbai offices for IIF Advisors. Anirudh previously served as a policy advisor to the Minister of State for Communications and Technology in the Government of India. Prior to that, he worked at McKinsey & Company and Goldman Sachs, serving clients in the consumer, retail, healthcare, energy and the public sectors. Named the Most Promising Young Indian Professional by India Empire and a Goldman Sachs Global Leader by the Goldman Sachs Foundation, Anirudh has also been the recipient of the Carnegie Endowment Fellowship, the C.V. Starr Fellowship and the Singapore Airlines Scholarship. Anirudh pursued a joint MBA-MPA degree at the Harvard Kennedy School of Government and the Wharton School at the University of Pennsylvania. He graduated from Haverford College with a BA in Economics and Political Science.

MR. MOE MYINT KYAW

Secretary General, Union of Myanmar Federation of Chambers of Commerce & Industry (UMFCCI), Myanmar

Mr. Kyaw is the Managing Director of Myanmar Makro Industry Co., Ltd. And Managing Director of Alligator Industry Co., Ltd.

MR. MUKUL SARKAR

Chief General Manager, Export-Import Bank of India

Mr. Mukul Sarkar is a Graduate in Mechanical Engineering from Indian Institute of Technology (IIT), Kharagpur, India and an MBA from Indian Institute of Management (IIM), Calcutta, India.

He has over 25 years of experience in Indian financial sector mainly in the area of investment banking, corporate finance, corporate credit, overseas investment finance, trade finance and risk management. He started his career in SBI Capital Markets Ltd. He is presently the Chief General Manager and Group Head, Corporate Banking Group of Export-Import Bank of India (Exim Bank). He is also heading the Bank's Infrastructure initiative in the SAARC region.

Mr. Sarkar spent 3 years in Milan, Italy as Exim Bank's Resident Representative in the Western Europe. Presently, he is on the Board of few Indian companies. Mr. Sarkar is also on the Board of African Export-Import Bank, headquartered in Cairo, Egypt.

MR. R.K. GUPTA

Chairman-cum-Managing Director, WAPCOS Limited

Mr. R.K. Gupta, Chairman-cum-Managing Director, WAPCOS Limited, a Government of India Enterprise under the aegis of Union Ministry of Water Resources, River Development & Ganga Rejuvenation has over 35 years of experience in ensuring and successfully accomplishing consultancy projects in the fields of Irrigation/Water Resources, Power & Infrastructure sectors in India and Abroad. A gold medalist, civil engineering alumni of the prestigious Regional Engineering College, Kurukshetra; he completed his post-graduation in Engineering (Structures, Civil) from Punjab Engineering College, Chandigarh. He holds Masters in Business Administration with specialization in Human Resource Management. He has acquired specialized managerial and technical training in India and abroad. He is a Fellow Member of Institution of Engineers (India), Indian Water Resources Society, Corporate Member, International Commission on Irrigation and Drainage, Member Consulting Engineers Association of India and Life Member of Indian Society for Rock Mechanics and Tunneling Technology. Shri Gupta is also President, India Water Partnership (IWP); Chairman of ASSOCHAM India -ASEAN Business Promotion Council; Co-Chairman of ASSOCHAM India-AFRICA Business Promotion Council. He has also been bestowed with Eminent Engineer Award by Institution of Engineers (India). He has exemplified WAPCOS at distinguished international and national forums.

H.R.H. NORODOM SIRIVUDH

Member of the Constitutional Council, Privy Counselor to His Majesty, the King of Cambodia

His Royal Highness Norodom Sirivudh is Founder & Chairman of the Board of Directors, Cambodian Institute for Cooperation and Peace (CICP). His political career began in 1971 when he joined the Paris-based royalist movement, GRUNC/ FUNK (Gouvernement Royale d'Union Nationale du Cambodge / United National Front of Kampuchea). He was in charge of laying the groundwork for FUNCINPEC's participation in the electoral process, mandated under the Paris Peace Agreement, in advance of the UN's 18-month Mission in Cambodia. In May 1993, as FUNCINPEC's Bureau Chief in Phnom Penh, Prince Norodom Sirivudh helped his party to its elections victory, after which he was appointed Co-Deputy Prime Minister and Minister of Foreign Affairs. In August 2001, HRH Norodom Sirivudh was elected as Senator. From March 2006 to present, HRH Norodom Sirivudh is a Privy Counsellor to His Majesty the King and a Member of Parliament. In May 2010, King Norodom Sihamoni appointed Prince Norodom Sirivudh as a new member of the Constitutional Council.

MS. NAVREKHA SHARMA

Former Indian Ambassador and Veteran Writer and Scholar

Ms. Navrekha Sharma is an Indian Foreign Services officer of 1971 Batch. She retired from the service in 2008. While in service her postings included Joint Secretary (SAARC) and Joint Secretary (ITEC) at Head Quarters and Ambassador in the Philippines and Indonesia. Since Retirement, Ms. Sharma has been writing and speaking extensively on Indonesia/South East Asia. She has recently published a book on India -Indonesia Relations in collaboration with Dr. Baladas Ghoshal. She now spends her time between Delhi and Ranikhet where she enjoys reading and gardening.

PROF. RENATO CRUZ DE CASTRO

International Studies Department, De La Salle University, Manila

Prof. Renato Cruz De Castro is a full professor in the International Studies Department, De La Salle University, Manila, and the holder of the Charles Lui Chi Keung Professorial Chair in China Studies. His research interests are Philippine-U.S. security relations, Philippine defence and foreign policies, U.S. defence and foreign policies in East Asia, and International politics of East Asia. He has written over 70 articles on international relations and security that have been published in a number of scholarly journals and edited works in the Philippines, South Korea, Canada, Malaysia, France, Singapore, Taiwan, Germany, the United Kingdom, Australia, and the United States.

BUNN SRI NA NAGARA

Senior Fellow, Foreign Policy and Security Studies, Institute of Strategic and International Studies, Kuala Lumpur, Malaysia

Mr. Bunn Nagara is a commentator on contemporary strategic issues and Consultant Editor of Moderation Monitor journal. He was Associate Editor and Foreign Editor of Star Publications (Malaysia), Senior Analyst and Visiting Fellow at ISIS Malaysia, Research Fellow at ISEAS (Singapore) and ASEAN Fellow at the Japan Institute of International Affairs (Tokyo). An award-winning journalist, he has held senior editorial posts at major Malaysian newspapers and magazines, and contributed widely to journals and other media internationally. He has also contributed to undergraduate, civil/public service and journalism courses. His research interests cover South-East Asia, the ASEAN Community, the South China Sea, national/ regional security and defence issues, East Asian integration, China, developing world, Gulf region, global power blocs and major power relations.

MR. YOGENDRA KUMAR

Former Indian Ambassador and Veteran Writer and Scholar

Mr. Kumar retired as Indian Ambassador to the Philippines, with concurrent accreditation to the Pacific Island countries of Palau, Micronesia and the Marshall Islands, in 2012. He was also High Commissioner to Namibia and Ambassador to Tajikistan (2000-2003) during which period he also handled Afghanistan affairs. He has been on the faculty of the National Defence College and, in Ministry of External Affairs, he has handled relations with multilateral organisations such as ASEAN, EAS, IBSA, IORA etc. He has been writing and speaking on foreign policy and security affairs and his book, 'Diplomatic Dimension of Maritime Challenges for India in the 21st Century', has just been published.

DR. JOEFE B. SANTARITA

Dean and Associate Professor, Asian Center, University of the Philippines

Joefe B. Santarita is currently the Dean and an Associate Professor of the Asian Centre, University of the Philippines. He completed his doctoral degree in South Asian Studies from the National University of Singapore. His research interests focus on Indian Studies, Migration Studies, Philippine Culture and Society, Maritime History, and Southeast Asian Political Economy. His Indian related publications include Growth and Government: The Rise of Information Technology Enabled Services' Centres in India and the Philippines; State, Society and Information Technology in Asia (Surrey: Ashgate, 2014); Capitalizing on

Cultural Connections: Indian Influences in the Philippines; Civilizational Dialogue: Asian Inter-connections and Cross-cultural Exchanges (New Delhi: Manohar, 2013); Construction, Negotiation and Reproduction of Identity: The Sikhs in the Philippines; Sikhs in Multicultural Southeast Asia - Negotiating an Identity (Singapore: Institute of Southeast Asian Studies (ISEAS), 2011); Contemporary Indian Communities in Western Visayas and Rising India and Indians in East Asia (Singapore: ISEAS, 2008).

DR. GIRISH GUJAR

Visiting Lecturer, Department of Logistics and Maritime Studies, The Hong Kong Polytechnic University

Dr. Girish Gujar has extensive sea going experience having served as marine engineer officer on numerous sea going vessels of different kinds for over a decade. Subsequently he gained further experience in the logistics, port operations and supply chain management over 15 years in India, Middle East and Europe. For the past 10 years he has been teaching various transport and supply chain management related subjects at the Faculty of Business at the Hong Kong Polytechnic University to under and post graduate students. He has published extensively in reputed peer reviewed journals and is a regular speaker at prestigious international conferences. His research interests include port economics, inland transport connectivity, competition regulation and container security. He has also published three books; "Essays on Dry Ports", "Shipping Today" and "Maritime Security: A New Outlook".

MR HONG HAN

The Hong Kong Polytechnic University, Hong Kong.

PROF. HIMANSHU PRABHA RAY

Former Chairperson, National Monuments Authority, Ministry of Culture, New Delhi

Himanshu Prabha Ray is Honorary Professor, Ludwig Maximilian University, Munich. She was the first Chairperson of the National Monuments Authority, Ministry of Culture, New Delhi from 2012 to 2015 and as Professor has taught at the Centre for Historical Studies, Jawaharlal Nehru University, New Delhi until 2012. Her research interests include Maritime History and Archaeology of the Indian Ocean, the History of Archaeology in South and Southeast Asia and the Archaeology of Religion in Asia. She is the Editor of the Routledge Series on Archaeology and Religion in South Asia.

MR. EDDIN KHOO

Founder Director of Pusaka Foundation, Malaysia

Eddin Khoo is a poet, writer, translator and journalist. He studied Politics at the University of Newcastle Upon Tyne, United Kingdom and Southeast Asian Art and Archaeology at the School of Oriental and African Studies, University of London, where he was a British High Commissioner's-Chevening scholar, graduating with distinction. He founded the cultural centre Pusaka and the publishing house, Kala, which devotes itself to publishing literary translations from the world's languages into Malay. Among his publications is a book of selected writings by the Malaysian artist and critic Ismail Zain, Intermediations: Selected Writings on Art, co-edited with the art historian T.K. Sabapathy and a book on traditional Malay Wood Carving, The Spirit of Wood, co-authored with the historian Farish Noor, as well as a translation of poems into Malay, Sajak-Sajak by the American poet Christopher Merrill. In recognition of his work in culture, Eddin Khoo was selected as one of Digi Telecommunications Amazing Malaysians in 2006 and as one of the Asians of the Year 2006 by the Channel News Asia, Singapore.

PROF. BALADAS GHOSHAL

Secretary General and Director (Academic), Society for Indian Ocean Studies (SIOS), New Delhi

Baladas Ghoshal was, until recently, ICCR Chair in Indian Studies at the Russian State University for the Humanities, Moscow; is also honorary Distinguished Fellow at the Institute of Peace and Conflict Studies. Professor Ghoshal is a former Professor of Southeast Asia and South-West Pacific Studies and Chairman of the Centre for South and Southeast Asian Studies at Jawaharlal Nehru University, New Delhi. Between 2004 and 2007, he was a Visiting Professor of International Relations first at the International Christian University, Tokyo and then at Nagoya City University; taught at the University of Illinois at Urbana-Champaign (1990-91) National University of Malaysia (1998-1999), University of Malaya (2000) and the University Utara Malaysia (2002-2003). He has held Senior Fulbright Fellowships at the Cornell and Rutgers Universities (1983-84); Fellow at the Institute of Southeast Asian Studies, Singapore (1985-86); Centre for Asian Studies, University of Hong Kong (Sept.-Oct. 2003), East West Centre (2010), Consultant to the United Nations Support Facility for Indonesian Recovery (November 2003-February 2004). His most recent publications include a book on India-Indonesia Relations, brought out by Institute of South Asian Studies, Singapore, and a monograph on China's Perception of India's Look East Policy, brought out by Institute of Defence Studies and Analyses, New Delhi.

PROF. SACHIDANAND SAHAI

Advisor, Preah Vihear National Authority, Royal Government of Cambodia, & UNESCO Expert for the Archaeological Complex of SamborPrei Kuk, Cambodia.

Sachchidanand Sahai specializes in cultural history of Southeast Asia. He is fluent in French, Laos and Khmer languages. Twenty monographs have been authored by him, besides a number of edited volumes. He is founder editor of Southeast Asian Review (1972). Sahai holds a doctorate degree from Sorbonne University (Paris). He is recipient of A.S. Altekar Gold Medal (1962), Pravasi Bharatiya Samman and Gold Medal (2012) and Padma Shree (2012). Currently he is advisor to Angkor Archaeological Park and Preah Vihear under the auspices of the Royal Government of Cambodia.

PROF. NGUYEN THAI YEN HUONG

Senior Research Fellow and Vice President, Diplomatic Academy of Vietnam (DAV)

Prof. Nguyen Thai Yen Huong was appointed as the Professor of History in 2014 by the National Committee for Professor Title. She has written and edited number of books. Her recent publications include The Analysis of "the Sino - US Economic, Strategic Dialogue" through the angle of Statistic, Journal of International Studies, No. 10, 2015; A Chapter - US balance to Asia offers opportunity for stronger Washington - Ha Noi ties, Strategic Vision for Taiwan Security, ISN 2227 3646, August 2014; Vietnam in the Context of Emerging Asia - Pacific within the Current International Politics: Opportunity and Challenges, International Conference on "Japan in the Age of Asia", Ha Noi, 2013; The 30 years of Sino-US relations under the theory of balancing of power, The Gioi Publisher, 2012; Confidence building Measures: One of the Solutions to Marine Security in Southeast Asia, Journal of International Studies, No. 26, 2012. In addition, she presented two papers about Sea Lines of Communication in Taiwan in 2012 and 2014. She was the CSCAP Co chair (2012- 2014). She has attended international conferences and workshops as a scholar and actively contributed to the enhancement of the Vietnam - US relations.

MR. R RAVINDRAN

Chairman, SAEA Research Group, Singapore

Mr. Ravindran is Chairman of SAEA Research Group based in Singapore. SAEA Research Group undertakes research on strategic and economic issues in the Asia Pacific region with a special focus on South Asia and ASEAN.

He is also a partner with Colin Ng & Partners LLP and has been in legal practice for more than 30 years. He sits on the boards of listed companies. He is a former MP is Singapore. His other prior appointments include Chairman of the Government Parliamentary Committee for Defence and Foreign Affairs. He holds a LL.B (Hons) and a LL.M.

MR. RAJIV BHATIA

Former Director General, ICWA, New Delhi

Mr. Rajiv Kumar Bhatia was the Director General of Indian Council of World Affairs (ICWA) till recently. As a career diplomat, he served India with distinction for over 37 years. He was India's Ambassador/High Commissioner in Kenya, Myanmar, Mexico and South Africa. Presently, he is also member of the Academic Council of Jawaharlal Nehru University, member of the Governing Council of National Institute of Design, and member-secretary of the Governing Council of ICWA. Since his retirement from the Indian Foreign Service in 2009, he has published over 125 articles on international affairs in India's national dailies, journals and periodicals. He has delivered lectures at the National Defence College, Foreign Service Institute, universities and other institutions in India. Since mid-2012, Ambassador Bhatia led ICWA delegations to Russia, China, Belgium, Australia, Indonesia, Vietnam and Myanmar. He also addressed Track-II conferences in Beijing, Shanghai, Port Louis and Paris, and interacted with leading academics in London, Kuala Lumpur and Jakarta.

PROF. PRABIR DE

Coordinator, ASEAN-India Centre (AIC), New Delhi

Prabir De is the Coordinator of ASEAN-India Centre (AIC). De works in the field of international economics and has research interests in international trade and development. He was a Visiting Fellow of the Asian Development Bank Institute (ADBI), Tokyo; and Visiting Senior Fellow of United Nations Economic and Social Commission for Asia and the Pacific (UNESCAP), Bangkok. He has been conducting policy research for the Government of India and several international organisations. De has a Ph.D. in Economics from the Jadavpur University, Kolkata. He has contributed several research papers in international journals and written books on trade and development. His recent publication includes "ASEAN-India Development and Cooperation Report 2015" (Routledge, New Delhi, 2015). He is the Editor of the South Asia Economic Journal, published by Sage.

DR. YANG PEOU

Permanent Secretary, International Relations Institute of Cambodia (IRIC), Phnom Penh

Dr. Yang Peou was educated at Royal Academy of Cambodia and completed his PhD in Political Science. He is a Lecturer at the Khemarak University from 2005. He worked as a Senior Researcher at the International Relations Institute of Cambodia of the Royal Academy of Cambodia too. He has many publications on Cambodia-Thai political conflict, border disputes between Thailand and its neighboring countries and South China Sea conflicts.

DR. GOPA SABHARWAL

Vice Chancellor, Nalanda University

Dr. Gopa Sabharwal is the founding Vice Chancellor, Nalanda University. She comes to Nalanda from India's foremost liberal Arts college, Lady Shri Ram College for Women where she founded the Department of Sociology in 1993. Her wide ranging research has focused on ethnic groups in urban India, visual anthropology, partition and the history of society. She obtained a PhD in Sociology from the Delhi School of Economics at University of Delhi.

Preface

Recognizing the need for greater engagement with the ASEAN region, India's Ministry of External Affairs (MEA) supported the inaugural Delhi Dialogue I, on 21-22 January 2009, which was organized by the Federation of Indian Chambers of Commerce and Industry (FICCI) and the SAEA Group Research (SAEA) with the institutional support of the Institute of Southeast Asian Studies (ISEAS), as an international conference to chart for leaders and business investors the issues and dynamics facing the Asia-Pacific Region. What emerged was an annual Track 1.5 forum for discussing politico-security, economic and socio-cultural issues between ASEAN and India. Since 2009 when the conference was first held, Delhi Dialogue has evolved into an important forum at which political leaders, policy makers, researchers, academicians, business leaders and media persons converge for brainstorming on a range of issues pertaining to ASEAN-India relations.

Background

The ASEAN-India relationship is one of the cornerstones of India's foreign policy and Act East policy, which has deepened across the three pillars of politico-security, economic and socio-cultural cooperation. The recently concluded 13th ASEAN-India Summit and 10th East Asia Summit in November 2015 in Kuala Lumpur, Malaysia, have defined a dynamic trajectory for ASEAN-India relations. The formalization of the ASEAN Economic Community (AEC) would also need a new approach towards India's engagement with ASEAN.

Keeping this context in mind and as India moved towards completing 25 years of its dialogue relationship with the ASEAN region, Delhi Dialogue VIII was appropriately themed "ASEAN-India Relations: A New Paradigm" and organized over a period of three days (17-19 February, 2016) at two venues. While the Business Session and the Ministerial Session were organised at The

Oberoi, the Academic Sessions were held at the IDSA Campus. This book tries to capture within its covers the thoughts and ideas that were generated during the conference.

The key themes of ASEAN-India relationship today will be highlighted in the Inaugural Session and its two panel discussions (with Indian and South East Asian leaders participating) relating to Connectivity and ASEAN Economic Community (AEC).

The first part of the book includes chapters pertaining to the Ministerial Session. The session began with the Welcome Remarks by the immediate past President of FICCI Dr Jyotsna Suri. This was followed by the Keynote Address by Hon'ble External Affairs Minister Mrs Sushma Swaraj who placed the significance of the Conference in its proper perspective. She recalled the key developments in ASEAN-India relationship such as the finalisation of the ASEAN-India Free Trade Area (AFTA), the ASEAN-India Plan of Action for the period 2016-2020 and the inauguration of India's dedicated Mission to ASEAN in Jakarta.

Indonesia, (also the headquarters of ASEAN) was represented by its Minister of National Development and Planning and Head of National Development Planning Agency, Dr Sofyan A Djalil. He said that Indonesia viewed India as a strategic partner in the promotion of maritime cooperation. Continuing with last year's format, the Conference organized two panel discussions. The first panel discussion was on 'Connectivity: Creating Pathways to a Shared Future' in which Heads of Delegation from Myanmar, Thailand and ASEAN Secretariat and Chief Ministers of the North Eastern States of India participated. The second panel discussion was on 'ASEAN Economic Community and India: Integrating Regional Value Chains and Production Networks'. The Ministerial Session concluded with a Vote of Thanks by Mr Jayant Prasad, Director General, Institute for Defence Studies and Analyses.

Encouraged by the success of the Business Session introduced last year at the Delhi Dialogue VII, it was decided that the range and depth of discussions merit a full day of discussions on matters economic. Delhi Dialogue VIII provided a larger canvas for the business chambers and the business community of both sides to paint their vision.

The second part of the book is devoted to the Business Session which saw the CEOs and business community of India and ASEAN spend a full day discussing problems and concerns which animated them. Deliberations focused on various issues including: Co-Manufacturing and Manufacturing Value Chains, Mega Trade Blocs, Infrastructure and sustainable Energy, Cross Border Trade and role of Startups and Digitization between India and the ASEAN region. The Business Session was addressed by the respective heads of chambers of commerce giving their own perspective. A Report summarises the proceedings of the session.

The third part of the book is devoted to the proceedings of the Academic Session, which included: ASEAN and Security of the Asia-Pacific; ASEAN-India and the Ocean Economy Dynamics; Reinvigorating the Civlizational Links between ASEAN and India; and the Way Forward towards 25th Anniversary of ASEAN-India Relations.

The Academic Session, held in the IDSA campus, opened with the Welcome Remarks by Director General, IDSA, Mr Jayant Prasad who drew attention to the paradigmatic change that had taken place in ASEAN-India relations and the Keynote Address by Secretary (East) in the Ministry of External Affairs, Mr Anil Wadhwa. Following the Remarks, the session on ASEAN and Security of the Asia Pacific was addressed by HRH Norodom Sirivudh from Cambodia who warned that an ASEAN without institutional reforms could lose its international role in maintaining peace. He saw a role for India and Mekong countries in working together for water resource security. Among the remaining three papers in this section that follow- the one by Bunn Nagara presents a historical perspective of ASEAN and the security of the region. Renato Cruz De Castro, who examines ASEAN's role in the context of the South China Sea tensions arrives at a somewhat pessimistic conclusion whereas Navrekha Sharma takes a more balanced approach in assessing ASEAN's role in the security of the Asia Pacific.

Another theme of the Academic Session was the blue economy. The idea of blue economy has come to constitute a critical component of national development strategy in many countries of the region. With growing acceptance of the idea that blue economy, there is greater willingness among states of the region to commit themselves to sustainable exploitation of living and non-living marine resources and deep seabed minerals with a view to enhance food and energy security. In order to overcome the technological and financial limitations constraining the development of the maritime sector nations of the region have to collaborate in devising appropriate national and regional strategies. That a blue water economy is vital to the success of a 'green economy' was an important take away from the UN Conference on Sustainable Development 2012 and Rio+20. This was followed by the first Blue Economy conference for member states of Indian Ocean Rim Association (IORA) held in Mauritius in September 2015. The session on ASEAN-India and the Ocean Economy Dynamics had three papers. Yogendra Kumar addresses the ocean economy dynamics in the South China Sea and the Indian Ocean and examines India-ASEAN initiatives and possible potential. Joefe B Santarita sees potential for collaboration in South China Sea where most see confrontation in his paper titled 'Beyond the Indian Ocean: India and its Blue Economy Partnerships in the South China Sea'. Girish Gujar and Hong Yan advocate that Indo-ASEAN evolve a blue economy strategy for their very survival in a highly mutating world.

The session on 'Reinvigorating the Civilizational Link between ASEAN and India' sought to link the present to the past even though admittedly many prominent discontinuities exist historically. The people to people contact between India and Southeast Asia dates back to the early centuries of the Christian era when religion and trade became the vehicle of spread of Indian culture and the Indianised kingdom of Sailendras, the Srivijaya Kingdom and the Majapahit kingdom flourished. As Europe dominated and colonial logic prevailed, migration of Indian labour businessmen and administrators followed. The anti-colonial freedom struggle further cemented the bonds which continued in the post-independence period. Beyond the cultural diffusion, the Bollywood films, and the democratic values lies the possibility of cooperation in capacity building in areas like education and health (of particular relevance to India's North East and Myanmar's west).

Sachidanand Sahai, an expert in cultural history of Southeast Asia and based in Cambodia, traced the forgotten Saka linkage between India and Southeast Asia. As there is a record of so many common historical strands and the Archaeological Survey of India has also played a constructive role in India's neighbourhood, the next presentation by Himanshu Prabha Ray 'Protecting and Preserving a Shared Cultural Heritage' becomes a valuable resource. Baladas Ghoshal seeks to provide contemporary relevance to the civilizational and historical linkages with Southeast Asia. By identifying the gaps and developing the hitherto underdeveloped sectors and regions, collaboration with the larger Asia-Pacific region could prove mutually beneficial.

Five papers - representing three ASEAN perspectives and two Indian - chart the future in the final session 'Way Forward: Towards 25th Anniversary of ASEAN-India Relations'. Nguyen Thai Yen Huong gives a Vietnamese perspective on India's Look East Policy and suggests the way forward. R Ravindran of Singapore relates the Plan of Action of India for ASEAN from 2015 to 2020 with ASEAN's Plan for the ASEAN Community up to 2025 and implications for the business and the strategic community. Yang Peou's paper on 'Cambodia-India Relations: Achievements and Way Forward' is important because it is a subject that is not sufficiently discussed or debated. Rajiv Bhatia provides the perspective of a policy maker and practitioner and indicates an optimistic direction despite the hurdles. Prabir De gives an economist's perspective on the way forward in shaping the ASEAN-India Partnership.

The views expressed in the papers are those of the participants in the Dialogue and have been reproduced without any significant change. We compliment them for their contribution.

The Ministry of External Affairs has led the Delhi Dialogue from behind with its experience. I thank Secretary East, Mr Anil Wadhwa for delivering the Keynote Address. I thank Joint Secretary (ASEAN Multilateral) Ms. Pooja Kapur and her team for the cooperation and support they provided us.

It is the Delhi Dialogue Partners and Associates who make this Conference possible. The Diplomatic Academy of Vietnam (DAV) is our latest Partner and we are proud to welcome it. I thank all other Partners: Federation of Indian Chambers of Commerce and Industry; Indian Council of World Affairs; ASEAN-India Centre at RIS; Economic Research Institute for ASEAN and East Asia, Jakarta; Institute of South Asian Studies, Singapore; SAEA Group Research, Singapore; Institute of Strategic and International Studies, Malaysia; Institute of Security and International Studies, Thailand; and Diplomatic Academy of Vietnam, Vietnam. I also thank our five Associates: All India Association of Industries (AIAI); The Associated Chambers of Commerce & Industry of India; Indian Chambers of Commerce, Kolkata; and Indian Council for Research on International Economic Relations.

Within IDSA I wish to thank DG, Mr Jayant Prasad for his encouragement and support. I thank DDG Brig. Rumel Dahiya who guided us and helped us overcome many difficulties. Dr Sampa Kundu, Research Assistant in the

Centre, dealt with many of the nitty gritties of the Dialogue. Niranjan Oak, Intern with the Centre, could be relied upon to finish the tasks quickly and efficiently. I thank also the four Rapporteurs during the Conference: Mr. Satyam, Dr. Pratibha, Ms. Rajbala Rana, and Ms. Gunjan Singh.

IDSA's Conference Cell is a pillar of support, especially, Ms. Aparna Krishna, Ms. Ameeta Narang, and Mr. Sumit Kumar. My thanks also to Mr. Pushkar Pathak for web support and Mr Mukesh Dabas for recording and photography.

It is our belief that participation of our Northeastern States is crucial for the success of Delhi Dialogue. I thank the Chief Minister of Nagaland and the Chief Minister of Mizoram for their participation.

The Academic Session was a success because of the frankness with which ideas were exchanged and the debate it generated. I thank the Moderators of the four sessions: Mr Nalin Surie (Session I), Prof Hidetoshi Nishimura (Session II), Amb. Shyam Saran (Session III) and Amb. Gopinath Pillai (Session IV). I am also grateful to Mr Vivek Kaushik and his team comprising Ms Vaijayanti Patankar and Ms Geeta for help in various stages of the publication process. I must also record my thanks to Mr Rajan and his team in the Pentagon Press for their professional efficiency in publishing this book.

New Delhi **Udai Bhanu Singh**

INDIA - ASEAN
INDIA
New Delhi
MYANMAR
Naypyitaw
LAOS
Vientiane
Hanoi
THAILAND
Bangkok
CAMBODIA
Phnom Penh
VIETNAM
PHILIPPINES
Manila
BRUNEI
Bandar Seri Begawan
MALAYSIA
Kuala Lumpur
SINGAPORE
INDONESIA
Jakarta
Arabian Sea
Laccadive Sea
Bay of Bengal
Andaman Sea
Gulf of Thailand
South China Sea
East China Sea
Philippine Sea
Sulu Sea
Celebes Sea
Java Sea
Banda Sea
Timor Sea
Arafura Sea
INDIAN OCEAN
© Institute for Defense Studies & Analyses
New Delhi, GIS Lab.
Map not to scale

PART I

MINISTERIAL SESSION

Welcome Remarks

Jyotsna Suri

Keynote Address

Sushma Swaraj

1

Welcome Remarks by Immediate Past President, FICCI, Dr. Jyotsna Suri

Hon'ble Minister of External Affairs Smt. Sushma Swaraj ji

Dignitaries and business leaders from ASEAN

Colleagues from Indian industry

Members of media from India and ASEAN

Sushmaji, we have had a great business session yesterday.

In the discussions, industry from India and ASEAN have unanimously welcomed efforts made by the Governments of India and ASEAN countries on creating an enabling environment for deeper economic ties.

As ASEAN is the core of India's 'Act East Policy', which has a strong economic agenda in addition to strategic and socio-cultural aspects, industry is enthusiastic to engage with ASEAN at the regional and bilateral level to achieve the combined trade target of 100 billion dollars.

For India's domestic agenda, there is special emphasis on cooperation with ASEAN on infrastructure, manufacturing, skills, urban renewal, smart cities, digital India and 'Make in India' programs.

Indian industry is ready to partner companies from ASEAN for all of these sectors.

Excellencies, the private sector of India is also with you in your endeavour to deepen our relationship on both Culture and Connectivity, in addition to Commerce.

Today, the India ASEAN partnership has emerged as a key driver of economic growth not just for the Asia-Pacific but the world as a whole.

As mentioned by our Hon'ble Prime Minister, India and ASEAN are two bright spots of optimism in the world.

Together, our combined regional significance in economic, demographic and strategic terms would be a catalyst to realise the dream of an Asian century and industry is with you every step along the way.

Thank you.

2

Keynote Address by Hon'ble External Affairs Minister Mrs Sushma Swaraj at the Ministerial Session of Delhi Dialogue VIII, New Delhi

H.E. Mr. Sofyan Djalil, Minister for National Development Planning and Head of National Development Planning Agency of Indonesia,

H.E. U Tin Oo Lwin, Deputy Minister of Foreign Affairs of Myanmar,

H.E. Mr. Vikasakdi Futrakul, Vice Minister of Foreign Affairs of Thailand,

H.E. Mr. Le Hoai Trung, Vice Minister of Foreign Affairs of Vietnam,

H.E. Mr. Somchith Inthamith, Vice Minister of Industry & Commerce of Lao PDR,

Dr. AKP Mochtan, Deputy Secretary General for Community & Corporate Affairs, ASEAN Secretariat,

H.E. Mr. Vikram Nair, Member of Parliament of Singapore and Chairman of the Singapore-India Parliamentary Friendship Group,

H.E. Kan Pharidh, Under-Secretary of State in the Foreign Ministry of Cambodia,

Heads of Delegations from Malaysia, Philippines and Brunei,

Mr. T.R. Zeliang, Hon'ble Chief Minister of Nagaland,

Mr. Lal Thanhawla, Hon'ble Chief Minister of Mizoram,

Distinguished Guests,

Ladies and Gentlemen,

It is my immense pleasure to welcome you to the 8th edition of the Delhi Dialogue.

A year has passed since the last Delhi Dialogue in March 2015, at which also I had the privilege of delivering the keynote address. This last one year has witnessed several important developments in the ASEAN-India relationship. During this year, the ASEAN-India Free Trade Area was completed, coinciding with the creation of the ASEAN Community. I formally inaugurated our independent Mission to ASEAN during my visit to Jakarta in April 2015. An ambitious new ASEAN-India Plan of Action for the period 2016-2020 was adopted in August 2015. All these positive developments paved the way for an exceptionally productive ASEAN-India Summit in Kuala Lumpur in November 2015.

Simultaneously, in the last one year a lot has changed in the global environment. The most significant is the escalation of terrorism, extremism and sectarianism. The rise of ISIS in particular and the displacement of millions of people from their homes, has caused enormous tensions and threatens the social fabric of many countries. The slowdown of the global economy has created its own set of issues for all our economies and development agendas.

Held against this backdrop, Delhi Dialogue VIII provides policy makers, business leaders and academics from both India and ASEAN with a multi-dimensional platform to discuss, debate and arrive at recommendations on how best to deal with these challenges. It gives an opportunity to intensify and broaden our constructive engagement to mutual benefit.

Excellencies,

In the context of the rapidly changing international scenario, the theme of this edition of Delhi Dialogue, 'ASEAN-India Relations: A New Paradigm', is especially pertinent. This is also because India is looking to chart a more ambitious and aspirational trajectory for its engagement with ASEAN.

ASEAN's achievements over the last five decades have been truly impressive, especially considering the diversity of challenges that it has been confronted with, both internally and externally. The centrality of ASEAN has become the fulcrum, around which the Asia-Pacific region has evolved and its importance has increased further in recent times. The establishment of the ASEAN Community last December is a commendable leap forward.

India, through its 'Act East Policy,' has been giving a renewed focus to its engagement with ASEAN and other friends in the East. It is not a coincidence that since Prime Minister Modi's government came to power in May 2014;

we have had visits by the President, Vice President and Prime Minister of India to 9 out of 10 ASEAN countries! The Hon'ble President Pranab Mukherjee visited Vietnam; the Hon'ble Vice President Hamid Ansari visited Cambodia, Lao PDR, Indonesia, Thailand and Brunei; and Hon'ble Prime Minister Modi visited Myanmar, Singapore and Malaysia. The Philippines, as the next Chair of ASEAN, will soon be on the list.

We are also looking forward to the year 2017, which will be a special year for ASEAN and the ASEAN-India partnership. As ASEAN celebrates its golden jubilee, India and ASEAN would also be commemorating the silver anniversary of their partnership.

India and ASEAN are two bright spots of optimism amidst ongoing global economic uncertainties. The ASEAN Community has opened up a whole new world of opportunities for shared socio-economic growth. India would like to be part of this growth and in this sense, the development of an ASEAN-India Economic Community would be a logical evolution. We also encourage the ASEAN member states which are yet to ratify the ASEAN-India Agreements on Trade in Services and Investments to do so at the earliest. The ASEAN-India Trade Negotiating Committee has also been commissioned to undertake a review of the ASEAN-India Trade in Goods Agreement. Together these will facilitate a qualitative shift in our trade and investment relationship.

A balanced and ambitious Regional Comprehensive Economic Partnership Agreement, which we hope will be concluded this year, will further boost our economic and commercial engagement with ASEAN and the wider Asia-Pacific. We hope that the Regional Comprehensive Economic Partnership and Trans-Pacific Partnership will not become competing regimes, but help in laying the foundation of an integrated economic community. I believe that yesterday's discussion in the business session on the impact of RCEP and TPP on ASEAN-India offered some interesting insights.

I am also pleased to note that the Business session of this Dialogue saw the participation of the Presidents of all three national business chambers of India as well as several regional chambers, alongside business leaders from ASEAN. The discussion on ways to create regional value chains and enhance cross-border trade was important as it holds the key to the future prosperity of our peoples.

Peace and stability are essential pre-requisites for progress and development.

In this context, we are all aware of the importance of ensuring maritime security, which has emerged as an important area of concern in recent times. The oceans and seas, including the South China Sea, are pathways to our prosperity and security. The security of sea routes in the Asia-Pacific is essential for India's economy as a majority of our global trade flows across the straits of Malacca and beyond. Moreover, the development of a Blue Economy and optimum utilisation of marine resources can only take place within the ambit of internationally recognised rules and norms.

The need for resolving disputes peacefully, without threat or actual use of force, cannot, therefore, be underestimated. In this regard I would also like to stress that we support the evolution of an inclusive, balanced, transparent and open regional architecture for security and cooperation in the Asia-Pacific. We continue to deepen ASEAN-India consultations and cooperation through various ASEAN-led fora including the East Asia Summit, ASEAN Defence Ministers' Meeting Plus, and the Expanded ASEAN Maritime Forum.

On the 10th anniversary of the East Asia Summit last November, we resolved to work closely with ASEAN member states to strengthen the EAS as the premier leaders-led forum for dialogue and cooperation on strategic, political and economic issues, with the aim of promoting peace, stability and economic prosperity in the region. We have also stepped up our consultations with the ASEAN mechanisms dealing with countering terrorism, piracy, drug trafficking and other transnational crimes, including by involving law enforcement agencies. We look forward to tomorrow's academic discussion on 'ASEAN and the Security of the Asia Pacific.' We also propose to host the first Government-to-Government ASEAN-India Cyber Dialogue in New Delhi in early 2016.

Enhancing connectivity is a strategic priority for both India and ASEAN. It is also an enabler for economic growth and people-to-people exchanges. For India's North Eastern region, it can be a game changer. India has been working with ASEAN to enhance physical connectivity via our North East as well as our eastern seaboard. A number of initiatives are underway for improving rail, road, water-ways and air connectivity within the region.

In the last one year, we have closely monitored the progress of our major connectivity projects—the Kaladan Multi Modal Transport project, India-Myanmar-Thailand Trilateral Highway and Rih-Tedim Project in Myanmar.

I am happy to share that the original waterways component of the Kaladan project has achieved a physical progress of close to 90 per cent and is scheduled to be completed in the next few months. The revised cost of the project was approved in October last year. The implementation of the road component and additional waterways items has been initiated. These are targeted to be completed by 2019.

As regards India-Myanmar-Thailand Trilateral Highway the tendering process for award of work for construction of 69 bridges and approach roads has been initiated. The project approval for this component was obtained in December last year. The implementation will start soon with the Friendship Bridge connecting Moreh and Tamu on the India-Myanmar border. The process for Kalewa-Yargi road has also been speeded up.

The Rih-Tedim Road project will provide all weather connectivity between eastern Mizoram and western Myanmar. The alignment for the road has been finalised. A Detailed Project Report will be completed by the second half of this year, and actual implementation will start soon thereafter.

Besides these projects, at the 13th ASEAN India Summit in November 2015, Prime Minister Modi announced a Line of Credit of One billion dollars to promote projects that support physical and digital connectivity between India and ASEAN. We will look forward to receiving proposals from ASEAN member states for utilisation of this Line of Credit.

We are also working for enhanced air connectivity for our North-East with our ASEAN friends. On the subject of connectivity, I also look forward to hearing the views of the Chief Ministers of our North Eastern states, who have so kindly graced today's event with their presence. I am pleased to inform you that we will be inaugurating very soon an ASEAN Studies Centre at the North-Eastern Hill University in Shillong, following Prime Minister Modi's announcement to this effect at the 13th ASEAN-India Summit. The Centre will include representatives from Universities in all North Eastern states and shall work to enhance mutual understanding and develop cross-border academic exchanges between India and ASEAN countries. We also look forward to the ASEAN-India Centre in New Delhi receiving ASEAN scholars and research fellows at an early date.

The deep and abiding socio-cultural links between India and ASEAN date back two millennia. It is important that as we further develop our political and economic relations we do not lose sight of our civilisational connect. With this objective, the first International Conference on ASEAN-India Cultural Links was organised in New Delhi in July 2015. The Conference deliberated on how to document our ancient and contemporary socio-cultural linkages, spanning our art and architecture, languages and religion, and mythology and folklore. I am happy that this Conference was not a one-off event and the 2nd ASEAN-India Cultural Relations Conference will be held in Jakarta in 2016.

We hope that such exchanges will engender research tie-up between our universities and think tanks to produce a credible repository of knowledge for the benefit of posterity. To further enhance understanding at the popular level, exchange programme of students, journalists, farmers, scholars, diplomats, parliamentarians and others are progressing apace. It was my pleasure to confer the ICCR Distinguished Alumni Award 2015 on Secretary General of ASEAN Mr. Le Luong Minh in December 2015.

I am also pleased to acknowledge the presence of 20 ASEAN journalists who are here today as part of the ASEAN-India Media Exchange Programme. The extension of the e-visa facility to all ASEAN countries will bring our peoples even closer. I also take this opportunity to invite ASEAN countries to be our partners and guests for the International Buddhist Conclave that we will be hosting later this year. We will be giving support to several leading Buddhist monks and scholars to visit India for this Conclave.

The Delhi Dialogue is a flourishing platform for exchange of ideas. This year's session will see nearly 50 speakers from India and ASEAN come together. This bears testimony to our common will and shared efforts to engage ever more deeply on issues of common interest and concern and to contribute to the overall peace, progress and prosperity of our countries and peoples.

As we prepare to celebrate 25 years of ASEAN-India Dialogue Relations and 15 years of Summit level interaction in 2017, I would welcome ideas from all speakers on how we can commemorate these landmarks suitably. Let me end by thanking you all for joining us. I wish you a fruitful and productive dialogue.

3

Address by Minister for National Development Planning and Head of National Development Planning Agency of Indonesia, Dr. Sofyan A. Djalil

Your Excellency Smt. Sushma Swaraj, Minister of External Affairs of the Republic of India, your excellencies Vice Ministers and senior officials of ASEAN member States, your excellencies high ranking officials of the Government of India, Your Excellency the Secretary General of ASEAN, honourable Dr. Jyotsna Suri, immediate past-president of FICCI, distinguished guests, ladies and gentlemen,

It gives me a great pleasure to join at the Delhi Dialogue VIII and to address this important issue in this meeting. On behalf of the Indonesian delegation, I wish to express our sincere appreciation to Government of India to this initiative and excellent arrangements and the generous hospitality extended to us. The Delhi Dialogue VIII became significant from being the first after the establishment of ASEAN community on 31st December 2015. I am glad that the discussion in this dialogue which bear the appropriate theme, 'ASEAN-India Relations—A New Paradigm' will focus on regional issues of common interest such as connectivity, global value chains and maritime issues. This is especially relevant and in line with efforts of ASEAN and India to achieve prosperity in the region. They are also in accordance with ASEAN Community Vision 2025 and its blueprint. It is therefore a unique opportunity for government officials, academia and business people to gather and engage in fruitful deliberations. This effort expected to forward a set of practical recommendations for building a concrete, meaningful and mutually beneficial ASEAN-India partnership.

Excellencies, distinguished ladies and gentlemen, our world today is characterised by inter-connectedness. For centuries people have been migrating to different lands exchanging goods and ideas to improve their lives. In the recent decade, technology advancement enabled us to close the distance between countries and the regions. The information and communication technology revolution has made it possible to coordinate and manage complex undertaking from a distance. Furthermore, the wage differences between countries and regions have created more business opportunities across the regions. This phenomenon has delivered new pattern of production, distribution and consumption. In response to this new trend, Indonesia has been encouraged to strengthen its national industries to be more competitive to produce high value added product as well as to participate more intensively in the global value chains. Therefore the government of Indonesia in its recent national medium term planning document gave priority to investment support to our industry's participation in global value chains. Furthermore, we also encouraged partnership between our local SMEs and foreign investors to ensure technology transfer, to improve the innovation capacity and to increase the product quality and standard. With this we can improve the ability of our SMEs to integrate themselves into global value chains.

Since September 2015 the Government of Indonesia has issued several economic packages to make the economy more efficient, resilient and business friendly. This, including deregulation and simplification of licencing and procedure for investment and doing business to increase the industrial competitiveness. It is obvious that the world interconnectivity has made countries dependent on each other. Our regional economic integration will be more resilient and constructive when it is founded on strong and productive regional value chains among our countries. It is therefore our responsibility to ensure sustainability and maintain progress in our regional value chains. This can be achieved by establishing a fair trade relationship bringing down tariff and non-tariff barriers and removing impediments to trade among countries in this region. High tariff barriers and some other non-tariff measures which are still applied to certain sectors in our region would hinder the development of our regional value chains in the long run. Hence, Indonesia supported the decision of ASEAN and Indian economic minister to review ASEAN India Trade in Goods Agreement (AITIGA) to further increase trade facilitation and reduce trade barriers. This arrangement will definitely strengthen our regional value chain particularly among ASEAN and India.

Indonesia also appreciates India's pledge to raise ASEAN India Science and Technology Fund. This will greatly strengthen ASEAN and India partnership as well as improve industrial capacities and human resource capacities. In order to fully take advantage of global value chains and compete in global market through improvement technology, innovation as well as research and development. Considering the importance of micro and small and medium enterprise in our region, encourage India to enhance cooperation in building the capacity of ASEAN SMEs in many areas such as productivity, technology and innovation, access to finance and market as well as entrepreneurship and human capital. Enhancing cooperation in those particular areas will increase the capacity of SMEs to participate in the regional value chain and contribute to the inclusive growth of prosperity in both ASEAN and India.

Excellencies, distinguished ladies and gentlemen, another keyword that should be borne in mind in this discussion is connectivity. As an archipelagic nation Indonesia puts great emphasis on connectivity, especially maritime connectivity. The development of maritime infrastructure can greatly enhance trade within the region. Should ASEAN and India share not only land and also sea borders, economic integration of ASEAN and India can be further accelerated through the development of maritime transport facilities. Increased maritime connectivity between ASEAN and India will lower cost of logistics and trigger the growth of trade in good and service between the two parties. Indonesia therefore support India's initiative to engage ASEAN in enhancing air and maritime connectivity cooperation. This is an area of cooperation that needs to be further developed.

Indonesia welcomes Indian allocation for one billion credit line for ASEAN member States that would launch projects under the ASEAN-India Strategic Partnership among others to realise the master plan of ASEAN connectivity. The implementation of master plan under ASEAN connectivity has been significantly progressive and expanding beyond ASEAN such as the framework of the East Asia Summit. Developing maritime connectivity is one of the five main elements in the ASEAN Economic Summit Statement on enhancing regional maritime cooperation which was adopted in the 10th East Asia Summit in Kuala Lumpur on 22nd September, 2015. This statement highlighted the important effort for developing sustainable and resilient infrastructure, port management and cooperation in navigation. This maritime infrastructure will accelerate economic growth, contribute to community building process as well as improve the mobility of people, goods and services.

Since Indonesia views India as a strategic partner in the promotion of maritime connectivity in the region, Indonesia therefore appreciate India's support for the East Asia Summit statement and its implementation particularly in provision and development of maritime connectivity. Moreover, Indonesia looks forward to India's continued involvement in maritime cooperation not only in the framework of the ASEAN-India Strategic Partnership but also in other ASEAN led mechanism such as the East Asia Summit, ASEAN Defence Ministers Meeting Plus, the Expanded Maritime Forum and the ASEAN Regional Forum.

Excellencies, distinguished guests, we believe that peace, security and stability is a precursor for the enhancement of ASEAN-India partnership. As the chair of the Indian Ocean Rim Association (IORA) from 2015 to 2017, Indonesia also seeks India's support for the adoption of IORA Concord which is scheduled to be adopted in the 1st IORA Summit in Indonesia in March 2017. The IORA Concord is expected to be a landmark document that will contribute to building a more secure, prosperous and stable Indian Ocean region. The concord highlights the principle of freedom, independence, non-interference, peaceful settlement of dispute as well as trust and confidence as a basis for strengthening cooperation. I trust with India's strong support the vision of IORA Concord will be successfully developed and finally adopted in 2017. Last but not least I am optimistic that with India's policy of not only looking East but also acting East and with India's continued support for ASEAN-India common values and goals our partnership will continue to grow from strength to strength in the years ahead.

Thank you.

4

Summary of Panel Discussions

Two panel discussions were held in the Ministerial Session on February 18, 2016.

Panel Discussion 1: Connectivity: Creating Pathways to a shared Future

Panel 1 dealt with the issue of Connectivity: Creating Pathways to a shared Future. The panelists stressed the following:

- Connectivity in all its aspects—physical, digital, institutional and people-to-people, is one of the foremost priorities in the ASEAN-India strategic partnership. Physical connectivity can be split into land, maritime and air connectivity. There is a need to discuss, analyze and try and synthesise the various components that would help us strengthen India's air transport linkages with Southeast Asia to mutual benefit.
- Connectivity is key to facilitating socio-cultural exchanges and an important priority as India shares both a land and maritime boundary with ASEAN. There is a need to connect geographic corridors with economic corridors.
- **Mr Virasakdi Futrakul, Vice Minister for Foreign Affairs of Thailand** stressed three modes of enhancing connectivity between India and the ASEAN region—Road, Rail and people-to-people connectivity. This will integrate the region for developing value chains and to enhance transport infrastructure and promote economic zones and corridors in the region and build industrial corridors and have India participate in the ASEAN supply chain. It is important that business government and academic communities work closely to achieve this transformation in connectivity in the regions.

- The importance of India's North East as the only viable natural land route that connects India with the ASEAN region. **The Chief Minister of Nagaland Shri T.R. Zeliang** stated that India's 'Act East Policy' aims to achieve this and pointed out that the most practical and convenient road and rain connection between India and ASEAN region should run through Nagaland to Moreh border town via Imphal. Hence, there is a need to extend the East West Corridor from Assam to Moreh via Nagaland. He stressed that what is required is better road connectivity between India and Myanmar and unlock land-locked border areas, remove restrictions on construction activities in border areas and need for better internet connectivity in India's North East.
- The **Hon'ble Chief Minister of Mizoram Mr Lalthanhawla** mentioned that closer cooperation between India and the ASEAN region is a potential growth force for India's North East. He stressed the need to improve infrastructure in the North Eats of India, develop the gateways between the North East and Myanmar besides Moreh to include Pangsu Pass in Arunachal and Zawkhathar in Mizoram; complete the 100 km long highway between Lowngtlai to Myanmar border as supplement to the Kaladan project, extend railways line to connect to Kaladan and improve rail and road connectivity between India's North East and the ASEAN region.
- It was stressed that Connectivity and Integration are two sides of the same coin.

Panel Discussion 2: Integrating Regional Value Chains and Production Networks in the ASEAN Economic Community and India

Panel 2 during the ministerial session of the Delhi Dialogue deliberated on Integrating Regional Value Chains and Production Networks in the ASEAN Economic Community and India and stressed the following:

- **Mr Hoai Trung, Deputy Minister of Foreign Affairs of Vietnam** stressed that India and the ASEAN region should be a common production market place with free flow of capital investment and labor, build a competitive economy, promote equitable development and integration in the region and link all aspects of the Strategic Partnership between India and the ASEAN countries. He also stressed that economic linkages are important in the region. For this integration building regional networks is important for each country to generate their production network.

- **Mr Vikram Nair, Member of Parliament** stressed that economic linkages are important and highlighted the importance of the FTA and RCEP agreements to realise connectivity (physical and air) and socio-cultural linkages between the two regions. He also stresses that to enhance trade, the Region needs to look at NTBs.
- **Mr Somnath Inthamith, Vice Minister, Ministry of Industry and Commerce** said that Regional Value Chains (RVCs) are important for regional cooperation. The communities should promote cooperation between the business communities of the two regions.
- **Mrs Teresita C. Daza, Ambassador of the Philippines to India** stated that the government is a catalyst for promoting regional value chains in the Region. She also stressed people-to-people connect—promote tourism, education linkages (medical student in the Philippines) between India and ASEAN.
- The Panel also stressed the role of SMEs in promoting RVCs in the region—SMEs can be a growth facilitator in this process of integration (if barriers are removed like finances, technology exposure and innovation) and for the government to create an enabling environment for collaboration and innovation.

Mr Jayant Prasad, DG IDSA gave the concluding remarks at the ministerial session of the Delhi dialogue and stressed that the need to deepen economic linkages—connectivity and value chains between India and ASEAN and the need to promote people to people linkages as an important tool for enhancing cooperation between India and the ASEAN. He concluded by inviting everyone to attend the Academic session in the Delhi Dialogue the following day.

5

Vote of Thanks by Director General, Institute for Defence Studies and Analyses, Mr. Jayant Prasad

Hon'ble Minister for External Affairs, Hon'ble Minister for Communications,

Excellencies,

Distinguished Guests,

Ladies and Gentlemen,

It is my honour to propose the vote of thanks on the conclusion of the final part of the Ministerial Session of Delhi Dialogue VIII.

We are grateful that in her Keynote Address the Hon'ble Minister for External Affairs, Smt. Sushma Swaraj has mapped out fully how India envisages a deeper, wider and more multifaceted relationship with ASEAN with whom we share a common civilisational space. We welcome and appreciate the presence of so many ASEAN dignitaries with us this evening. Some among them have had an arduous itinerary because of the ASEAN-US Summit held in California over the preceding two days. The Delhi Dialogue has evolved into a composite and productive annual forum over the past seven years for discussing key strategic and economic issues between ASEAN and India. That the Dialogue has grown in importance is shown by the robust participation this year of diverse stakeholders.

We began yesterday with a meeting of the captains of business and industry and their associations. A meeting that stretched a whole day for the first time in eight years. We heard from Jyotsna Suri how productive that meeting was. Today we heard from ASEAN dignitaries and the Chief Ministers of Nagaland

and Mizoram. And tomorrow practitioners, political/public personalities and academicians will explore more fully the new paradigms of ASEAN-India relations. They will consider ways to impart momentum to these relations as we approach the silver jubilee of India's relations with ASEAN next year. ASEAN is the fulcrum of India's Look East Policy and the keystone of a new security architecture in Asia. The core focus this year has been the deepening of economic linkages throughout the region. Our exchanges have been constrained in the past by connectivity gaps and the absence of value chains. We heard much about these during the discussions this evening. Implementation of the agreed Plan of Action for the ASEAN India Partnership for Peace Progress and Shared Prosperity over the next five years should help us overcome these constraints. India is committed to working creatively on all aspects of connectivity, whether commercial exchanges, and investments, transportation or energy or information and communication technologies or the most important of all, the people to people linkages. And now it is my pleasant duty to record our deepest appreciation to Excellencies:

HE Dr Sofyan A Djalil, Minister for National Development Planning of Indonesia;

HE U Tin Oo Lwin, Hon'ble Deputy Minister of Foreign Affairs, Myanmar;

HE Mr Somchith Inthamith, Vice Minister of Industry and Commerce, Laos;

HE Mr Le Hoai Trung, Hon'ble Deputy Minister of Foreign Affairs, Vietnam;

HE Mr Vikasakdi Futrakul, Hon'ble Vice Minister for Foreign Affairs of Thailand;

HE Mr Vikram Nair, MP, Chairperson of the Government Parliamentary Committee for Defence and Foreign Affairs of Singapore

HE Kan Pharidh, Under-Secretary of State, ASEAN-Cambodia, Ministry of Foreign Affairs, Cambodia.

HE Claro S Cristobal, Director General, Foreign Service Institute of the Philippines

HE Datuk Naimun Ashakli, High Commissioner of Malaysia to India

HE Dato'Paduka Sidek Ali, High Commissioner of Brunei Darussalam

HE Dr AKP Mochtan, Deputy Secretary General of Community & Corporate Affairs, ASEAN Secretariat and

HE Mrs Teresita C Daza, Ambassador of the Philippines to India

And continuing the previous tradition of the past two years of inviting key North Eastern Chief Ministers from there. This evening we had the honour of having two leaders of India's North Eastern States. Our thanks are due to Hon'ble Chief Minister of Nagaland, Mr TR Zeliang, and Hon'ble Chief Minister of Mizoram, Mr Lal Thanhawla.

I would like to express my sincere thanks to Secretary (East) in the Ministry of External Affairs, Mr Anil Wadhwa, Joint Secretary (ASEAN Multilateral) Ms. Pooja Kapur and their team and to thank all our Partners and Associate Institutions:

Federation of Indian Chambers of Commerce and Industry

ASEAN India Centre at RIS

Economic Research Institute for ASEAN and East Asia, in Jakarta

Institute of South Asian Studies (ISAS), Singapore

Institute of Strategic and International Studies, Malaysia

Institute of Security and International Studies, Thailand

SAEA Group Research, Singapore

Diplomatic Academy of Vietnam, Vietnam

Indian Council of World Affairs

All India Association of Industries

The Associated Chambers of Commerce & Industry of India

Confederation of Indian Industry

Indian Chamber of Commerce, Kolkata

Indian Council for Research on International Economic Relations

They have all contributed to the Dialogue in myriad ways and I thank them all.

Tomorrow on 19th February, the IDSA is holding the Academic Session of the Delhi Dialogue VIII at the Institute at 9 AM. We feel privileged in inviting all of you to join in this Session as well. In the end I would like to thank you for your participation in this Dialogue and for the investment all of you are making to promote closer relations between ASEAN and India. It has been a real pleasure to have you with us. Thank you all very much. Namaste and Good Evening.

PART II
BUSINESS SESSION

Welcome Remarks

Jyotsna Suri

Remarks

Sumit Mazumder

Sunil Kanoria

Shiv Siddhant Narayan Kaul

Vijay Kalantri

Special Remarks

Anil Wadhwa

6

Welcome Remarks by Immediate Past President, FICCI, Dr. Jyotsna Suri

Shri Anil Wadhwa, Secretary East, Ministry of External Affairs, dignitaries and business leaders from ASEAN, my colleagues from the Indian industry, Excellencies, members of media from India and ASEAN, ladies and gentlemen, namaskar. I have great pleasure in welcoming you to the 8th Edition of the Delhi Dialogue which is an annual initiative of FICCI in partnership with the Ministry of External Affairs. The theme this year as is mentioned is ASEAN-India Relations—A New Paradigm and for the first time ladies and gentlemen, we have a full day dedicated to the business session at Delhi Dialogue. Indian industry partners have come together with five panel discussions on sectors of complementarity between India and ASEAN.

Over the past two years, there has been a growing convergence between India and ASEAN on security, economic, social and cultural fronts. Prime Minister Modi observed at the 13th ASEAN-India Summit in Kuala Lumpur and I quote, "We meet at a time of multiple global challenges, economic uncertainties, political turmoil and security threats, and in this difficult moment India and ASEAN are two bright spots of optimism." Excellencies, we live in exciting times with great promise which we should leverage to create opportunity for the youth that dominate our regions. As two of the world's growth centres, India and ASEAN have great potential for bilateral and multilateral cooperation.

An enabling environment has been created for us by the new ASEAN-India Plan of Action and the establishment of the ASEAN Economic Community. A balanced and ambitious Regional Comprehensive Economic

Partnership or RCEP which would hopefully conclude this year will open common doors into the Asia-Pacific as well. Ladies and gentlemen, there are great opportunities for investment as well as trade expansion and diversification. However, we are restrained because of poor connectivity. We need to improve our connectivity via land, air and sea, so as to facilitate trade, business travel and tourism. We share a rich heritage of Buddhist pilgrimage sites which can give a tremendous boost to tourism within the regions.

Thank you all for coming here ladies and gentlemen and I wish the Delhi Dialogue all success.

7

Remarks by President, CII, Mr Sumit Mazumder

Mr Anil Wadhwa, Secretary East, Ministry of External Affairs, my colleagues on the dais from different chambers and industry associations, distinguished guests, Excellencies, ladies and gentlemen, CII is delighted to be a part of the Delhi Dialogue process. The ASEAN region has been demonstrating steady economic growth coupled with dynamic growth that we are witnessing in India at the moment. Indian industry believes that we could leverage each other's capabilities to form a formidable economic force. India's bilateral trade with ASEAN has grown in the last 5 years.

The India-ASEAN economies complement each other. India has comparative advantage in IT and ITES, medical tourism, education, space science while ASEAN is strong in the energy sector, automobile industry and financial sectors. A special mention needs to be made of Cambodia, Laos, Myanmar and Vietnam or CLMV economies. During the last ten years India's total trade with the CLMV countries has had a ten-fold increase. ASEAN investments in India over the last eight years amounted to US $28 billion while Indian investments in ASEAN reached US$ 32 billion. ASEAN accounts for around 13 per cent of the investment inflows into India.

There are lot of potential for substantially enhancing engagement between India and ASEAN, some of these I will mention. First of course is energy and resources sector. India can harness untapped energy potential in CLMV countries. For instance, Lao PDR has a hydro power capacity of 26000 MW but the installed capacity there is just about one-fourth of what they require. It is now looking for foreign investments in its power sector. Cambodia and Myanmar are also inviting private investments in their energy sectors.

Information and communication technology is the other area. In terms of ICT the economies of India and ASEAN are complementary. India's expertise as a software services provider coupled with ASEAN's ICT manufacturing prowess can lead to a win-win situation.

Agriculture, India's expertise in agri-business and horticulture will be of direct relevance to agriculture dependent CLMV countries. India and ASEAN can collaborate in climate resistant high yield rice hybrids, capacity building in farm mechanisation and so on.

Tourism, while a large number of Indian tourists frequent countries such as Thailand, Malaysia, Indonesia, there is enormous scope to promote tourism to the other countries in the ASEAN region, especially in the CLMV region. Similarly there is enormous scope for tourists from ASEAN to visit India not only for recreation but also for health.

Investments, India and ASEAN need to take advantage of the opportunities created by India-ASEAN FTA in services and investments. They can promote cross border investments by linking investment promotion agencies, foreign investors and local entrepreneurs. In addition, Indian companies can seek to connect with ASEAN's well developed regional value chains.

Now, what role could CII play? CII has been actively working to strengthen relations with South East Asia. The CII South East Asia office was opened in Singapore in 1994 which coincided with the government's announcement of the Look East Policy. The focus has been to work both with corporate and governments in the ASEAN region to devise a strategy which promotes an enduring and mutually beneficial economic relation spanning trade, investment, technology transfer and so on. CII has established ties with 34 institutional partners in the ASEAN region to further bilateral and multilateral cooperation. CII also provides key support to forums like Indo-Myanmar Joint Trade and Investment Forum. The ASEAN-India car rally is another key initiative of CII which was undertaken in 2004 and 2012. This aimed to strengthen people to people contacts and business engagements.

Thank you very much ladies and gentlemen.

8

Remarks by President, ASSOCHAM, Mr Sunil Kanoria

Dignitaries on the dais, members of the Diplomatic Corps, ladies and gentlemen, a very good morning to all of you. Friends, in a world also marked by volatility, ASEAN and India can be each other's insurance policies, courtesy the size of the combined captive market, their fast growing economies and a young population. At this Delhi Dialogue I have three thoughts for discussion. In agriculture and other primary sectors, we need a better dialogue between all stakeholders in India and in ASEAN, between our food safety regulators, between our agriculture scientists who share common challenges, between our agri-business companies, between highly efficient commodity producers in ASEAN and farmers in India, between those who market ASEAN's flowers, fruits and food and India's food processing companies. Only then can we learn from each other's successes and failures.

Both ASEAN and India have a young population. To reap this demographic dividend it is imperative to forge partnerships at the institutional levels for various disciplines like finance, R&D, education, healthcare, legal, ITES, tourism, etc. With movement of professionals within ASEAN, India, already liberalised, thanks to the Services Pact, this would be instrumental in strengthening the human resources development in this region. Imparting the right skill sets to a young, aspiring workforce can unleash huge entrepreneurial talent. In addition, improvement in the institutional structures helps in unifying interest standards and actions amongst member States. A specific idea is to encourage the top business schools of India to meet with the top business schools of ASEAN in competitions and case studies. Similarly, the accountants and lawyers and doctors should meet and create a true dialogue.

A third area of dialogue is around the shared challenge of climate change. As urbanisation picks up in our two regions, we face the issues of air pollution and water pollution and carbon emissions. The city of Delhi itself is trying a brave experiment in combating air pollution. Perhaps there is something we can learn from Jakarta and Singapore in this.

All these areas hold immense potential in the private sector. ASSOCHAM and its members will be happy to benefit from and contribute to this dialogue, thus increasing prosperity for all in this region. Thank you very much.

9

Remarks by President, ICC, Mr Shiv Siddhant Narayan Kaul

Mr Anil Wadhwa, Secretary East, distinguished colleagues from Chambers of Commerce and Industry, distinguished delegates and friends from the media, very good morning to all of you. I believe that there are three pillars that highlight and base India's engagement with the ASEAN region. They are politico-security relations, economic ties and socio-cultural relations.

In the context of economic relationships, as India's economy continues to grow and progress, the ASEAN group is becoming increasingly important. With the India-ASEAN FTA in Services and Investment coming into force only last year, I believe that there will be a meaningful increase in our mutual engagement. As the countries now move towards discussion on the RCEP, it is essential for us in the business community and private enterprise to make full use of the existing FTA that is now in place and make sure that we can establish and strengthen using this framework of economic ties. To do this, I believe it is essential that connectivity is enhanced. Physical and digital connectivity needs to be a strategic priority and it has to serve as one of the lynchpins of the new paradigm that we are discussing here today.

India is now established as a dynamic economy. We have a vibrant startup ecosystem, we have enlightened efforts such as Make in India, Skill India and Digital India. These efforts will serve to energize not just large enterprises but also smaller and medium enterprises as well as enterprises that are just starting up. We have already seen significant interest from the large group of international large firms who are willing to come here and invest here. That a strong connectivity framework will present an opportunity for all these groups of enterprises and entrepreneurs to grow rapidly and truly make use of the entire region as a common market, as a common resource pool and as a common supply chain. This I believe is the future to which we all have to work.

Along with the existing sea and air networks, I believe that it is imperative to establish a robust highway network. This kind of infrastructure between India and ASEAN will only serve to improve the quality of the linkages and will also serve to highlight the geographical proximity between the ASEAN nations and India. As the world pivots East it is essential that we strengthen our own linkages and as we introspect to do this, there are a few things I believe that have been done recently that will help significantly. Foremost is the introduction of the e-visa framework which now covers almost all the ASEAN countries. This will lead to greater people to people linkages and will again serve to highlight the enormous traditional and ancient cultural, socio-cultural linkages that are present. This has to be dovetailed into vibrant business and economic cooperation networks. India's North East and East regions are placed strategically to be a vital part of this engagement and connectivity. As part of the new paradigm it is also imperative that these regions are developed as gateways and hubs from which trade and commerce ties can blossom in additional to the traditional cultural linkages.

India-ASEAN dialogues go back to 1992 and commenced with the sectoral partnership, a part of the erstwhile Look East and now Act East policies. This association has strengthened into something that is extremely firm and is an edifice of India's foreign and trade policy. The Delhi Dialogue forum captures this energy and allows us to think of where we can go to from here. In this sense, the theme for this year's dialogue which is, a new paradigm, is extremely apt.

The Indian Chamber of Commerce is extremely privileged to be a part of this dialogue. We have been working for the last several years to strengthen economic and business ties between India and ASEAN and with a special focus on the Eastern and North Eastern regions of India. We are confident that based on these efforts and based on what has already been done there would be significant enhancement of these three pillars that I mentioned at the beginning and the policies that are in place now will be standing us in good stead for the time to come. Thank you all very much.

10

Remarks by President, All India Association of Industries, Mr Vijay Kalantri

Good morning friends, Mr Wadhwa, my colleagues on the dais, diplomatic fraternity and friends from ASEAN countries. We are very happy to be associated with ASEAN Dialogue and we had been last year also associated with that. I have been organising regular meetings to promote trade between India and ASEAN countries. I feel we have been always looking at West, Europe and US, we should look more seriously at ASEAN continent because this is very closer to us, more proximity and it could deliver lot of things. Today in view of global crisis, I feel ASEAN is one of the areas where we could seriously work together for promoting trade. Of course the maritime connectivity, road connectivity, air connectivity needs to be improved but these are the areas where even our prime minister has announced some of the schemes where we could work together.

In regard with FTA we have not taken any advantage from the ASEAN countries. We feel that we need to work more and explore more possibilities. We in AII have more than 20 MoUs with various counterparts from ASEAN countries and we seriously work with them including exchange of delegations and sending delegations but we feel that regularly as we have one year conference, we can work together quarterly or some times on having some think tank where we could see that which are the concentrated areas like renewable energy, solar energy, digital India, whatever areas of working together could be identified and those focus areas could be taken forward. I think that will make a lot of difference in times to come.

Today of course we are doing a session on Startups and Digital India.

I think that is one area which needs to be explored more. We in MSME feel that there is lot of scope for small scale industries to collaborate and work together with ASEAN countries. Thank you for an opportunity associated with this ASEAN Dialogue. Thank you very much.

11

Special Remarks by Secretary (East) Ministry of External Affairs, Mr Anil Wadhwa

Dr. Jyotsna Suri, Immediate Past President, FICCI

Mr. Sumit Mazumder, President, CII

Mr. Sunil Kanoria, President, ASSOCHAM

Mr. Shiv Siddhant Narayan Kaul, President, ICC

Mr. Vijay Kalantri, President, AIAI

Distinguished Speakers and Delegates,

Ladies and Gentlemen,

1. I am delighted to address the Business Session of the eighth edition of the Delhi Dialogue.
2. India is currently undergoing economic and social transformation on a scale and a speed that is unmatched in history. The Indian economy is the fastest growing major economy with a growth rate of 7.3 per cent in 2014-15.
3. We have undertaken a number of steps to improve the business climate which have resulted in FDI inflows going up by 40 per cent; we have become world's 7th most valued nation brand with a 32 per cent sprint in brand value; we have improved our UNCTAD ranking of investment attractiveness from 15th to 9th place; and Moody's have upgraded our rating as positive.
4. We have started liberalising the FDI regime along with other reforms. We allowed 100 per cent FDI in railways and enhanced the FDI limit to 49 per cent in Defence and Insurance. We are also actively addressing the last mile operational issues in such policies.

5. At the same time, with the formal establishment of the ASEAN Economic Community (AEC) in December 2015, ASEAN is forging ahead as a community by deepening its economic integration. Collectively the third largest economy in Asia and the seventh in the world, the AEC offers many prospects and opportunities, including a middle income market of 622 million people. It will further enable our businesses to jointly explore opportunities in the wider South East Asian region.
6. At the last ASEAN-India Summit in November 2015, Prime Minister, Shri Narendra Modi, called India and ASEAN "two bright spots of optimism" amidst ongoing global economic uncertainties.
7. ASEAN is India's fourth largest trading partner. Bilateral trade between ASEAN and India has crossed US$ 76.53 billion in 2014-15, with India's exports amounting to US$ 31.82 billion, and imports amounting to US$ 44.72 billion. Among the ASEAN member states, Indonesia is the largest trading partner of India, with bilateral trade of US$ 19.03 billion in 2014-15, followed by Malaysia, Singapore and Thailand.
8. Singapore leads among ASEAN countries in inward investments, emerging as the second largest source of FDI for India globally, with inflows amounting to US$ 38.8 billion till September 2015, which is 14.6 per cent of total FDI inflow. Singapore is followed by Malaysia (US$7.6 billion) and Indonesia (US$6.2 billion). In turn, Singapore is a huge recipient of Indian investment, with outflows from India amounting to US$37.8 billion.
9. Enhancing India-ASEAN trade is a priority area under the new Plan of Action to implement the ASEAN-India partnership for peace progress and shared prosperity (2016-20). The Plan of Action envisages a number of steps in the areas of Trade and Investment, Finance, Transport, Food, Agriculture, Forestry, Information and Communication Technology, Tourism, Science, Technology and Innovation, and Mining and Natural Resources Management.
10. In the past year, a significant achievement has been the completion of the ASEAN-India Free Trade Area with the entry into force of the ASEAN-India Agreements on Trade in Services and Investment on 1 July 2015. So far, India, Brunei Darussalam, Malaysia, Myanmar, Singapore, Viet Nam and Thailand have ratified the Agreements. Lao PDR has ratified the

Agreement on Trade in Services. We request you to use your good offices to encourage the remaining ASEAN countries to ratify the Agreement at an early date.

11. Furthermore, the ASEAN-India Trade Negotiating Committee has been tasked to undertake a review of the ASEAN-India Trade in Goods Agreement, which came into effect on 1 January 2010. The review will help optimise its utilisation and bring it up-to-date with today's standards.
12. Negotiations on the Regional Comprehensive Economic Partnership have moved satisfactorily, with modalities being agreed in August 2015. If the technical negotiations, which are underway, are completed swiftly, RCEP may turn into a dynamic reality very soon, particularly if we simultaneously succeed in forming regional value chains and production networks. With the TPP becoming a reality, expediting RCEP is in our interest.
13. Confronted with global economic slowdown, we need to develop our common value chains and production networks. To encourage the same in CLMV countries, which comprise a special category within the ASEAN, Hon'ble PM has announced a Project Development Fund with a corpus of INR 500 crores to develop manufacturing hubs in CLMV countries.
14. In order to fully utilise the potential offered by the ASEAN-India Free Trade Area, we can focus on building complementaries which can generate the necessary goodwill and trust. We need to undertake capacity building programmes, workshops and seminars that focus on the ASEAN-India FTA, Rules of Origin, services liberalisation, regulatory aspects of E-Commerce, elimination of non-tariff barriers, Competition Policy and Intellectual Property Rights, SMEs cooperation and promotion. I trust that today's discussions will throw up practical recommendations in this regard.
15. Our Government is keen to facilitate cross border trade between our North Eastern States and neighbouring ASEAN countries by setting up more border trade points and border haats. Under the MOU on Border Haats along the India-Myanmar border signed in 2012, it has been agreed to set up 9 Border Haats in the states of Arunachal Pradesh, Nagaland, Manipur and Mizoram. We have two Lands Customs Stations at Tamu-Moreh in Manipur and Rhi-Zowkhathar in Mizoram, and the LCS at Moreh is being upgraded into an Integrated Check Post.
16. Our efforts at promoting cross border trade at the micro level need to

supplemented at the macro level by enhancing physical connectivity. We have announced a Line of Credit of US$1 billion to promote projects that support physical and digital connectivity between India and ASEAN. Along with the construction of the India-Myanmar-Thailand Trilateral Highway and the Kaladan Multimodal Project, we are also at the final stages of a Motor Vehicles Agreement between India, Myanmar and Thailand which will address soft connectivity issues.

17. Science and technology is an important component of our cooperation. We have enhanced the ASEAN-India Science and Technology Fund from US$ 1 million to US$ 5 million w.e.f. this year, which will go towards setting up of an ASEAN-India Innovation Platform to facilitate commercialisation of low cost technologies and collaborative R&D projects. We also need to collaborate in development of infrastructure and sustainable energy by promoting private sector cooperation in the development and utilisation of renewable and alternative energy sources; clean energy technologies and energy efficient technologies through institutional capacity building; the facilitation of trade and investment in the energy sector; and liberalisation of power trade among ASEAN Member States and India. I welcome ideas and suggestions in this regard.

18. We have a session on the 'Start-up India, Stand Up India' initiative. We have announced a 19 point action plan in January this year for setting up of Start-ups which would work towards innovation, development, deployment or commercialisation of new products, processes or services that are driven by technology or intellectual property. I hope the session will come up with the broad contours of an ASEAN-India ecosystem to facilitate the convergence of technology, integration across diverse fields, distributed architecture and people willing to back an idea.

19. I am confident that today's Business session will provide an insight into the changes that are currently taking place in India on the investment and economic front as well as into the potential which India holds for greater engagement with ASEAN Member States. Let us use this opportunity to collectively shape our post-2015 agenda for greater progress and prosperity of our peoples.

Thank You.

12

Report of Business Session of Delhi Dialogue VIII held on 17 February, 2016

India-ASEAN Relations

Delhi Dialogue VIII at its Business Session discussed co-manufacturing, mega trade blocs, Infrastructure and sustainable energy, cross border trade and Start-ups and digitisation

The destinies of South-East Asia and India are intricately linked. As the two sides work to bolster their relationship, especially against the backdrop of India's renewed commitment to ASEAN with its action-driven and result-oriented 'Act East Policy', we recognise that economic cooperation between India and ASEAN must go hand in hand with better understanding between our peoples and deeper integration of our societies.[1] Trade between India and South East Asia remains an important aspect of our engagement in the 21st century, with ASEAN being India's fourth largest trading partner.

Today India and ASEAN are at the threshold of a qualitatively substantive relationship. As India and the countries of the ASEAN set new goals to move the ASEAN-India Strategic Partnership forward all pillars of engagement—political, economic and socio-cultural are crucial for enhancing this relationship. India and South East Asia constitute a community of 1.9 billion people, representing one-fourth of humanity and account for a combined GDP of US$ 4.75 trillion—substantive and invigorating relationship.

Regional Cooperation: India is an active participant in the East Asia Summit, ASEAN Regional Forum, ADMM+ and Expanded ASEAN Maritime Forum which are important initiatives for creating an open and inclusive regional architecture.

Delhi Dialogue VIII

Delhi Dialogue is an annual Track 1.5 forum for discussing politico-security, economic and socio-cultural issues between ASEAN and India. Since 2009 when the conference was first held, Delhi Dialogue has emerged as an important forum at which political leaders, policy makers, researchers, academicians, business leaders and media persons converge for brainstorming on a range of issues pertaining to ASEAN-India relations.

Delhi Dialogue VIII Business Session

Keeping this context in mind and as India moves towards completing 25 years of its dialogue relationship with the ASEAN region, Delhi Dialogue VIII is appropriately themed "**ASEAN-India Relations: A New Paradigm**".

The eighth edition of the Delhi Dialogue comprised a full day Business session on the following themes: Co-Manufacturing and Manufacturing Value Chains, Mega Trade Blocs, Infrastructure and Sustainable Energy, Cross Border Trade and role of Start Ups and Digitisation between India and the ASEA Region.

The key take aways for the deliberations at the Business Session were:

RCEP

The session on "What do Mega Trade Blocs—RCEP, TPP mean for ASEAN and India" provided details about the rise of mega regional trading blocs and their impact on the regional and global trade architecture. It was shared that while NAFTA and ASEAN are extremely successful in promoting intra-regional trade and investment, a few more mega FTAs including the Trans Pacific Partnership (TPP), The Regional Comprehensive Economic Partnership (RCEP), etc are under various stages of negotiations which are expected to have major impact on trade and investment front.

The RCEP, on the other hand, is a Free Trade Agreement between ASEAN and its 6 FTA partners, namely Australia, China, India, Japan, Korea and New Zealand. India supports a high quality, modern, comprehensive and mutually beneficial RCEP.

Regional Value Chains and Production Networks

This business session reiterated that Regional Value Chains (RVCs) and Production Networks are crucial for the economic integration of India with the countries of the ASEAN region. It was noted that the India-ASEAN FTA and the RCEP are setting the tone for forming RVCs and PN in the Region.

In addition to this the need to cooperate in capacity building and enhancing common skill sets, developing an enabling banking infrastructure—building a Consortium Bank and strengthening SME cooperation and promoting connectivity between the ASEAN Region and tier 2 and tier 3 cities in India was stressed between Indian and the ASEAN region. It was also stressed during the Delhi Dialogue that standards and quality is going to be the key negotiating tools in all upcoming mega trading bloc negotiations. Both India and ASEAN need to develop a comprehensive strategy to deal with standards and quality.

Sustainable Energy

Recognising the need to collaborate in development of infrastructure and sustainable energy, the business community from India and the ASEAN region stressed private sector cooperation and further cooperation in the development and utilisation of renewable energy and alternative energy sources along with power trade. Solar Energy, Hydro Power and Geo Thermal initiatives were highlighted during the session at the Delhi Dialogue.

Other areas: Startups and Cross Border Trade

The Dialogue defined the broad contours of an ASEAN Indian ecosystem to facilitate the convergence of technology, integration across diverse fields in the region. The ASEAN region has excellent potential for startups from India to cooperate with ASEAN. Young talent, SMEs and their integration are forces that will shape the future markets.

The role of India's North East in enhancing cooperation between India and the ASEAN region was emphasised as well as furthering investments in physical infrastructure projects, people-to-people connect and tourism between India's North East and the ASEAN region was stressed.

NOTES

1. Secretary (East) at Inaugural Session of the International Conference on 'ASEAN-India Cultural Links: Historical and Contemporary Dimensions, New Delhi (July 23, 2015).

PART III

ACADEMIC SESSIONS

Welcome Address: Jayant Prasad

Keynote Address: Anil Wadhwa

13

Welcome Address by Director General, IDSA, Jayant Prasad

Secretary East in the Ministry of External Affairs, Shri Anil Wadhwa,

Excellencies,

Distinguished Guests,

Panelists,

Presiders,

Ladies and Gentlemen.

I am privileged to welcome you to the Academic Session of the eighth edition of the Delhi Dialogue. The Dialogue has evolved dynamically over the last seven year. In the Delhi Dialogue there have been many firsts this year. It is for the first time that the Business Session involving the captains of business and industry and the principal associations met for an entire day. And it is not for the first time really that the Ministerial Session included interactive sessions but these were very productive last evening—on connectivity and integrating value chains and production networks. That session was graced by Hon'ble Minister of External Affairs, Smt Sushma Swaraj in which the visiting ASEAN dignitaries spoke together with Chief Ministers of two States of North East India—Mizoram and Nagaland. ASEAN Countries and India share the same civilisational space. Their cultural consonance and trading links go back to ancient times when Buddhism first, Hinduism and Islam went to South East Asia from the Indian subcontinent. The Srivijaya Kingdom from the 8th to the 12th centuries established a robust relationship between India and Southeast Asia not by force of arms or military adventure but by forging cultural and trading links creating a Sino-Indic confluence in that entire region. Its natural that the ASEAN-India relationship has become a cornerstone of India's Act East Policy with its three pillars resting on greater economic cooperation, deepening cultural ties, and developing strategic relationships with countries in the Asia Pacific region.

India is an active participant in many ASEAN forums, the East Asia Summit, the ASEAN Regional Forum, the ASEAN Defence Ministers' Meeting Plus (the ADMM Plus). This is how India demonstrates the centrality of ASEAN in the practical articulation of its Act East Policy. As ASEAN countries begin to construct the building blocks of a new security architecture in Asia ASEAN's cohesion and continued progress would make it the pivot around which the norms of cooperative security might be developed. Meanwhile the core focus for ASEAN and India must continue to be accelerating their social and economic transformations. While ASEAN and India are blessed by their cultural connect, the 21st relationships beat to a different pulse. They prefer the rhythm of commerce and investment and innovation and entrepreneurship. At the last ASEAN-India Summit meeting held last year, Prime Minister Narendra Modi described the two regions—ASEAN and India as the two bright spots of optimism amidst ongoing global economic uncertainties. Even so, the two way commercial exchange and investments have remained quite modest and below their potential. These can grow exponentially perhaps within certain parameters. The first of course would be the early conclusion of Regional Comprehensive Economic Partnership (RCEP) agreement. Discussions over the preceding two days would have underlined that this must go hand in hand with efforts to forge greater integration of the ASEAN and Indian economies for which harmonisation of standards and norms are a prerequisite. Connectivity and infrastructure lie at the heart of integration efforts as it key enablers. The pursuit of these objectives involves creating a range of regional public goods including investments in inter and intra-regional connectivity projects in five distinct clusters—trade, transportation, energy, infrastructure and communication technology and peoples. All these together with infrastructure building will facilitate the free and unfettered flow of goods, services, investment, persons, ideas, and technology between India and the ASEAN countries. Permeation of knowhow and technology through various connectivity network have a distinct bearing on the lives of the people by enabling their access to health, education, social insurance and improved state support and social solidarity for coping with the impact of climate change and natural disaster. ASEAN and India are committed in principle to meet these challenges by implementing their Five Year Plan of Action about which Secretary Shri Wadhwa has been speaking over the past two days. India has also conceived focused initiatives to incubate manufacturing hubs in the CLMV countries (Cambodia, Laos, Myanmar and Vietnam), through dedicated funding and EXIM bank loans. It is a good augury that the Plan of Action coincides with the establishment of the ASEAN Economic Community. It presents an opportunity for deepening our partnership with both ASEAN countries and India expected to grow at a healthy pace over the next decade. The Academic Session will focus on themes ranging from security of the Asia Pacific, to ocean dynamics, reinvigorating civilisational links and charting the way forward in order to give momentum to these relations as we approach the silver jubilee year next year. Our speakers include a mix of academicians, practitioners, and domain experts, and this should enable productive discussions.

The last two days of fruitful deliberations at the Business Session and the Ministerial Session is testimony to the fact that Delhi Dialogue has established itself as an important annual track 1.5 forum for discussing politico-security and economic issues between India and ASEAN. By allocating a full day exclusively for the Business Session, we have sought to provide a regular platform for the CEOs from India and ASEAN to share their experiences and suggest ways to move forward with accelerated B2B interactions. The Academic Session is the icing on the top. It is spread over four sessions: ASEAN and the Security of the Asia-Pacific; ASEAN-India; the Ocean Economy Dynamics and Reinvigorating the Civilisational Links and a final session on the Way Forward: Towards 25th Anniversary of ASEAN-India Relations.

For the Academic Session alone we have 12 speakers from nine ASEAN countries. Our attempt is to have a balanced representation from the ASEAN countries.

The Act East policy enunciated in 2014 is the culmination of India's growing economic, strategic and cultural linkages with the region to its east. India has been a consistent advocate of ASEAN centrality. Prime Minister Narendra Modi made it a point to attend the ASEAN-India Summits—in Nay Pyi Taw (2014) and then in Kuala Lumpur (2015). What the Act East policy has done is to bring into focus India's North East while reaffirming our linkages with the larger Asia-Pacific or the Indo-Pacific. The Indian diaspora in the region has an important role to play. Indian culture found a fertile ground in Southeast Asia where it was creatively adapted and modified into a unique syncretic whole. It is this which has imparted them the national and regional resilience.

India's accession to the Treaty of Amity and Cooperation and the Free Trade Agreement in goods and the entry into force of the Trade in Services and Investment Agreements in July 2015 has further cemented the relations. India also looks to progress in the negotiations on the Regional Comprehensive Economic Partnership Agreement (RCEP). While the growth of India-ASEAN trade to about $77 billion in 2014-15 is a promising development, there is scope for improvement through 'Make in India", 'Skill India' and 'Smart Cities'projects. ASEAN businesses could also look at investing in projects in North East India and Western Myanmar which are on the threshold of a transformation.

The growth in the economic partnership has paralleled the growth in the India-ASEAN political relationship which moved from sectoral partnership in 1992 to Full Dialogue Partnership and ARF and EAS membership later.

This event would not have been possible without active collaboration and cooperation among the Dialogue Partners. The Ministry of External Affairs deserves special mention for their unstinted support for the event. In this connection, I would like to thank Secretary (East) Mr Anil Wadhwa and Joint Secretary Ms. Pooja Kapur and her team for their help and support.

Thank you.

14

Keynote Address by Secretary (East), Mr Anil Wadhwa

Mr. Jayant Prasad, DG, IDSA;

Distinguished Academics & Opinion Makers from ASEAN Member States and India;

Ladies and Gentlemen,

It is a distinct privilege for me to address the academic session of Delhi Dialogue VIII in front of such a distinguished audience from India and ASEAN countries. In the last two days we have deliberated extensively on the economic, political and business aspects of India's engagement with ASEAN and, I am sure, the organisers would be able to cull out a number of recommendations from Delhi Dialogue VIII. We now turn our attention to Security, Maritime and Cultural issues.

2015 was an eventful year for the Asia-Pacific region in terms of regional security issues. The security issues of terrorism, moderation, cyber-crime, South China Sea were addressed throughout the year culminating in the 10th East Asia Summit (EAS), which was held in November, 2015. Counter-Terrorism and South China Sea issue dominated the proceedings in the wake of rise of ISIS, Paris Attacks and activities carried out in some of the islands of South China Sea. EAS participating countries, including Malaysia and Indonesia, rejected the brand of Islam being propagated by ISIS, and advocated undertaking effective counter-measures against ISIS, including promoting moderation and awareness about the true nature of Islam. Three Statements/

Declarations were adopted by EAS on counter-terrorism related issues, viz. on Countering Violent Extremism; Global Movement of Moderates, and on Information and Communication Technology (ICT) Security.

The adoption of a statement on countering violent extremism is to be seen as a continuation of the common resolve to counter terrorism and violent extremism displayed, during the 9th EAS in 2014, by way of adoption of a statement expressing deep concern on the rise of violent extremism and brutality committed by terrorist organisations in Iraq and Syria. The need to prevent the use of technology, communications and resources for criminal or terrorist purposes was also reflected in the statement on Information and Communications Technologies. The declaration on Global Movement of Moderates recognised that moderation can be a tool to counter violent extremism and supported education as an effective medium to prevent spread of violent extremism and to address its root causes.

India's peaceful settlement of the boundary with Bangladesh under UNCLOS was hailed as an example worthy of emulation by EAS participating countries during discussions on maritime security. They also called for resolution of dispute in the South China Sea in accordance with international law; upholding of Declaration of Conduct on South China Sea agreed between ASEAN and China; and early conclusion of a legally binding Code of Conduct on South China Sea, based on consensus.

In the very first month of 2016, we were confronted with terrorist attacks in Jakarta, Indonesia and in Pathankot, India. Terrorism has become a truly global scourge today. India has displayed early initiative in building a global resolve and new strategies for combating terrorism by tabling a Comprehensive Convention on International Terrorism at the United Nations almost two decades ago. The initiative has now gathered greater traction at a time when the spectre of global terrorism appears more threatening. We encourage a 'whole of the world' approach in countering terrorism.

We undertook several initiatives to promote greater cooperation with ASEAN on terrorism and security related issues in 2015. We sent a multi-agency delegation to visit ASEAN law enforcement institutes in June 2015. We jointly hosted, with Cambodia, an EAS Workshop and Dialogue on Regional Security Architecture at Phnom Penh in July 2015. We have also organised an ASEAN-India Cyber Security Conference in January 2015 in

New Delhi. We aim to host the first G-2-G ASEAN-India Cyber Dialogue in New Delhi in early 2016.

Maritime Cooperation has emerged as a significant priority area of cooperation. The Leaders adopted a statement on Enhancing Regional Maritime Cooperation in the Asia-Pacific at the 10th EAS which emphasised sustainable marine economic development. The EAS Conference on Maritime Security and Cooperation which India organised at the ASEAN-India Centre in November 2015 prior to the 10th EAS called for a more cooperative and integrated future for the region through overall development of an ocean-based blue economy. There is a need to ensure long-term sustainability of the coastal and marine ecosystems and the economy by moving from an ocean economy, to a blue economy the sustainable development of which requires careful balancing of human needs and ecosystem protection.

Developing a blue economy in our region would mean integrating its goals into our social, economic and environmental development. This is also the requirement of the 2030 Agenda for Sustainable Development. The new Sustainable Development Goal 2014 refers to the need to conserve and sustainably use marine resources.

We can develop a common regional vision for a blue economy through public private partnerships. Leveraging of technology, such as marine spatial planning, to harvest marine resources in a sustainable manner, is a priority. So also is the need to encourage the private sector to act more responsibly in its use of marine resources while participating in nine key marine resource based industries: Fisheries and Aquaculture; Ports, Shipping and Marine Transport; Tourism, Resorts and Coastal Development; Oil and Gas; Coastal Manufacturing; Seabed Mining; Renewable Energy; Marine Biotechnology; and Marine Technology and Environmental Services.

Sustained historical ties, culture and knowledge have continued to underpin India's interactions with South East Asia over two millenia. India's linkages with South East Asia, which came to be called Indo-China by Occidental scholars, date back to ancient times. The geographical peninsula that now contains most ASEAN nations was referred to as *Suvarna Bhumi* (Golden land) and *Suvarna Dwipa* (Golden Island) in the Ramayana. Indian influence spread to South East Asia via both land and sea routes. Traders, travellers, scholars and priests travelled far and wide from India, bringing the language, mythology, culture and religion of India with them. Evidence of linkages between Ancient India and South East Asia are found in many texts and in the folklore of the region. The Malay Annals, Burmese chronicles and ancient inscriptions in Vietnam, dating back to the 6th century AD in Sanskrit and Cham language at My Son Wat, demonstrate strong Indian linkages. Tamil literature of 2nd Century AD during Pandya and Chola Kingdoms, too, records trade with Malaysia.

Recognising these civilisational linkages, the ASEAN-India Vision Statement adopted at the ASEAN-India Commemorative Summit held in December 2012 encouraged the study, documentation and dissemination of knowledge about the civilisational links between ASEAN and India. In accordance with this mandate, we organised an International Conference on "ASEAN-India Cultural Links: Historical and Contemporary Dimensions", which was held in New Delhi on 23-24 July 2015.

One of the recommendations of the Conference was to continue the dialogue with renewed emphasis on history and culture. The Chair's statement on the 13th India-ASEAN Summit held in November 2015 has also encouraged holding a second conference. We intend to organise the 2nd ASEAN-India cultural relations conference at Jakarta in 2016. Eminent scholars and academicians, as well as the senior officials from both India and South East Asia will be invited to take part in this conference. I would like today's session to deliberate upon ways to document our cultural linkage by undertaking joint research projects.

Today's final session will discuss the way forward, bearing in mind that we are a year away from celebrating 25 years of ASEAN-India Dialogue Relations and 15 years of Summit level interaction in 2017.

It would be of immense interest to us to hear from all of you, creative suggestions on how we can commemorate this landmark in a befitting manner. I would like to contribute my two cents. Why don't we consider holding a year-long India-ASEAN commemoration, with a wide range of activities such as retracing journeys undertaken by Buddhist pilgrims, travelers and scholars of ancient times; re-enactment of historical events; and staging of performing arts which brings into life our shared cultural heritage. On this thought, let the academic session begin.

Thank you.

ASEAN AND SECURITY OF THE ASIA PACIFIC

Chaired by

Nalin Surie

15

Address by Founder and Chairman, Cambodian Institute for Cooperation and Peace

H.R.H. Norodom Sirivudh

ASEAN founded five decades ago is facing mounting strategic pressures and challenges. Without institutional reforms and capacity at the regional and national levels, ASEAN may loose its international role in maintaining peace and development.

The increasing strategic competition between China and the US and its allies in the Asia-Pacific is threatening regional peace and stability. China and US are the two main actors in the region. Peace or conflict depends very much on how they can co-exist and accommodate each other's core interests.

ASEAN's centrality in shaping the evolving regional security and economic architectures is critical to regional peace and development but that centrality role needs to be earned by each member of ASEAN and the whole ASEAN family. If the members of ASEAN are not resilient in the face of major power competition and rivalry, its future is bleak.

Uncertainty and unpredictability are hampering economic development prospect of the region. The rising tensions in the East and South China Seas, the irrationality and unpredictability of North Korea, and the water security and conflict in the Mekong region are the sources of regional security concern.

Now the question is who will be responsible to maintain regional order and peace. The answer is clear. Every state, regardless of their size and power, shares responsibility in maintaining peace and stability. International law and rules-based international relations need to be strictly observed.

So far no superpower has been the role model in promoting rules-based international relations. The hegemonic power, the US, has low record in respecting international laws. While the US is intervening in the South China Sea under the purview of freedom of navigation, it has not acceded to the United Nations Convention on the Law of the Sea (UNCLOS). The US's intervention in regional affairs is counter-productive to regional peace and stability.

China, as an emerging power, is learning from the US in expanding its global influence. China is trying to create a new world order featuring emerging powers. China promotes a multipolar world in which global and regional actors can act in unison to collectively address global issues. However, China has not proven to be the global leader, which adheres to the principles of international law. The way China is handling the disputes in the South China Sea is damaging China's global image as a peaceful-development-oriented global power.

Regardless of its past record of successfully going through the storm of the Cold War, ASEAN is facing a new turn in its history. Complex power competition and interdependence put ASEAN at serious test. The differences among the members with regards to regionally sensitive issues such as the South China Sea, haze, and the Mekong River need to be holistically addressed. National and regional interests need to be balanced and harmonised.

Japan and India are other two main actors in regional security issues. India's Look East policy and Japan's Proactive Pacifism demonstrates a more assertive approach towards the Indo-Pacific region. A complex interaction and interdependence among China, India, Japan, and US is critical to regional peace and development.

ASEAN plays crucial role in creating safe space for these countries to interact and build trust. The region would be more uncertain and risky if ASEAN is not in existence. ASEAN does not only build the habit of cooperation but also a habit of respect of international laws and rules-based international relations.

Creation and promotion of norms and rules-based international relations should be the two main functions of ASEAN in coming decades. Socialising major power, deepening complex interdependence, and building common norms are essential to peace and stability.

India and other major powers should invest more in strengthening the capacity and role of ASEAN. It is not for the interest of ASEAN and its member states but for all countries in the region. ASEAN-centric regional order should be promoted and nurtured.

Our security is interconnected. My security is your security. Your security is my security. A strong and relevant ASEAN serves the interests of all. India-ASEAN strategic partnership plays important role in strengthening the role of ASEAN. India should further support ASEAN on maritime security, water-energy-food security nexus, cyber security, climate change, and transnational crimes.

India and the Mekong countries should work closer together on water resource security and sustainable governance of trans-boundary water resource. The Mekong River is being threatened by a series of hydropower dams construction along the mainstream of the Mekong River.

Thank you.

16

ASEAN Centrality and the Security of Asia Pacific

Navrekha Sharma

Since 1967, ASEAN (led in all but name by Indonesia) has gained a formidable reputation as an inclusive and consensus based forum for multilateral diplomacy. It has spawned a sophisticated array of sometimes overlapping institutions to promote peaceful interaction among its stakeholders who include the world's most powerful (or potentially most powerful) countries. In comparison to them, all ASEAN countries—except Indonesia—are like minnows among whales! Yet, at the Chulalongkorn University, Indian Vice President Hamid Ansari only recently expressed India's firm faith in ASEAN and its related institutions to help with promoting India's growing engagement in the Asia Pacific under the Act East Policy. He also reminded his audience that India has some very special civilisational links with the ASEAN, which makes her a comfortable and trusted international partner.

Perhaps it is appropriate at this stage to remember that half the world's merchandise shipping and a quarter of its petroleum passes through the Straits of Malacca, while a significant amount of bulk carriers, too big to use the Malacca Route, pass through the Straits of Lombok and Makassar, and that all these are in ASEAN controlled waters.

As the flow of trade and energy—vital for development of South, South East, and East Asia (and of countries across the Pacific)—increases, so will the potential for historical disputes over sovereignty and ownership. Will they be contained? Or, will they reach a point of no return? Will ASEAN remain centre stage in managing on going rapid developments, both external and internal? Or, will it, as some people fear, collapse from institutional overload?

How long will ASEAN continue to display the robustness, capacity, and willingness to shape the "Asian Century" which India so much wants it to do?

ASEAN has grown slowly and steadily over nearly fifty years to become today the world's most successful regional organisation. Its success rate in forging intra-ASEAN economic integration has been positive; but even more positive has been her management of cross cutting pressures which have been growing in tandem with the region's complex security needs. During, but especially after, the Cold War, ASEAN's role as architect of the parameters of the dialogue between stakeholders in the Asia Pacific, her capacity to anticipate shifting world trends and to shape the agenda accordingly, and its capacity to re-imagine itself with changing external circumstances, has been nothing short of remarkable. Mandated by the Treaty of Amity and Cooperation (TAC) to forgo war as a means of settling disputes, ASEAN has succeeded in making the idea of war unthinkable: an achievement which SAARC next door could emulate. The proof, if proof be needed, of ASEANs wisdom and far sightedness can be gauged from the puny defence budgets of member States in comparison with the boom in their populations and economies.

Undoubtedly, the security umbrella of the USA and its alliance system during (and even after) the Cold War helped; but even so, ASEAN's success in equitable economic growth was by no means guaranteed: witness there cord of many countries in other parts of the world who have also been recipients of US largess.

The credit for ASEAN's early success goes to its leadership and its distinct style. This has sometimes been criticized for its ambivalence and indirect approach, but which succeeded because it was understood and broadly accepted by ASEAN's many diverse and often disputatious members, who became even more diverse in ideology and economic standards after they were joined by Cambodia, Vietnam, Laos, and Myanmar in the early 1990s. By honing a familial culture of trust and confidentiality, non-interference in internal affairs and decision by consensus, ASEAN built up formidable political capital. Indonesia went even further, deliberately keeping a low profile and leading, so to say, "from behind". This strategy set the stage for interpersonal trust and group harmony which, in turn, fostered inclusive and broad based growth in each member country, not only of its elite (wherein corruption has also thrived, alas!). This was the secret of the national resilience which was so admirably displayed by ASEAN (and Indonesia in particular), in the Financial Crisis of 1997-8.

In 1993, with the Cold War over, ASEAN added a Security forum (ARF) to allow "Dialogue Partners" to engage in discussions of Traditional, and increasingly, Non Traditional Security—that is, piracy, drug trafficking, oil spills, haze, uncontrolled migration, child trafficking, diseases of various kinds, and later and most disturbing of all, Islamic terrorism. All these and more followed the contraction of USA's full spectrum dominance of the waters of the Asia Pacific. ASEAN, which was used to seeing these problems as domestic (hence not to beaired openly) now recognised the need for inter-state cooperation in sensitive areas. In the centre of ARF it placed itself to do what it does best: that is, use its accumulated credibility and diplomatic prowess to encourage all stakeholders to bring their security problems to a common table. Unlike NATO, ARF is inclusive, and prevents no one, regardless of size or ideological persuasion, from expressing his/her views. It has been sometimes criticized as a talk shop; but it has nonetheless been used gratefully by all major powers.

After the financial crisis, ASEAN introduced some even more drastic changes to its institutional structure. As Chairman of ASEAN, in 2003, Indonesia (now a democracy and determined to make up for lost time), proposed at the Bali Summit to dilute the earlier culture of ambivalence, and institutionalise ASEAN's aims and objectives through a Charter, which would also provide for a Human Rights Watchdog. The earlier informal approach had outlived its usefulness, and had indeed cost the country and its neighbours dearly by failing to provide early warning signals of the impending crash. The Bali Summit also launched a proposal for an ASEAN Community by 2020 (later advanced to 2015) which was conceptualized in three ways: the Politico-Security Community, the Economic Community, and the Socio-Cultural Community. These three Bodies were expected to encourage the gradual replacement of National identities with a Regional or ASEAN identity, necessary to prevent ASEAN from pulling indifferent directions (as had happened during the Crisis).

Another major change in response to the financial crisis was APT: that is, ASEAN plus Three (China, Japan and Korea), an institution set up in gratitude for help given in ASEAN's hour of need with the setting up of a Currency

Swop Arrangement for ASEAN. China in particular had refrained from taking advantage of the Crisis by devaluing her currency. APT is today the most energetic of ASEAN-spawned Institutions; but it is exclusive, and several Asia Pacific players are not in it.

A few years later, in 2005 therefore—perhaps to hedge against the possibility of China's rise not being as peaceful as promised, or may be to ensure that it would be as peaceful as promised!—ASEAN was persuaded by Indonesia and Singapore (disregarding strong Chinese objections) to set up yet another Institution: the EAS or East Asia Summit. It comprises ASEAN, plus APT, plus Australia, New Zealand and India, to which were added the USA and Russia in 2011. The ADMM Plus and the RCEP are the last two institutions to be established (or at least conceived of), for Security consultations at the Defence Ministerial level as well as to bring the different FTAs of ASEAN under one umbrella, respectively.

This in brief, is the trajectory which ASEAN has followed to arrive at where it is today. At each stage, it has ensured the continuity of two central ideas: decisions are arrived at by consensus; and that no stakeholder, however small and powerless, fails to get a hearing. It is the world's only known multilateral organisation in which the weak lead the strong. More accurately, ASEAN "persuades" and "socializes" its dialogue partners; it does not lead them! It persuades by example, and ensures that it remains focused on the common good. Amitav Acharya even says that Asia's changing regional environment is more likely to change Chinese and Great Power behaviour, than vice versa. This may sound audacious, but one can hardly not agree.

Paradoxically, in 2016, when the ASEAN Community has supposedly arrived, the exuberance one would expect is nowhere to be seen! Instead there is apprehension—perhaps a crisis of confidence—as ASEAN members are expressing doubts about ASEAN's longevity and capacity to cope with demands on its time and resources. According to newspaper reports, the goalpost of "ASEAN Community Vision" has now been moved to 2025, to allow time for deeper public identification with the concept. Reducing sovereignty is apparently too radical a concept still for many ASEAN members to whole heartedly support.

As with several crises which have faced ASEAN in the past, the key to unlocking this one too may lie in Indonesia. A feeling has emerged of late—

encouraged by Indonesian officials themselves—that Indonesia has outgrown ASEAN, and that she neither cares about ASEAN concerns nor is giving the priority to smoothening ruffled feathers within the organisation as she did earlier. In his election campaign, President Jokowi said that the South China Sea dispute is "other countries' problem"; and recently, a key Indonesian official declared that ASEAN is no longer "the" pillar of Indonesia's Foreign Policy, but only "a" pillar. Indeed, the same official has gone public to declare his pique at the lack of sympathy which Indonesia receives from ASEAN on issues that concern herself, despite her bending backwards to meet other ASEAN concerns. One example of the lack of sympathy he cites is Indonesia's proposal (as Chairman made at Bali in 2003) for a Peace keeping Force for ASEAN. Recent newspaper reports are suggesting that this may be set up now.

I am confident, however, that these signals are not life threatening for ASEAN. President Jokowi is by nature a bi-lateralist, and a change of style is expected with a change of Presidency. He has launched a bold new initiative for Indonesia: a vision of a Global Maritime Fulcrum spanning the Indian and Pacific Oceans and, by drawing in massive Chinese investments for it, he is not only realising his vision but hedging against the possibility of a China upping the ante on Natuna. He wants to connect the far flung Provinces of Indonesia, which will only secure Indonesia and her neighbourhood from Jihadi terror. The boosting up of Indonesia's puny defence and naval capabilities will no doubt help. By becoming a "realist" (as reports suggest) and seemingly warming upto China, it does not necessarily follow that Indonesia under President Jokowi has forgotten the imperative of a Free and Active Foreign Policy or the idea of "Strategic Autonomy". De-prioritising the neighbourhood would surely only jeopardize Indonesia's own security in the long run!

Perhaps, Indonesia's foreign policy advisors are only suggesting to ASEAN that she need no longer be willing to keep a low profile and "lead from behind", as she has been doing earlier. Maybe, the confident and democratic Indonesia under a new President is unwilling to continue merely as the "thought leader" of ASEAN—that is, *without* open acknowledgement of her leadership status. I have no doubt that the ASEAN countries will be able to sort out their existential problems sooner rather than later. Without Indonesia, ASEAN may as well cease to exist just as, conversely, without ASEAN Indonesia will surely carry less international weight!

More important is the problem of the lack of resources to run the ASEAN Secretariat and the work overload from organising over 1000 meetings annually, an ever growing agenda, and insufficient powers for the SG. Suggestions for trimming the workload, prioritizing projects, upgrading the SGs role, and even creating a new Secretariat for EAS have been made, and are no doubt being considered. Many countries, including India, have posted an Ambassador to ASEAN who is available for consultations if required. Strengthening EAS certainly seems like a good idea.

As for external pressures on ASEAN, the most serious of these is the possibility of its cracking up under the opposing pulls of the USA and China. That ASEAN will not be able to withstand such pressure was clear in Cambodia in 2012 when a Communiqué citing the South China Sea failed to be adopted. There are also strains building up from TPP and AIIB which have divided the members of ASEAN. Singapore's Prime Minister Loong hopes that, eventually, China will join the TPP, and that the USA and Japan will join the AIIB. India—which doesn't belong to any Alliance system (however closely her interests may lie with some powers)—must surely endorse Loong's view. Indeed, for all her Dialogue partners, especially those in rival camps, to manage Security without ASEAN at the centre is unthinkable.

As a permanent member of UNSC, China is actually quite comfortable with the world order, and unlikely to want it changed (except in some details). It has much to lose in terms of access to the global commons itself if there is too much volatility in the South China Sea. Every major power in the world, including the USA and China, is today too intimately connected with the world's financial, production and manufacturing networks to want to risk the rupture of the existing order.

India fully supports the ASEAN route to peace and community building in the ASIA Pacific through inclusivity and consensus. Aiming to gain legitimacy rather than exercising raw power is always better policy. The alternative scenario of carving out exclusive spheres of influence is too grim to contemplate and, in any case, it is anomalous in today's interconnected world.

In conclusion, ASEAN will no doubt deliver peace as wisely in the Asia Pacific in the future as it has in the past. However, that in today's scenario, she will need the wisdom and support of all other stake holders more than ever. If there has been a feeling that India has not lived up to its role as security provider, it should have been put to rest since Prime Minister Modi came to power. Today, the Indian Government is collaborating fully with regional players in the security domain. Evidence of India's prowess and willingness to serve the cause of Peace and Security in the Asia Pacific was fully on display at the second edition of the International Fleet Review at Visakhapatnam (4-8 February 2016), where India's Prime Minister affirmed that the security and growth of all in the Indian Ocean region is one of his government's top priorities. In other words, ASEAN should have no doubts about India's support to its goals.

17

ASEAN's Diminishing Role in East Asian Regional Security Architecture[1]

Renato Cruz De Castro

This paper examines the Association of Southeast Asian Nations' (ASEAN') diminishing security role in East Asia in the light of the South China Sea dispute. Since the early 1990s, ASEAN member states have tried to address the dispute by trying to embed China into the association's system of diplomatic consultations and confidence-building measures aimed at building mutual trust on a multilateral basis, with the eventual goals of mitigating existing disputes and finding means of resolving them. Unfortunately, China has prevented the ASEAN member states from pulling it into this diplomatic process. In fact, China has succeeded in dividing these small powers and, in effect, weakening ASEAN as a regional organisation. Alarmed by China's growing strategic clout in the South China Sea, and the ASEAN's eroding role in managing this territorial row, the USA and Japan have strategically balanced this emergent power from realising its long-term objective in the South China Sea—total sea control. In the long run, the current strategic impasse between China on the one hand, and the USA and Japan on the other hand can lead to a major armed confrontation that can effectively divide ASEAN, and cause its weakening as a regional association committed to peace and stability.

The South China Sea Dispute

The South China Sea is a semi-enclosed sea surrounded by China as well as several small and militarily weak Southeast Asian powers such as the

Philippines, Vietnam, Malaysia, and Brunei. For almost three decades, these littoral states have been involved in a chronic competition as each one seeks to extend its sovereignty and jurisdictional claims over more than a hundred islets, reefs, and rocks and their surrounding waters. The dispute became dormant in the late 1990s and the early 21st century, after China and the Association of Southeast Asian Nations (ASEAN) signed the 2002 Declaration on the Conduct (DOC) of Parties in the South China Sea. A non-binding political statement, the DOC set out for trust and confidence-building measures as well as five voluntary cooperative activities among the claimant states. The parties reaffirmed that "the adoption of a code of conduct in the South China Sea would further promote peace and stability in the region and agree to work, on the basis of consensus, towards the eventual realisation of this objective."[2] The parties also agreed to exercise restraint, and refrain from activities that would complicate the dispute.[3]

However, tension arising from this maritime row increased again in 2009 when China discarded its tactic of delaying the resolution of the dispute, and asserted instead its sovereignty over the contested waters. In an assertive posture, China consolidated its jurisdictional claims in the South China Sea by expanding its military reach, and pursuing coercive diplomacy against the other claimant states.[4] Since 2009, Chinese leaders have felt confident that, with its political and economic clout and its strong People's Liberation Army (PLA), China can boldly advance its "core interests" in the maritime domain. This thrust is reflected in China's insistence on the "Air Defense Identification Zone (ADIZ)" in the East China Sea, the conduct of live-fire exercises by the People's Liberation Army Navy (PLAN), the People's Liberation Army Air Force (PLAAF) in the West Pacific, and the hard-line response of PLAN and other maritime law enforcement agencies during several confrontations with Philippine and Vietnamese civilian ships in the South China Sea.[5] This shift in diplomatic tactics is aimed to deter other smaller claimant states like the Philippines and Vietnam from cementing their claims, and to enable China to negotiate with these small powers from a position of strength.

This maritime dispute caught the attention of the USA early on, and it has been trying to maintain its naval primacy in East Asia, especially in the face of China's emergence as an economic and military power. In 2011, the Obama Administration announced the US strategic rebalancing to the Asia-

Pacific region. The move was made to ensure that the US diplomatic initiative of a comprehensive "rule-based" system to resolve the East Asian states' clashing claims in the South China Sea is backed by American military power.[6] Interestingly, Japan has also become interested in the dispute. As China's geo-strategic rival and USA's key ally in East Asia, Japan is bent on playing a balancing role in the dispute by helping other claimant states build up their respective naval capabilities. Alarmed by the PLAN's actions in the contested sea, the USA (with the support of Japan and other allies) displays its naval and air power to prevent China from establishing its primacy in the region.[7] This situation enables these two naval powers to demonstrate their maritime prowess and draw their long-range surveillance and strike capabilities to maintain their 'forces over-horizon' and projecting power against an expansionist China in the South China Sea.[8] The growing involvement of the USA and Japan in the South China Sea dispute has generated a strategic balance in the region with respect to the South China Sea dispute.

Trapped in this potentially dangerous strategic balance in East Asia are the small claimant states—the Philippines, Vietnam, Brunei Darussalam, and Malaysia. These small powers find themselves in a classic security dilemma in which the actions of China—the most powerful claimant state in the dispute—are viewed as extremely threatening by the other claimants.[9] Since the early 1990s, these small powers, through the Association of Southeast Asian Nations (ASEAN), have tried to peacefully manage the dispute by relying on the association's methods of conflict avoidance and management to de-escalate the tension without resolving the dispute. This involves fostering the habit of constructive dialogue and consultation on political and security issues of common interests and concerns in order to make significant efforts towards confidence-building and security cooperation in the Asia-Pacific.[10] Unfortunately, the above-mentioned developments have squarely pushed the small Southeast Asian states in the middle of a strategic stand-off between China and the USA/Japan that has the potential of igniting into a major systemic conflict in the 21st century.

This paper examines the limits of the ASEAN's approach in managing security matters in general, and in particular, maritime security issues in the light of the growing involvement of the great powers in the South China Sea dispute. It addresses this main question: how has the involvement of the great powers in the South China Sea dispute diminished ASEAN's role in addressing maritime disputes in East Asia? It also explores the following questions: What is the nature of ASEAN's methods of managing security issues in general, and maritime security issues in particular? What are the strengths and limitations of these methods? How has China successfully exploited the limitations of the ASEAN approach in handling maritime security issues? What will be the long term implications of ASEAN's diminishing role in the management of the South China Sea dispute?

The Limits of the ASEAN Approach to Security: A Focus on the ARF

The ASEAN approach to security is reflected in the formation of the ASEAN Regional Forum (ARF) in 1995, and its subsequent foray into regional security affairs. The ARF was formed during a three-hour, low-key gathering in July 1994, immediately after the Association of Southeast Asian Nations (ASEAN) Foreign Ministers' Meeting. It is ASEAN's first and tentative venture into the field of regional security. The ARF is not an institution for collective defense; nor is it a concert for the management of regional security.[11] It is based on the ASEAN-derived approach of cooperative security which involves the building of trust on a multilateral basis with the goal of mitigating existing disputes, and eventually finding means of resolving them.[12]

Figuratively speaking, the ARF was created to tame or domesticate the foreign policy behavior of the People's Republic of China (PRC). The forum was originally envisioned as a way to entrap China—then a potentially rising hegemon and an extra-regional state with territorial claims in the waters surrounding Southeast Asia—into accepting the ASEAN's set of regional norms. This strategy hoped to temper China's hostile stance against the other claimant states, enhance defense transparency, and promote peaceful and cooperative solutions to existing disputes. China's current behavior is a dream come true for the founders of ARF. It joined the ARF to avoid being left out of the regional grouping, and has since supported the ASEAN's central role and its incremental approach to problem-solving. Since the late 1990s, it has highlighted the importance of the ASEAN states' leading role in the ARF in pushing forward regional security dialogues and confidence-building measures. Furthermore, Beijing has ushered the regional forum in further exploring as well as developing dialogues and cooperation in addressing non-traditional security challenges (such as terrorism) and in expanding the forum to include the participation of defence officials.[13]

However, the small powers in Southeast Asia are realistic enough to know that an effective engagement policy with China requires the involvement of other regional powers.[14] These small powers have been more than willing to engage Beijing in several cooperative undertakings. However, at the same time, they also recognise the importance of keeping the USA and Japan involved in regional affairs. The presence of these two other powers is insurance for constraining and balancing China just in case the small powers' engagement policy fails to socialise this emerging power into a *status quo* power. As a group of small powers with limited military and economic capabilities, the ASEAN states have had no choice but to

> exploit the tendencies of the big powers to both cooperate and compete among themselves, as well as their physical presence in the region, to make it possible and desirable for them to monitor each other's activities while keeping an eye on developments in Southeast Asia.[15]

And in doing this, they have also seen the need to form a multilateral security forum that can hopefully mitigate post-Cold War era's strategic uncertainties that were revolving around two major dynamics: a) the changing weight and position of the major powers in the region; and b) the changing pattern of their relationships in the light of the withdrawal, and eventual disappearance, of Soviet power from East Asia.

In the mid-1990s, the ASEAN countries were concerned about the implications of China's growing economy and military power. They feared that China's military assertiveness could set the stage for an intense Sino-Japanese rivalry.[16] Furthermore, they believed that a strong American response to Chinese belligerence could stoke nationalist and hard-line sentiments in China and destabilise the region.[17] The realists, for their part, also acknowledged the ARF as a balance-of-power mechanism to which most member states defer in managing the trilateral China-USA-Japan relations.[18]

Both the liberals and the realists discerned the ARF merely as an instrument, and ignored its primary but indirect objectives. Whether fostering norms, inculcating values, or maintaining the balance of power, the ARF's end goal is to create a regional order based on 1) transparency in strategic intent and threat perceptions; 2) mutual trust and confidence with regard to the member-states' military capabilities and deployment; and 3) habit of cooperation which will facilitate the peaceful resolution of existing and future conflicts.[19] The late Michael Leifer observed that "the ARF aims to contribute to the promotion of a predictable and constructive pattern of relationship in the Asia-Pacific."[20] As such, the ARF is similar to other forms of behavior and mechanisms that regulate relations among states.

Such patterns of managing interstate relations include the Concert of Europe, alliance systems, crisis management, bipolar alliance structures, spheres of influence, and systems with features resembling the more traditional balance of power.[21] However, what differentiates the ARF from these examples is its objective to foster an international (or regional) order that deviates from the use of force in settling interstate disputes. Like in collective security, arms control, and the development of international law, the ARF wants a certain degree of institutional or cultural constraint on the use of force in effecting change in the system.[22] As Amitav Acharya succinctly pointed out, "a major goal of the ARF is to discourage the use of force by its member states to settle disputes."[23]

However, the ASEAN or its offspring organisations (like the ARF), possess no significant centralised mechanism to enforce agreements signed by their members, monitor domestic events in member countries, or anticipate emerging problems. The bottom line of the "ASEAN Way" in foreign affairs is moral persuasion.[24] This orientation restricts the forum's ability to maintain the status quo or effect a gradual and peaceful change in the regional system. Many regional security problems cannot be solved through ARF's dialogues, or through the ASEAN method of consensus-building because of the historical origins of and the stakes involved in these disputes. The ASEAN and the ARF assume that most disputes arise because of simple misunderstanding and lack of trust, and that these squabbles can be mitigated by communication and confidence-building. Actually, many historic and lingering conflicts stem from competition over scarce resources, strategic advantage, control over a certain population, tilting the balance of power, or from the desire to be the major hegemonic power. These issues can only be resolved when the states involved (usually the great powers) agree to compromise or settle them through a systemic conflict or a hegemonic war.[25] Neither communication nor confidence-building by themselves can never redefine what vital interests are involved; nor will they resolve the clash of national interests.

The small powers of Southeast Asia, even acting collectively and cohesively within the ASEAN and the ARF, cannot definitively manage any security challenge or any unexpected change in East Asia. The best they can do is to influence the major powers in ways that may further their interests and manage any changes in the status quo. These small powers still need to obtain the tacit support of the great powers to let them occupy the ARF's driver's seat. However, occupying the driver's seat does not automatically mean that they can steer the forum's course and agenda to where they want it *without* the concurrence of the great powers in the ARF. Being on the driver's seat also means seeking consultation as well as recognising the great powers' various positions and competing interests on regional security issues, and managing their own collective affairs as small powers. The ASEAN states must be able to manage the conflicting and sometimes converging interests of the great powers and their support and participation in the ARF. As Jurgen Haacke observes,

> to uphold ASEAN's on position in the ARF and to ensure that the Forum remains central to security cooperation in the wider East Asia, ASEAN decision-makers accept that it is necessary to steer a middle path between defending the ASEAN way and embracing new understanding of some of its norms.[26]

The general stability of the inter-great powers relationship is critically important to the ARF's survival as well as viability as a regional security forum for East Asia. Any regression to any adversarial relations among the great powers may cause this group of small powers to take sides or be paralyzed into a form of passive neutrality. Furthermore, this forum can only make substantive progress if there is cooperation among the great powers. Cooperation among the great powers means that they all accept the status quo—or at least they all believe in the importance of a "peaceful change" in East Asia.[27] However, the limits of the ASEAN approach to maritime security would be tested by China's incremental efforts to alter the status quo in the South China Sea, and in the process of pursuing this goal, it created fissures within this regional association.

The South China Sea Dispute and the Limits of the ASEAN's Way

Among the claimant states, China poses the biggest challenge to any efforts to either resolve/manage or escalate the South China Sea dispute and the tension associated with it.[28] Needless to say, China is the largest and most powerful of the littoral states, which has established sovereign control of the southernmost islands of Hainan and the Paracel Islands in the South China Sea. It has also declared full sovereignty over most of the contested sea based on an old and official Chinese map featuring a nine-dotted line that extends as far south as the northern Malaysian and Bruneian coast.[29] In effect, by consolidating its claim over the South China Sea, China enhances its territorial integrity and national security. Nevertheless, from the viewpoint of the small Southeast Asian states, this move is clearly an ominous act of Chinese expansionism in an area of key strategic location and potential economic resources.[30]

Confronted by China's incremental efforts to alter the status quo in the South China Sea, ASEAN member states have applied the ASEAN-derived regional diplomacy to embed China in a regional maritime consensus.[31] Initially, China refused to be part of the ASEAN way of managing the dispute as it considered the South China Sea dispute as a bilateral rather than multilateral issue.[32] Eventually, it changed its position, and rhetorically adopted ASEAN's norms and principles as its style of informal diplomacy.[33] On 2 September 2002, ASEAN and China signed the "Declaration on a Code of Conduct (DOC) for the South China Sea." This was primarily a political statement of broad principles of behavior, aimed to stabilise the situation in the South China Sea and prevent any accidental outbreak of conflict in the disputed areas. In addition, the two sides pledged to practice self-restraint in activities that could escalate the disputes, and to deepen their efforts to "build trust and confidence between and among them."[34]

Interestingly, when it was signed in 2002, the DOC was considered as an interim accord as well as the first step for further cooperation between China and the ASEAN member states. The two sides, therefore, were expected to continue working on the eventual adoption of a binding code of conduct in the South China Sea. ASEAN's goal is to move from a DOC to a legally binding Code of Conduct, and not just a broad statement of principles. However, China has resisted such efforts.[35] Consequently, little progress has been made towards the implementation of the DOC as well as the eventual negotiation of a legally binding COC. Ten years after China and the ASEAN signed the DOC, the two parties have not even started the negotiations for the COC for the simple reason that China has declared that the time is not yet ripe to do so.[36] This impasse stems from the fact that the ASEAN member states and China do not share the same objectives on the COC. On the one hand, the Southeast Asian states would like to conclude a COC as quickly as possible so that China would be drawn deeper into the ASEAN process of peaceful consultations and conflict-avoidance. On the other hand, as a great power, China doesn't want to be embedded into any diplomatic system created by small powers. Interestingly, it wants first the full implementation of a non-binding DOC before any formal negotiations on the COC could begin. It supports a step-by-step approach whereby the conclusion of a legally binding COC is perceived as a long-term rather than as an immediate goal.[37]

In 2013, Foreign Minister Wang Yi declared that China is in no hurry to conclude an agreement on a COC as he insisted that cooperative activities and confidence-building measures in the DOC must first be implemented.[38] This process, however, could take years.[39] China's efforts to delay any negotiation with ASEAN for a legally binding COC stem from two reasons. Firstly, it is part of China's delaying strategy in resolving territorial disputes that involves maintaining a state's claim to a piece of land but neither offering concessions nor outright use of force.[40] This strategy is premised on maintaining existing claims in a dispute. The goal is to consolidate China's claims, especially to maritime rights or jurisdiction over these waters, and to deter other states from strengthening their own claims at China's expense, including resource development projects that exclude China.[41] Secondly, Chinese officials have argued that since the South China Sea is a Chinese territory anyway, a COC with the smaller claimant states is not relevant to their eventual goal in the dispute territory—total sea control.

China has not only prevented ASEAN from effectively embedding it into the association's way of managing security issues by stonewalling the Southeast Asian states' efforts to negotiate a multilateral and legally binding COC. More importantly, it has also effectively neutralised the regional organisation by creating division within ASEAN by slicing off its member states one by one. Called Salami strategy by a noted American academic, this tactic involves offering each claimant state a joint development venture as a means of resolving the South China Sea dispute.[42] This is an important component of China's diplomatic initiative—that is, of "setting aside disputes and pursuing joint development" with a claimant state on the disputed maritime territories that from China's perspective actually belong to it.[43]

China was able to apply this tactic when it convinced the Philippines and Vietnam to join a Joint Maritime Seismic Undertaking (JMSU) in the South China Seas. However, by joining the JMSU, the Philippines and Vietnam became complicit in China's Salami Strategy for two reasons:[44]

> a) the agreement undercuts the position of two ASEAN member states—Malaysia and Brunei—since it tacitly lends validity to China's extreme claims to islands and maritime space in the South China Sea; and b) by signing a trilateral deal, the Philippines and Vietnam derogated the united front that ASEAN had successful formed to deal with China in the South China Sea. Accordingly, the forging of the original bilateral agreement with China bereft of any consultation with the ASEAN members states could be seen as a violation of the spirit, if not the letter, of the 2002 ASEAN-China Declaration on the Conduct of Parties in the South China Sea (DOC). As one Australian analyst notes:
>
>> the Philippine government has broken ranks with the Association of Southeast Asian Nations, which was dealing with China as a bloc on the South China Sea issue.... Through its actions, Manila has given legitimacy to China's legally spurious "historic claim" to most of the South China Sea.[45]

In 2012, China again applied the Salami tactic against the Southeast Asian states during the 45th ASEAN Annual Meeting in Phnom Penh. This was the first time in ASEAN history when the ministerial meeting was not able to issue a formal communiqué. This unfortunate incident was the result of Cambodian Foreign Minister Hor Nam Hang's objection to any mention of the 2012 stand-off between Filipino and Chinese civilian vessels near the Scarborough Shoal and to the Vietnamese and Filipino proposals that the communiqué should refer to the various marine incidents involving their ships and Chinese patrol boats.[46] Despite efforts by Indonesia and Singapore to broker a compromise over the wording of the South China Sea section of the communiqué, Hor Nam Hong rejected the wording of several successive drafts.

He insisted that bilateral disputes with an outside power were not an appropriate subject for an ASEAN communiqué, although such disputes have been discussed in various ASEAN meetings.[47] Acting as the ASEAN chair, Cambodia sought to appease Beijing by taking into account its concerns, and minimising the internationalisation of the South China Sea dispute.[48] Consequently, for the first time in ASEAN's 45 years of existence, a joint AMM communiqué was not issued.

By vetoing any reference to the 2012 Scarborough Shoal stand-off, Cambodia took China's position that the South China Sea dispute should not be discussed in an international forum, especially when it involves external powers, preferring instead to negotiate bilaterally with the Southeast Asian claimant states.[49] Consequently, the possibility of ASEAN becoming more divided over the South China Sea issue is a real possibility given the member states' divergent views of this issue as well as, more significantly, China's creeping influence within the association as a result of its growing economic and military capabilities. Observing the cleavage within ASEAN over the South China Sea dispute, Professor Sheldon Simon notes the following:

> In retrospect the absence of ASEAN agreement on such a politically sensitive topic as the SCS should not have been surprising—disappointing perhaps but not surprising... When it comes to dealing with China, they vary considerably, all the way from serving as a diplomatic surrogate for Beijing (Cambodia) to being willing to directly confront PRC and attempt to obtain open military support of the U.S. (Philippines) to points in between, where keeping a low profile and adopt a hedging strategy is followed (Malaysia).[50]

The East Asian Regional Balance of Power and its Dangers

China's adroit ability to prevent the Southeast Asian states from embedding it into its system of peaceful consultations and conflict avoidance as well as its efforts to divide this regional association have diminished ASEAN's role in managing the South China Sea dispute. In effect, it has weakened the ASEAN-centric security institutions as part of the emerging security structure in East Asia. This trend continues as the disparity of economic and military power between China and the ASEAN member states become wider and obvious. Consequently, this has alarmed the other great powers in the region that have been warily observing ASEAN's diminishing role in the South China Sea dispute in particular, and in regional security affairs in general. In November 2011, the Obama Administration announced a strategic pivot to the Asia-Pacific region. Accordingly, this refocusing of American strategic attention to the Asia-Pacific is "to ensure that the USA will play a larger and long-term role in reshaping the region and its future." The main gambit is backed by the diplomatic strategy of constraining China with a stick. It does not envision a Cold War type containment of China which is deemed simplistic and wrong, but to make China acknowledge "America's strength, determination, and strategy."[51] Its ultimate goal is to shape the norms and rules of the Asia-Pacific region, to ensure that

> international law and norms be respected, that commerce and freedom of navigation are not impeded, that emerging powers build trust with their neighbors, and that disagreements are resolved peacefully without threats of coercion.[52]

The USA's strategic rebalancing to Asia provides further impetus for Japan (China's traditional rival in East Asia) to balance China in the South China Sea. It entails strengthening American presence in Japan and South Korea—the cornerstone of the strategy—even as the USA also builds up its security relationship with other states in and around Southeast Asia.[53] Specific to the maritime issue, the USA always underscores that the freedom of navigation in the disputed sea that can only be guaranteed if the South China Sea remains a global common—that is, it belongs to all states, and is not subject to sovereign control by a single powerful regional state. Hence, in line with this policy, the Obama Administration supports the coalition of states that can constrain China in the South China Sea dispute.

China claims almost 80 per cent of the South China Sea. However, it cannot exercise complete territorial control over the Spratlys and its surrounding waters since basically these land features are occupied by the other claimant states, and more significantly, because of the growing involvement of the USA and Japan in the maritime dispute. The USA is troubled by China's bullying behavior towards the small claimant states. By all appearances, it assumes that any Chinese use of force against the Vietnam and the Philippines (formal treaty allies of the USA) challenges American military supremacy and diplomatic influence in East Asia. Meanwhile, Japan, pressured by China over the Senkaku Islands dispute, has become involved in the South China Sea dispute as well. The stable but fragile security situation can be described as an old-fashioned strategic balancing of an emergent regional power by two small powers that depend on other external major maritime powers to maintain a precarious status quo in the South China Sea for the present and the foreseeable future.[54] On the dynamics of this balance of power system in Southeast Asia, the Australian-based Lowy Institute for International Policy notes the following:

> The system assumes competition between states and hence the ever-present risk of aggression and conflict...in which participants agree, if only tacitly to curb competition for influence in the interest of maintaining system-wide stability.

The key to the system is its inherent dynamism. If the power of one state grows disproportionately, the system adjusts through a realignment of the relationships among the others. Some states—those most susceptible to the gravitational pull of the growing power—will be attracted closer to it. Others will respond by drawing closer to each other, and to an alternative pole or poles in the system. Some states will attempt mix of both, as is evident in Southeast Asia. The choice states make in response to a balance of power dynamic need not be based solely on power considerations; questions of how benign they perceive a powerful state to be also influence their decisions about balancing or bandwagoning.[55]

Thus far, this balance of power system in the South China Sea has averted an armed conflict among the claimant states, prompting Professor David Scott to quip that "the benefits of such balancing may become apparent because balancing is itself a stabilising process."[56] However, the balance of power situation has two major flaws. One, it generates a very fluid situation wherein any error or miscalculation by any claimant state may trigger an armed confrontation that may escalate or may drag the other maritime powers into a major systemic war. Two, while the balance of power system has stabilised the situation, it has simply failed to resolve the dispute, creating a tense and protracted impasse. The claimant states are using this lull to build-up their respective military capabilities for any eventuality.

As a case in point, China has intentionally delayed the resolution of the dispute to fortify its control of the contested areas, and dissuade the other states from pursuing their claims.[57] These rules out any possibility of compromise. As a counter-measure, the Philippines and Vietnam adopt a balancing strategy that draws the USA and Japan into the fray. Interestingly, these external maritime powers are anxious to curtail China's growing strategic clout in East Asia. At present, China finds itself trapped in its own security dilemma as it faces increasing American and Japanese naval presence and pressure in the South China Sea. Despite almost decades of restructuring and modernisation, the Chinese leadership is not yet entirely confident that its untried (and inexperienced) armed forces can win wars under high technology conditions when confronted by the US Navy supported by Japan's MSDF.[58] The International Institute for Strategic Studies observes that despite the PLA's ambition for a blue-water navy, China has yet to put in place all the assets necessary to form an effective carrier task group for blue-water capability.[59] However, if the balance of power works against its interests, China might use force on any of the claimant states who have cemented their security ties with the USA and Japan. Nonetheless, such maneuvering by China will surely invite possible intervention by these two maritime powers, especially if Chinese forces make the strategic push against American (and Japanese) naval presence in the first-island-chain. In effect, the current balance of power system can become the proverbial "calm before the storm."

Conclusion

Since 2009, China has taken an aggressive approach in pursuing its expansive maritime claim in the South China Sea. Initially, it used a delaying tactic in the resolution of the dispute while it consolidated its claims over disputed maritime territories, deterred small claimant states from strengthening their own claims and, in the process, has weakened ASEAN. Eventually, the USA and Japan have shown their interests in the dispute, and have projected their naval prowess in East Asia. These two naval powers have also extended military assistance to the small claimant states in the South China Sea dispute—Philippines and Vietnam. This, in turn, has raised the possibility of a major naval confrontation between an emergent power and two major naval powers in the South China Sea. These developments have created a potentially volatile balance of power situation in the South China Sea. So far, this balance of power has prevented an armed conflict among the claimant states. Consequently, many International Relations scholars and analysts have elevated the South China Sea dispute from a simple territorial row to a high-level geo-political concern since the disputed area is "a dangerous ground" for a "future of conflict." As a "future of conflict," the South China Sea becomes an arena where states with powerful navies will jockey for strategic and diplomatic positions with their warships in the high seas, pursue their conflicting claims for natural resources, and strive for supremacy in the Western Pacific.[60]

This dangerous and unfortunate situation is partly a result of ASEAN's inability to influence security developments in the South China Sea. Since the early 1990s, in the face of China's southward expansion to the South China Sea, ASEAN sought to establish a conflict management mechanism through the negotiation of a legally binding code of conduct to lower the risk of conflict among the claimant states. However, China has prevented ASEAN from establishing this mechanism by delaying the negotiations for the COC, and applying the Salami strategy among the member states. This has weakened the ASEAN, and created a strategic vacuum in East Asia. Currently, the USA and Japan are filling this space by strategically balancing China in the South China Sea. Beyond an immediate heightening of tension in the disputed waters, increased strategic competition between China on the one hand, and the USA and Japan on the other hand, has complicated the peaceful management of the South China Sea dispute, and has effectively diminished ASEAN's role on this issue. As the great power rivalry over the South China Sea intensifies, the smaller Southeast Asian states will ultimately make a choice between a superpower bent on maintaining the status quo and an emergent regional power determined to alter the current territorial arrangements in maritime East Asia. This, in turn, will erode not only ASEAN's clout in East Asian security matters but also threaten its very existence as a regional association of small powers committed to peace and stability in Southeast Asia.

NOTES

1. This paper was first read in the conference on 'Confidence-Building in Asia,' Ballroom Plaza, 2nd Floor, Sofitel Plaza Hanoi, 4 December 2015. Preliminary draft. Please do not quote without permission of the author.
2. Carlyle A. Thayer, 'ASEAN, China and the Code of Conduct in the South China Sea,' *SAIS Review*, XXXIII, No. 2 (Summer-Fall 2013), p. 77.
3. Sheldon W. Simon, 'ASEAN and the New Regional Multialteralism: The Long and Bumpy Road to Community,' *International Relations of Asia* (Eds.) David Shambaugh and Michael Yahuda (Lanham, Maryland: Rowman and Littlefiled Publishing Group, Inc., 2008), p. 205.
4. Clive Schofield and Ian Storey, *The South China Sea Dispute: Increasing Stakes and Rising Tension* (Washington DC: The Jamestown Foundation, November 2009), p. 1.
5. National Institute for Defense Studies, *NIDS China Security Report 2014* (Tokyo, Japan: National Institute for Defense Studies, 2015), p. 3.

6. See Mark E. Manyin et al, 'Pivot to the Pacific? The Obama Administration's "Rebalancing" toward Asia,' *Congressional Research Service* (Washington, D.C.: Congressional Research Service, 28 March 2012).
7. Ibid., p.33.
8. See Malcolm Cook, Raoul Heinrich, Rory Medcalf, and Andrew Shearer, *Power and Choice: Asian Security Futures* (Sydney, Australia: Lowy Institute, June 2010), p. 36.
9. Taylor, *op. cit.*, p. 296.
10. Michael Yahuda, *The International Politics of the Asia-Pacific* (London; New York: Routledge, 2011), p. 199.
11. Michael Yahuda, *The International Politics of the Asia-Pacific* (New York; Oxon: Routledge, 2013), p. 199.
12. Ibid., p. 215.
13. Liu Xucheng, 'Strengthening ASEAN-China Cooperation in the ASEAN Regional Forum,' *ASEAN-China Relations: Realities and Prospects* (Eds.) Saw Swee-Hock, Sheng Lijun and Chin Kin Wah (Singapore: Institute of Southeast Asian Studies, 2005), p. 43.
14. Small or minor powers are generally small or even medium-sized states whose territory, population and resource base make it difficult for them to defend themselves against external military attacks or other forms of big power intervention. To insure their security, this type of states is generally compelled to adjust its bilateral relations with the big powers and to deal with changes in the regional balance of power. There is no general pattern of behaviour on how small powers relate with the big or major powers. Rather, each of this state maintains a specific pattern of relation with the major or big powers, each has been affected differently by changes in the latter polices, and each has responded in various ways. See Laura Neack, *The New Foreign Policy: U.S. and Comparative Foreign Policy in the 21st Century* (Maryland: Rowman and Littlefield Publishers, 2003), pp. 108-159.
15. Chien-Peng (CP) Chung, 'Southeast Asia's "Hedging" Relationship with Major Powers of the Asia-Pacific,' in *Seeking Alternative Perspectives of Southeast Asia* (ends) Andrew TH Tan, Michael L.R. Smith and Dato Khoo Kay Kim (Ipoh, Malaysia: Perak Academy, 2004), p. 292.
16. Ibid., p. 203.
17. Ibid., p. 203.
18. Sheldon Simon, 'ASEAN and Multilateralism: The Long, Bumpy Road to Community,' *Contemporary Southeast Asia* (August 2008), vol. 30, No. 2, p. 278.
19. Ibid., p. 190.
20. Michael Leifer, *The ASEAN Regional Forum: Extending ASEAN's Model of Regional Security*, (London: New York Oxford University Press, 1996), p. 45.
21. Ian Clark, *The Hierarchy of States: Reform and Resistance in the International Order* (Cambridge: Cambridge University Press, 1989), p. 13.
22. Ibid. p. 23.
23. Amitav Acharya, *Regionalism and Multilateralism: Essays on Cooperative Security in the Asia-Pacific* (Singapore: Times Academic Press, 2002). p. 190.
24. Simon, 'ASEAN and Multilateralism,' p. 267.
25. This type of wars can be defined as large-scale severe wars among major or great powers that involve the leading states at some point in the war and most other major states in a struggle to resolve the most fundamental issues on the global political agenda. See John Vasques, The *War Puzzle* (The UK: Cambridge University Press, 1993), p. 63.
26. Jurgen Haacke, *ASEAN's Diplomatic and Security Culture: Origins, Development and Prospects* (London and New York: Routledge Curzon, 2003), pp. 221-222.

27. Daljit Singh, 'Evolution of the Security Dialogue Process in the Asia-Pacific Region,' *Southeast Asian Perspectives on Security* (Ed) Derek da Cunha (Singapore: Institute of Southeast Asian Affairs, 2000), p. 50.
28. Alice D. Ba, 'Staking Claims and Making Waves in the South China Sea: How Troubled are the Waters?', *Contemporary Southeast Asia* 33. 3 (December 2011), p. 269.
29. Marc Lanteigne, *Chinese Foreign Policy: An Introduction* (Oxon and New York: Taylor and Francis Group, 2009), p. 121.
30. David Scott, *China Stands Up: The PRC and the International System* (Oxon; New York: Routledge, 2007), p. 104.
31. Sheldon W. Simon, 'Conflict and Diplomacy in the South China Sea: The View from Washington,' (November-December 2012) 52, 6, p. 1000.
32. Ralf Emmers, 'ASEAN's Search for Neutrality in the South China Sea,' *Asian Journal of Peacebuilding*, 2 1 (2014), p. 64.
33. Ibid., p. 64.
34. Ibid., p. 64.
35. Leszek Buszynski, 'The South China Sea Maritime Dispute: Legality, Power and Conflict Prevention,' *Asian Journal of Peacebuilding* 1, 1 (2013), p. 54.
36. Emmers, *op. cit.*, p. 64.
37. Ibid., p. 73.
38. Carl A. Thayer, 'ASEAN, China and the Code of Conduct in the South China Sea,' *SAIS Review* XXXIII, 2 (Summer-Fall 2013), p. 82.
39. Ibid., p. 82.
40. M. Taylor Fravel, 'China's Strategy in the South China Sea,' *Contemporary Southeast Asia* 33, 3 (2011), p. 297.
41. Ibid., p. 293.
42. Weatherbee, *op. cit.*, p. 146.
43. Yang Mingjie, 'Sailing on a Harmonious Sea: A Chinese Perspective,' *Global Sea* 4, 5 (Winter 2010), p. 25.
44. Mark Valencia, 'The Philippines' Spratly Bungle,' *UPIA Asia Online* (28 March 2008), p. 2. http://www.upiasia.com/Politics/2008/03/28/the-philippines/spratly_bungle/3227/?view=print
45. Barry Wain, 'Manila's Bungle in the South China Sea,' *Far Eastern Economic Review* 171, 1 (January 2008), p. 2, http://proquest.umi.ciom/pqdweb?index=12&did=1423249481& Src
46. Simon, *op. cit.*, p. 1016.
47. Ibid., p. 1016.
48. Emmers, *op. cit.*, p. 67.
49. Ibid., p. 67.
50. Simon, *op. cit.*, p. 1016.
51. Mark Landler, 'How Obama Switched to Tougher Line with China,' *International Herald Tribune* (21 September 2012).
52. Mark E. Manyin et al., 'Pivot to the Pacific? The Obama Administration's "Rebalancing" toward Asia,' *Congressional Research Service* (Washington, D.C.: Congressional Research Service, 28 March 2012), p. 1.
53. Michele Flournoy and Janine Davidson, 'Obama's New Global Posture,' *Foreign Affairs* 91 4 (July/August 2012), p. 59.
54. Scott, *op. cit.*, p. 1041.
55. See Malcolm Cook, Raoul Heinrich, Rory Medcalf, and Andrew Shearer, *Power and Choice: Asian Security Futures (Sydney,* Australia: Lowy Institute, June 2010), pp. 25-26.
56. Scott, *op. cit.*, p. 1042.

57. Taylor, *op. cit.,* p. 12.
58. See Huai-Feng Ren and Fu-Kuo-Liu, 'Transitional Security Pattern in the South China Sea and the Involvement of External Parties,' *Issues and Studies* 49, 2 (June 2013), pp. 107-145.
59. The International Institute for Strategic Studies, *The Military Balance 2012: The Annual Assessment of Global Military Capabilities and Defence Economics* (London: The International Institute for Strategic Studies, 2012), p. 213.
60. See Robert Kaplan, 'The South China Sea is the Future of Conflict,' *Foreign Policy* 188 (September/October 2011): 76-88. http://search.proquest.com/docview/888030576?accountid=28547

18

ASEAN and the Security of the Asia-Pacific: A Historical Perspective

Bunn Sri na Nagara

Introduction

Southeast Asia is among the world's most intriguing regions, and one of the most watchable segments of the Asian continent. At one level, it is a geographical region which, for generations, has been in search of the right kind of geopolitical regionalism. At another level, it is a key component of the wider East Asia (with Northwest Asia) which remains the world's most economically dynamic and promising regions. At yet another level, Southeast Asia consists of fewer than a dozen sovereign nations which exist in close proximity, and yet have, perhaps, the most diverse cultural, economic, political, and historical features of any region in the world.

This is also a region that has seen decades of external major power posturing and competition, but not Cold War rivalry per se. It is also virtually synonymous with the Association of Southeast Asian Nations (ASEAN), which is—the European Union aside—arguably the most successful regional organisation of nation states today. Currently, ASEAN is set on developing an ASEAN Community with greater economic integration and socio-political harmonisation. However, compounding some uncertainty and confusion, there are some persistent misperceptions of ASEAN and its member states.

Of the 11 sovereign nations in Southeast Asia, 10 are now members of ASEAN. And of the 10, four have been colonies of Britain. The British influence in these countries (Brunei, Malaya/Malaysia, Myanmar, and Singapore) remains until today in the form of constitutional practice, juridical institutions, and use of the English language. However, this does not mean that ASEAN or its predecessor—the short-lived Association of Southeast Asia (ASA)—is pro-Western or pro-British. These are, after all, groupings of newly independent nations, each proud and protective of their own respective national sovereignties.[1]

However, early perceptions of ASEAN by such countries as Burma, Cambodia, and China—that it was a pro-Western organisation were misplaced though were unexpected. Thailand and the Philippines were allies of the USA; Malaysia's Prime Minister Tunku Abdul Rahman was an Anglophile; the 1954 Manila Pact, which led to the formation of the Southeast Asia Treaty Organisation (SEATO), was indeed a product of the Cold War as SEATO was intended to be Southeast Asia's version of NATO. But only two of SEATO's eight members—Thailand and the Philippines—were in Southeast Asia. ASA comprised Malaysia, the Philippines, and Thailand; but without regional heavyweight Indonesia, it did not gain traction.

The Earlier Years

When SEATO was formed in 1954, the various motivations of member countries virtually ensured that it would not endure. Six of the eight members that were not of Southeast Asia—Australia, Britain, France, New Zealand, Pakistan, United States—tended to see their common purpose and chief objective as fighting the global communist scourge. However, the two Southeast Asian nations, Thailand and the Philippines, did not exactly share the view of the region as being dominoes set to fall to global communism's sway. Thailand saw SEATO as a bulwark against its traditional regional rival Vietnam, and the Philippines hoped SEATO could be wielded against its own domestic communist insurgency—or at least serve to generally provide more foreign security assistance to shore up the state.

Both Thailand and the Philippines were soon disappointed by SEATO's inability or reluctance to deliver on those fronts. Thailand found that even after the Viet Minh had invaded buffer nation Laos earlier in 1954, SEATO offered no means to neutralise the perceived threat this posed to Thailand. The Philippines also found that being part of a Western-defined and directed SEATO had limited its options in identifying with the rest of Southeast Asia while compromising its nationalist credentials. Manila could not get what it wanted from SEATO; nor could it do whatever it wanted in the region as a Southeast Asian nation.

Thus, initially hailed as an organisation for Southeast Asia if not also of and by Southeast Asia, SEATO failed to be credible within Southeast Asia. Bereft of regional support, and given the disconnect between transnational communist ideology and domestic insurgencies and other concerns, SEATO's development slowed down and stagnated. Meanwhile, other countries in Southeast Asia showed a lack of interest, if not outright hostility. Burma was concerned that SEATO might unduly provoke China; Indonesia was opposed to what it saw as a Western manipulation of the region; and then British Malaya (and Singapore), and subsequently Malaysia, also kept its distance. Thus, SEATO effectively became dysfunctional in the 1960s before withering away in the 1970s.

In their separate ways, Thailand and the Philippines discovered that they needed a regional organisation of Southeast Asia that did not involve the participation and direction of Western powers. This would functionally be a regional organisation that was also for and by Southeast Asia. Such an autonomous and truly regional entity would not incur opposition by Indonesia, or indifference by Malaya. Thus, in 1961, Malaya, the Philippines, and Thailand came together to form the Association of Southeast Asia (ASA).

However, Indonesia proved difficult to convince. Thailand aggravated Jakarta's suspicions of ASA's innate pro-Western bent by declaring the hope that ASA would become a military alliance—implicitly, an alliance at variance with China. For its part, the Philippines stepped up its territorial claim to Sabah (British North Borneo)—a territory then on the verge of gaining independence from Britain to join Sarawak, Singapore, and Malaya to form Malaysia. When these domestic exigencies flared in ASA member nations, as they inevitably would, ASA clearly became inexpedient, and then also dysfunctional.[2]

As Malaya moved towards the formation of Malaysia, Indonesia announced a policy of confrontation (*konfrontasi*) against Malaya in January 1963. In July, the Philippines convened a summit with leaders of Indonesia, Malaya, and the Philippines in Manila to form a Greater Malayan Confederation, called MAPHILINDO. Ostensibly to unite the three countries where the Malay ethnic community predominates, the proposed confederation was said to be non-political; however, its intentions were nothing but political. Indonesia and the Philippines had the common objective of stymieing the formation of Malaysia. The Philippines was still bent on pursuing Sabah to Sukarno's Indonesia—for Sabah, Sarawak, and Singapore to join Malaya in forming Malaysia was a threat to its regional dominance.

For Malaysia, MAPHILINDO seemed inoffensive and innocuous; but was fundamentally flawed and hazardous. Territorially, it would set back the formation of Malaysia. Demographically, it threatened the national unity and stability of the fledgling multi-racial nation by emphasising the primacy of a single ethnic community nationally as well as regionally—to the benefit of a suspicious Indonesia. Given its internal contradictions, MAPHILINDO—or the moves towards realising it—lasted only one month.

In September 1963, Malaya had grown into Malaysia. President Sukarno of Indonesia promptly escalated *konfrontasi* until it became an undeclared war against Malaysia. Although much of the military engagement was conducted in Borneo, particularly across parts of the Sarawak-Kalimantan border, Indonesia also made incursions into the Malay Peninsula as well as Singapore. At the same time, however, Indonesia was experiencing instability owing to the Indonesian Communist Party (PKI), splits within its military, Sukarno's shaky hold on power, and the rise of the army faction led by General Suharto.

ASEAN and Beyond

By 1965, the PKI had become the strongest political party in Indonesia, and the most influential communist party in the region. Sukarno the nationalist had tried to maintain his grip on power by juggling between the contending interests of the PKI and the military. But, as the economy declined, PKI influence came to be of concern to the military, the nationalists, and the Islamists. At that time, Sukarno's policy of *konfrontasi* against Malaysia also peaked, and became a source of regional concern.

The new administration—instituted in stages by Suharto—had effectively displaced Sukarno's government by early 1966, but it was still an unknown quantity to much of Southeast Asia. Although its character and regional intentions might not yet have been clear to neighbouring countries, Malaysia knew that it did not want to revert to the days of *konfrontasi*. To this end, senior Malaysian officials worked quietly behind the scenes with their

Indonesian counterparts (such as General Ali Murtopo, a close aide of Suharto) to transcend this bitter legacy of Sukarno.[3] In May 1966, Indonesian and Malaysian officials in Bangkok jointly declared *konfrontasi* over.

Between them, Malaysian officials and their newly empowered Indonesian counterparts agreed that this new era of improved relations between their countries had to be cemented and institutionalised. This had to take the form of a new regional institution where membership had to be of, by, and for the sovereign nations of Southeast Asia, and where membership meant equal rights and privileges for all members, regardless of size, status, power or wealth. This could not merely be a modified version of an existing institution such as ASA from which Indonesia had been excluded, by simply admitting it as a member. This had to be a completely new regional organisation in form, spirit and purpose.

This was the Association of Southeast Asian Nations (ASEAN). From the beginning ASEAN had to be pragmatic, regionally focused, non-aligned, and demonstrably so. It sought to include all the countries of Southeast Asia eventually, regardless of their national, economic or political systems or their individual inclinations with respect to the major world powers. Although Suharto's New Order regime had fully displaced Sukarno's by early 1967, Indonesia still placed an appreciable degree of importance on non-alignment. Thus, such universal principles as enshrined in the UN Charter and highlighted in the Declaration of the 1955 Bandung Conference as "Abstention from intervention or interference in the internal affairs of another country" formed the core of ASEAN concerns.

Furthermore, another fundamental aspect of ASEAN's concerns may be traced to another Bandung principle: "Abstention from the use of arrangements of collective defence to serve any particular interests of the big powers." ASEAN's founding document, the Bangkok Declaration, acknowledges the presence of foreign military bases in some ASEAN countries. However, it states that member states "are determined to ensure their stability and security from external interference in any form or manifestation," and that

> all foreign bases are temporary and remain only with the expressed concurrence of the countries concerned and are not intended to be used directly or indirectly to subvert the national independence and freedom of States in the area or prejudice the orderly processes of their national development.[4]

However, as in previous attempts at regional organisations in Southeast Asia, the prime motivating factor of political cooperation was down played to the extent of emphasising cooperation in other fields.[5] This is formally reflected in the Bangkok Declaration's prioritizing "economic growth, social progress and cultural development"[6] over political cooperation. This coyness in Southeast Asian diplomacy predates ASEAN, and is likely to remain a feature of the region indefinitely. It informs and characterises the gamut of ASEAN's dealings—from its stated intentions to its modus operandi to its acknowledgement of its own achievements. It also expresses ASEAN's pragmatism in openly focusing on the low-hanging fruits of economic and cultural cooperation so as to facilitate political cooperation.[7]

That ASEAN grew from a need to repair Indonesia's dangerously hostile relations with Malaysia was evident from the start. Over time, ASEAN also became a vehicle for Indonesia's neighbours to feel more confident in their relations with the regional giant, Indonesia. ASEAN would afford Indonesia a commonly acceptable channel for regional leadership, while also assuring Indonesia's relatively smaller neighbours that it would abide by universal norms and conventions. Thus, in effect, ASEAN is the most significant confidence-building measure in Southeast Asia, the wider East Asia, and possibly also the Asia-Pacific.

At the same time, ASEAN also affords other benefits to its members. The creation of a common market within the ASEAN area became more of a reality as the more established original member states became more economically developed. Intra-ASEAN trade, long underdeveloped owing to the stronger ties between member nations and more industrialised countries outside ASEAN, was just 5 per cent of their total external trade in the early 1990s. Two decades later, it multiplied nearly five-fold, and continues to grow as a proportion of member nations' total external trade.[8]

Meanwhile, the newer and less developed CLMV member nations (Cambodia, Laos, Myanmar, and Vietnam) look upon ASEAN as a means to accelerate their economic development and enhance their international diplomacy. In practice, this also means they would keep any mutual historical rivalries and border issues in check. ASEAN's promotion of regional, and intra-ASEAN security also remains significant for its original members: the Philippine claim to Sabah is dormant and manageable, since ASEAN and all that it represents and offers are much more than any single historical dispute can signify. Similarly, ASEAN also ensures that the disputes among the four ASEAN member nations (Brunei, Malaysia, Philippines, and Vietnam) over claims to the Spratly Islands in the South China Sea do not present a threat to any of them.

Understanding ASEAN entails realising that, as a truly indigenous organisation for Southeast Asia, it is essentially internally focused. Its norm of decision-making through consensus is also a regional attribute, with roots in the concepts of *musyawarah* and *mufakat* or deliberations and confabulations among community elders and leaders in traditional Malay society. This nuanced, rather loose, and somewhat informal mode of negotiating, despite the official fanfare of ASEAN Summits, remains a feature distinct from the more formal and contractual mode typical of occidental culture.[9] It explains why ASEAN member nations prefer other means than formal ASEAN instruments such as its dispute settlement mechanism when the need for such instruments arises.

That the adherents of the occidental culture to fail to understand or appreciate Asian culture may be understandable; but it is not acceptable. ASEAN does not work like an invasive drug against a perceived ailment in the manner of an antibiotic in Western pharmacology. Rather, it works to create an environment and an atmosphere in which the balance of constructive diplomacy may thrive, and where the imbalance of injustice or aggression is curtailed or avoided. In this way, the well being of the rest of the body politic remains in a healthy balance and stays uncompromised. Therefore, the ASEAN way is more akin to traditional Chinese herbal remedies and Indian Ayurvedic medicine in Asian pharmacology. ASEAN does not insist that its method is better for all regions; but merely practises it for its own needs as a complementary method.

Misunderstanding ASEAN is still common, particularly when presumptions and assumptions are made from an occidental perspective. Critics have assailed ASEAN for a variety of alleged failures: from not resolving the 1997–98 Asian financial crisis to not effectively policing its region against strategic challenges. But ASEAN is not—and was never meant to be—a transnational financial institution or an Asian equivalent of NATO.[10] Even when ASEAN never sought to be involved in the Cold War, some analysts would attribute Cold War concerns to the ASEAN region.[11] However, where clear challenges such as piracy exist, ASEAN countries have not hesitated to rise to them, as Indonesia, Malaysia, Singapore, and Thailand did in launching the "Eyes in the Sky" integrated patrols in the Straits of Malacca in 2005.

Cold War concerns—such as a country's political ideology or its international affiliation—was never an issue so long as no security threat is posed. The basic principle of non-intervention in the internal affairs of other countries ensured that Vietnam and Laos were admitted into ASEAN without hindrance. What have always been of concern to ASEAN are security and stability, such that Cambodia's membership was delayed on account of its internal problems at the time. That several ASEAN countries had fought domestic communist insurgencies (the Philippines continues to do so) was their own respective internal issue, and they did so primarily because these were armed insurgencies threatening the state and the status quo rather than simply because they were communist. A part of ASEAN's success may be attributed to its Southeast Asia-specific nature in finding regional solutions to regional problems in both approach and outcome, such that the applicability of its example as a template for other regions remains moot.[12]

The Likely Future

An inescapable fact for the countries of Southeast Asia is that whatever their culture, history or aspirations, they occupy a region beset by the interests and concerns of major world powers. In East Asia as a whole today, these happen to be China and the United States. To be caught in the midst of the sometimes contending interests and often rival perspectives of the world's most important bilateral relationship, or "G2," is not necessarily advantageous or reassuring. The situation becomes more vexing when one or the other major power expects smaller countries located between them to oblige or conform in certain ways—particularly when these prefer to remain non-aligned.

For ASEAN countries, Japan is also a major power. Moreover, their region has lately come to the heightened attention of another two major powers: India and Russia. The concept of a "balance of powers" tends to work better and more clearly in theory rather than in practice. Being the focus of attention of more major powers complicates the prospect of regional security. This is where the principle of non-intervention in the internal affairs of other countries becomes more pertinent; but it is a principle to which ASEAN member nations are more attached than the external major powers impinging on the region. Internally, this is not a problem for member nations since ASEAN allows for interventionist approaches when needed without seeing them as such.[13] Externally, differences with any ASEAN Dialogue Partner are mitigated by their being obligated to abide by key ASEAN norms and conventions.

It would not take long for any ASEAN member nation to realise that even when working well and cohesively as a unified ASEAN, Southeast Asian countries have very limited means in addressing transnational issues that impact them when major powers decide to assert themselves. Therefore, ASEAN has sought to reach beyond Southeast Asia in engaging major external powers, if only to better ensure regional security for Southeast Asia. To this end, ASEAN countries have, individually or collectively as ASEAN, embarked on institutional development transcending Southeast Asia. The response, however, has been mixed from both within and outside ASEAN.

Soon after ASEAN's establishment, South Korea (Republic of Korea) in 1970 proposed the formation of an Asian Common Market. However, the countries of Southeast Asia were still relatively underdeveloped, while the CLMV countries in particular were still mired in conflict. The original five ASEAN countries themselves (Indonesia, Malaysia, Philippines, Singapore, and Thailand) had yet to experience significant economic impetus brought on by foreign investment, such as the relocation of Japanese manufacturing industries in the 1970s. Then, in 1988, Japan proposed the formation of an Asian Network; but Southeast Asia still cast around looking for a suitable regional entity that was larger than ASEAN.

In 1990, Malaysia proposed the formation of the East Asia Economic Grouping (EAEG) comprising the countries of ASEAN (Southeast Asia) and those of Northeast Asia (China, Japan and South Korea). This was on the occasion of Chinese Prime Minister Li Peng's visit to Kuala Lumpur in December. Li Peng promptly accepted the proposal from Prime Minister Datuk Seri Dr. Mahathir Mohamad. However, Singapore was reportedly lukewarm to the proposal; Indonesia was apparently unhappy that it was not consulted beforehand; and Japan rejected it as the USA had opposed it on account of it not being included. Australia saw it as a bad idea since it was excluded, but it would be good if it were in it.

Months of rationalising by Malaysia followed; but eventually, the EAEG failed to materialise despite Malaysia remaining firm. Singapore then proposed a compromise in revising the EAEG into the EAEC (East Asian Economic

Caucus), essentially to assure the USA that this would only be a caucus within the US-led APEC, and thus would not compete against it. The EAEC would then be a joint ASEAN project, enjoying the support of all ASEAN countries. However, since it meant little change from the status quo, with Malaysia remaining indifferent, the EAEC was also left by the wayside. Once more, regional institutions billed as "economic" were seen as possessing significant geopolitical implications, and being "excluded" from these institutions was taken to mean being excluded from the region.

However, such setbacks did not restrain ASEAN in reaching out. By now ASEAN had also grown in stature and credibility. More regions wanted to have dealings with it—a situation no doubt helped by ASEAN's potential as a regional market. But for its part, ASEAN knew that economic priorities—important as they are—could not be separated from security considerations, particularly when they were complementary.

Besides its own meetings (including summits) among national leaders, ASEAN has been holding ministerial-level meetings with its ten Dialogue Partners. ASEAN also has separate annual summits with the heads of government of India, Russia, and the USA. As an outgrowth of its ministerial meetings with Dialogue Partner countries, the ASEAN Regional Forum (ARF) was established in 1994. Originally conceived as an ASEAN-led security forum comprising member countries in East Asia and the Pacific, ARF membership in time grew to 27.

The first Asia-Europe Meeting (ASEM) was held in Bangkok in 1996. Although more countries, including India, Pakistan, Russia and Australia, subsequently joined, the focus has been on EU and ASEAN countries. Soon after that inaugural ASEM event, China and Japan also sought regular summits with ASEAN leaders. In 1997, the Asian financial crisis struck East Asia, severely afflicting South Korea, Thailand, and Indonesia in particular. Critics outside the region blamed ASEAN for being ineffective against this regional contagion, but had the EAEG been allowed to proceed from 1990, regional measures and safeguards would have been in place to mitigate if not avoid the crisis.

Subsequently, the same 13 countries of the EAEG—those of ASEAN plus China, Japan and South Korea—came together to form ASEAN Plus Three (APT) in December 1997. Much of the canvassing work to realise the APT came from South Korea. By then, Japan had allowed itself to be persuaded to join the APT. Unlike the ARF with more than twice the number of member countries, the APT remains more manageable and focused. By 1999, the APT was formally established, with new safeguards against further crises as the effects of the 1997–98 disaster subsided. Protecting against such catastrophes remains paramount, since security for ASEAN and other East Asian nations is equated with freedom from economic and other severe vulnerabilities.

The APT has given rise to the East Asia Summit (EAS), an annual series of summits of leaders from member countries. Initially comprising 16 countries—the 13 APT countries with India, Australia, and New Zealand—membership broadened further to include Russia and the USA. Like the ARF, the EAS is centred on ASEAN. To the extent that both relate to regional security matters, questions have been raised about possible duplication in their functions. Rather than conceive of these regional institutions as competitive, it may be better to regard them as complementary in the pattern of concentric rings: with ASEAN at the centre, they radiate outwards from the APT, EAS, and ARF.

This may be taken as an example of "ASEAN Centrality," with ASEAN itself held together from within and without. ASEAN will continue to remain highly pertinent to its members, particularly when old suspicions and rival interests remain between them. But, as the world generally becomes more competitive, globalisation increasingly impacts on Southeast Asia, and as rivalries between major external powers also escalate, ASEAN needs to be more unified, focused, and purposeful. Therefore, the security architecture for Southeast Asia, East Asia, and the Asia-Pacific is vital, and it becomes reassuring for ASEAN members if ASEAN remains at the centre.

It would also be reassuring to ASEAN's partner countries. ASEAN, comprising relatively weak nations, possesses no extra-regional ambitions other than fostering peace and prosperity. It represents a non-strategically competitive region governed by international norms and conventions, and imbued with the principle of not interfering in the internal affairs of other countries. It has stood the test of time in its continued importance to the countries of its region. As a constructive and non-threatening entity, it stands ready to assist in building positive relations among the countries of Northeast Asia—its "Plus Three" countries.

At the same time, ASEAN continues to build strong foundations for itself in constructing the ASEAN Community. The three pillars of the ASEAN Community—Political-Security, Economic and Socio-Cultural—are formal in nature, but nominal in scope because they are all security-related. As it was, since the beginning for ASEAN, and ever since Southeast Asia sought a regional organisation for itself, security in both traditional and non-traditional forms is paramount. Without security, there can be no peace, stability, or development. The security-development nexus is evident everywhere.[14]

However, an ASEAN weakness is its state-centrism which has long bedevilled its activities and priorities. While conceived as an association of nations, ASEAN has functioned more as an association of nation states—and in practice, a congregation of national governments. This has led to such anomalies as citizens being more familiar with the societies and cultures of their former colonial powers than with other ASEAN member nations. However, change is on the way. A result of the 1997–98 Asian financial crisis was the realisation that ASEAN needed to broaden its base, its appeal, and its popular constituency.

This meant broadening ASEAN participation to include ASEAN civil society organisations. It led to the inclusion of the phrase "a people-oriented ASEAN" in formal ASEAN deliberations in order to signify the intended direction of the ASEAN Community. However, such expanded inclusiveness in ASEAN societies has experienced uneven support across ASEAN member nations. The more authoritarian and state-centric countries were not so receptive to the idea.

The original "people-oriented" accent was developed by Malaysia into a "people-centred" ASEAN when Malaysia was the ASEAN Chair in 2015. But some countries indicated that "people-oriented" was as far as they would go. In the Kuala Lumpur Declaration from the 26th ASEAN Summit, it became "a people-oriented, people-centred ASEAN."[15] ASEAN's innate pragmatism and accommodation triumphed again. However, the future of ASEAN as a regional security device, in whatever formal shape it would take, still depends on greater inclusiveness for the myriad components of a diverse regional community.[16]

NOTES

1. For a discussion of the backgrounds of ASA and ASEAN, see Vincent K. Pollard, 'ASA and ASEAN, 1961–67: Southeast Asian Regionalism,' in *Asian Survey*, Vol. 10, No. 3, University of California Press, March 1970; see also, Russell Hunt Fifield, 'National and Regional Interests in ASEAN: Competition and Cooperation in International Politics,' Occasional paper no. 57, Institute of Southeast Asian, Singapore, 1979; for a fuller discussion of the sentiments, perceptions and nuances of the countries of the region at the time, see Leng Thearith, *ASEAN Security and Its Relevency* (sic), CICP E-Book No. 1, June 2009, Cambodian Institute for Cooperation and Peace, Phnom Penh.
2. Ibid., Leng Thearith.
3. Personal communication with former Malaysian Foreign Minister, Tan Sri Ghazali Shafie, 1991.
4. The ASEAN Declaration (Bangkok Declaration), Bangkok, 8 August 1967.
5. Ibid., Tan Sri Ghazali Shafie.
6. Ibid., The ASEAN Declaration.
7. Rizal Sukma, 'ASEAN And Regional Security In East Asia,' in *Security Politics in Asia and Europe*, Panorama 02/2009 – Insights into Asian and European Affairs, Konrad Adenauer Stiftung, Singapore, 7 June 2010.
8. ASEAN Merchandise Trade Statistics Database (compiled/computed from data submission, publications and/or websites of ASEAN Member States' national ASEAN Free Trade Area [AFTA] units, national statistics offices, customs departments/agencies, or central banks), at asean.org/storage/2015/12/table18_as-of-10-June-2016.pdf
9. Amitav Acharya, *Constructing a Security Community in Southeast Asia: ASEAN and the Problem of Regional Order*, Psychology Press, 2001; see also, Shaun Narine, *Explaining ASEAN: Regionalism in Southeast Asia*, Lynne Rienner Publishers, 2002; also, Taku Tamaki, 'Making Sense of 'ASEAN Way': A Constructivist Approach,' Institute of Asian Cultural Studies, International Christian University, Tokyo, paper presented at the Annual Conference of the International Political Science Association, Fukuoka, 2006; see also, Bunn Nagara, 'Cross-cultural Approaches To Security, Peace and Development', paper presented at the 18th ASEM (Asia-Europe Meeting) Think Tank Dialogue, 'The Age of Connectivity, ASEM and Beyond: Asia-Europe Cooperation on Quiet Diplomacy and Conflict Mediation,' Ulaanbaatar, May 2016.
10. Bunn Nagara, 'Building A New East Asia,' in *Regional Order in East Asia: ASEAN and Japan Perspectives*, Issue 1 (ed.), Jun Tsunekawa, NIDS Joint Research Series, National Institute for Defence Studies, Tokyo, 2007.
11. Katja Weber, 'ASEAN: A Prime Example of Regionalism in Southeast Asia,' in European Union Miami Analysis (EUMA), Special Series, Vol. 6, No. 5, April 2009, Published with the support of the EU Commission.
12. Ibid.
13. Lee Jones, 'ASEAN and the Norm of Non-Interference in Southeast Asia: A Quest for Social Order,' Nuffield College Politics Group Working Paper, March 2009.
14. Ibid., Bunn Nagara, 'Cross-cultural Approaches To Security, Peace and Development'.
15. 'Kuala Lumpur Declaration On A People-Oriented, People-Centred ASEAN,' Kuala Lumpur, 27 April 2015.
16. Noel M. Morada, 'APA And Track 2½ Diplomacy: The Role of the ASEAN People's Assembly in Building an ASEAN Community,' Singapore, 31 July – 1 August 2007; see also, Kelly Gerard, 'From the ASEAN People's Assembly To The ASEAN Civil Society Conference: The Boundaries of Civil Society Advocacy,' at www.tandfonline.com/doi/abs/10.1080/13569775.2013.835113?journalCode=ccpo20

ASEAN-INDIA AND THE OCEAN ECONOMY DYNAMICS

Chaired by

Hidetoshi Nishimura

19

ASEAN-India: The Dynamics of the Ocean Economy

Yogendra Kumar

The current era of technological revolution promises to unfold a vast scope for harnessing the immense oceanic resources by transforming the 'Ocean Economy'—or the Blue Economy from being a more-or-less cottage industry to becoming the locomotive power for global socio-economic progress. The march of technology has also led to existential global and regional challenges which also originate from the seas. Addressing both the opportunities and challenges has come to constitute a major national, regional, and, even global endeavour. At the same time, these national and regional endeavours face a complex environment of geo-political flux, systemic fragility, and governance issues as well as a host of traditional and non-traditional security threats. It is here that burgeoning, multi-dimensional India-ASEAN relations hold considerable promise.

The prevailing geo-political setting for the Blue Economy is crucial as it impacts the level of trust, the quality, and effectiveness of regional governance mechanisms, and heightens the exposure of the region to the full spectrum of traditional and non-traditional security threats. The South China Sea is a representative example of the geo-political fluidity negatively impacting collaboration in developing a robust regional blue economy. In recent times, the tension and distrust levels there have only grown due to great power naval rivalry, and there is a possibility that these tensions might spill over into the Indian Ocean Region (IOR).

The Importance of the Oceans

The UN report on the state of the world's oceans warns that "(h)uman activities now have so many and great impacts on the ocean that the limits of its carrying capacity are being (or, in some cases, have been) reached."[1] The urgency of steering the development of the blue economy cannot be gainsaid as challenges grow due to the hurtling pace of technology, the security downside of the disruptive effects of climate change, demographic and urbanisation imbalances in the littoral regions and countries, failing states/regions, and the destabilising impact of pandemics and natural disasters. Coral reefs provide a habitat for fish, mangroves minimise coastal erosion and act as a natural barrier against storms and flooding, and seagrass beds help regulate climate change by sequestering carbon dioxide from the atmosphere up to twice as much as the world's temperate and tropical forests. The growing awareness of the increasingly fragile ocean ecology is translating into business risks such as the higher volatility of resource prices, higher taxation for companies with poor environmental performance, and the market requirements of the sustainability reports of companies.[2]

The Blue Economy—or the New Economy as it is being increasingly called—aims at tapping the resources of the ocean and the ocean-dependent littoral economy to complement the larger national economy for social-economic progress in an ecologically sustainable manner. Although the oceans have been a part of human history, including India's and south-east Asia's, it is only recently that the recognition of its criticality has triggered serious national as well as multi-lateral attention. Larger communities, especially coastal and small island nations, are dependent on oceans for fishing, minerals, oil and gas, rare earth metals, renewable energy, and other resources. Since a large part of oceanic activities are fishing and trade, a robust blue economic regeneration would be equitable and inclusive for the dependent communities. The pressing quest for sustainable, economic growth is bolstered by newer technology for the exploitation of deep sea resources such as hydro-carbons, rare earths, and poly-metallic nodules, marine bio-diversity, etc. Moreover, the Indian Ocean's importance in monsoon forecasting and weather modelling has long been recognised. An important aspect of this scientific interest is the understanding of the climate change phenomenon, and the vulnerabilities due to increasing frequency and severity of extreme weather events for littoral states. This aspect has implications for the capabilities of the littorals to cope with the disasters, with the potential adverse consequences of administrative collapse, spread of radicalism, societal break-down and, most importantly, regional stability.

The challenges arising from the seas—and how these interact with the circumstances obtaining in the littoral settlements—can have devastating effects if they are mishandled as a result of governance deficit or capability inadequacies. The current state of oceanography—with better monsoon study capabilities and better understanding of climate change trends—is helping in devising geo-hazard coping capability from the point of view of the vulnerability mapping of the littoral areas and vital onshore and offshore infrastructure. Better meteorological capabilities have implications for coastal marine ecology: these involve island development activities, drugs from the sea, integrated coastal marine area management, as well as coastal monitoring and protection systems. They also have implications for sea-level rise, the natural sinking of lands in relevant areas, sustaining isolated communities, integrated coastal communities[3] as well as for geo-engineering responses to climate change. For India, climatologist, Stephen Harrison, speaks of a distinct possibility about future climate change being abrupt and non-linear.[4] Due to large migration flows of people from the hinterland belonging to diverse social strata, the coastal urban demography is likely to be predominantly young and thus result in constituting the population of unplanned megacities. The pressures on infrastructure in terms of transport, education, and health will have implications for security as well as Blue Economy governance onshore and offshore.

Indian and ASEAN Efforts

Regional Blue Economy: Objectives and Strategic Challenges

Since a robust Blue Economy is increasingly being recognised as the sole economic basis for many, especially island, states and as an economic accelerator for the others, it has been listed as Goal 14[5] of the 17 UN-mandated Sustainable Development Goals (SDGs) to be achieved by the comity of nations by 2030. The targeted activities are the following: to achieve significant reduction of marine pollution; directly manage and protect marine and coastal ecosystems; minimise the impacts of ocean acidification; effectively regulate harvesting; end overfishing (including illegal fishing); conserve at least 10 per cent of coastal and marine areas; prohibit forms of fisheries subsidies contributing to overcapacity; increase economic benefits to Small Island Developing States (SIDSs) and least developed countries (LDCs) from sustainable use of marine resources; increase scientific knowledge and the transfer of marine technology; provide access to small-scale artisanal fishers to marine resources and markets; and enhance conservation and the sustainable use of oceans as reflected in UNCLOS. The objective of developing a strong Blue Economy is to ensure food security; meet the demand for protein; increase coastal and marine tourism, seaborne trade, and supporting infrastructure; preserve non-renewable and renewable energy, develop ecological and sustainable coastal urbanisation as well as ocean technologies.

The realisation of the critical complementarity of a Blue Economy to the national economy as well as the extreme seriousness of challenges arising from the sea have focused on broader attention on caring for them better in the international community. This has also focused attention on the governance mechanisms for the various oceanic water bodies. The implementation of the above stated tasks still needs a reality check by taking into account the prevailing circumstances in the South China Sea and the Indian Ocean. A stable strategic environment for the oceans implies that the 'maritime order' is successfully defended by international navies, with well understood 'rules of the road' to avoid misunderstanding the intentions of each other as they carry out their normal functions. Cooperation in maritime security and the development of a wholesome Blue Economy go hand in hand.

South China Sea Ecology

The South China Sea's ecology is under threat, and the recent assertion of national claims on the Spratlys and the Paracels has been seen as aggravating conditions further. John McManus (University of Miami) is of the opinion[6] that, apart from the damage through over-fishing, reclamation, and the creation of artificial islands causes irreversible damage to reef ecology. Coral reef fisheries along the coasts of the South China Sea have been heavily over-fished, especially along the coasts of southern China, Vietnam, Malaysia and the Philippines, often by using destructive fishing methods.[7] South China Sea hosts one third of world's bio-diversity. This is under threat, affecting coral reef, mangrove forests, seagrass, estuaries, and wetlands. According to the UN, 88 per cent of coral reefs in south-east Asia are under threat; mangrove forests have been reduced to 30-50 per cent of their historical coverage.[8]

Indian Ocean Ecology

Much the same threats to the Indian Ocean ecology, including acidification, exist as in the South China Sea. More than 65 per cent of coral reefs in the Indian Ocean are at risk from local threats like coastal development, overfishing/destructive fishing, marine pollution, and/or watershed-based pollution. There is sharper threat focus on areas along continental shores where more than 90 per cent are threatened.[9] According to Wikipedia, increasing ocean temperatures are taking a toll on the marine ecosystem.[10] An assessment of phytoplankton changes in the Indian Ocean shows a decline of up to 20 per cent in the marine phytoplankton during the past six decades. Tuna catch rates have abruptly declined during the last half century due to industrial fisheries and ocean warming. Amongst other endangered marine species are dugongs, seals, turtles, and whales. In 2010, an Indian Ocean garbage patch covering at least 5 million km^2 was noticed; this garbage patch circulates with the ocean current from Australia to Africa, down the Mozambique Channel, and back to Australia in a period of six years.

South China Sea Governance

The concept of a Blue Economy within the ASEAN framework finds a place in the ASEAN Economic Community Blueprint which came into effect in 2015. Item A7 deals with Food, Agriculture, and Forestry. The necessity of streamlining the overarching regional security architecture to address issues concerning the maritime commons has been stressed by strategic experts, such as Prof Carlyle Thayer.[11] The latest EAS (East Asia Summit) Statement on Enhancing Regional Maritime Cooperation (issued at its summit meeting in Kuala Lumpur dated 22 November 2015) outlines numerous decisive steps in this direction. They include a detailed Track I Forum in addition to the existing Track 1.5 of Expanded ASEAN Maritime Forum, and emphasise the necessity of maritime security through dialogue as well as building synergies with other regional forums.[12] It affirms complementarity between sustainable maritime economic development (covering fisheries, community empowerment, marine-based renewable energy, tourism, and cooperation with other regional frameworks on shipping, infrastructure, etc.), as well as maritime security and cooperation (UNCLOS and other international laws, CBMs, anti-piracy cooperation with other organisations including IORA), implementation of DOC[13] and early conclusion of COC,[14] cooperation through ADMM Plus, safety of navigation, trans-boundary challenges, etc. As ASEAN moves forward energetically to develop its Blue Economy agenda, the maritime security dimension of this would be seen as critical to its successful implementation. India could be expected to play a role in both these aspects.

Indian Ocean Governance

A similar process is underway in the Indian Ocean Region (IOR) also, although the circumstances are quite different from those in the South China Sea. The security challenges in the by-and-large placid Indian Ocean waters allow concerted regional efforts to bolster a regional Blue Economy. No doubt naval tensions could grow as a result of present challenges inhering more in littoral instability and jihadist extremism leading to conflict (or near-conflict) situations on its vital, northern periphery. IORA is developing structures which meet both the strategic as well as growth requirements in the current strategic environment which is highly conducive for this process. India is also a major player in the Indian Ocean Region which can uphold a favourable, facilitative maritime order. IORA is aiming for regional maritime safety and security through capacity-building, and through a regular dialogue forum between stakeholders in this respect. It aims to strengthen capabilities for maritime search and rescue in the Indian Ocean, including the development of standard operating procedures (SOPs) to cover joint patrolling by maritime security forces.[15] It is in the early stages of developing institutional linkages with the recently created dialogue forum amongst the various navies—namely, the Indian Ocean Naval Symposium (IONS).

At its Perth meeting (October 2014), IORA's Council of Ministers adopted the Blue Economy as its top priority for regional cooperation. This comprised fisheries and aquaculture; renewable energy from ocean, sea ports and shipping; seabed exploration and minerals; marine bio-technology and R&D; tourism; ocean knowledge clusters, as well as SIDS and LDCs.[16] It is expected to boost coastal and national economies, new employment and skill sets, regional interconnectedness, tapping of ocean resources, economic sustainability, and climate change mitigation. A ministerial Blue Economy conference (September 2015), deliberated on these aspects of the IORA agenda. The issues emerging are in terms of funding constraints and skill upgradation; maritime safety and security issues relate to the formulation of guidelines and regional maritime surveillance system. Projects are being identified through a series of seminars being held to develop the agenda of IORA.

Additional Common Governance Mechanisms

Two other organisations also need to be taken into account. They are ASEAN-related, and act as a bridge between the two regions: the BIMSTEC (comprising Bangladesh, India, Myanmar, Sri Lanka, Thailand, Bhutan and Nepal), and the Mekong-Ganga Cooperation organisation (comprising Cambodia, Myanmar, Laos, Vietnam and India). Both these have major connectivity (including maritime) programmes as well as for cooperation in the Blue Economy-related spheres such as food security, fisheries, environment, and natural resource management. The India-ASEAN Vision Document issued at the summit level (December 2012), envisages a Mekong-India Economic Corridor (MIEC) connecting the two regions through the Andaman Sea. The Indian government is already operating two shipping services between Indian ports on its eastern seaboard and Myanmar and, most recently, also with Thailand.

India-ASEAN Initiatives

The initiatives for forging partnerships between India and ASEAN in a Blue Economy are synchronous with Prime Minister Modi's own direct engagement with the Indian Ocean island countries, as well as his articulation of the 'SAGAR' ('Security and Growth for All in the Region') policy (12 March 2015), its strong Blue Economy component being set within a larger strategic framework for the Indian Ocean Region. He also emphasised this aspect during his speech at the India-ASEAN summit in Kuala Lumpur (21 November 2015) in which he considered it an "increasingly important driver of our future economy, and a source of food security, medicines and clean energy." The India-ASEAN Plan of Action (2016-2020) includes areas such as maritime security/safety and co-cooperation, food, agriculture, forests, and fisheries as well as disaster management and emergency response, environment, climate change, bio-diversity, and narrowing the development gap within ASEAN. India has already initiated the process of fleshing out the implementation of various agenda points by convening a conference on maritime security and related issues. Presently, the collaboration between IORA and ASEAN is only envisaged with regard to anti-piracy operations. However, the IORA Secretariat has made an approach to the ASEAN for a dialogue on cooperation in the Blue Economy sector. This is expected to gain traction during the presidency of Indonesia of IORA.

Suggested Approach

IORA is developing an extensive agenda for Blue Economy for the region for multilateral cooperation as well as for incorporation into the programmes of the member countries. Unlike the South China Sea situation, the IOR has seen a modicum of 'defence of the (maritime) system' cooperation against piracy where both the structured and the non-structured coordination amongst the different regional as well as extra-regional navies/coastguards—even belonging to adversarial countries—has been quite extensive. The scope of this developing interoperability and the comfort of experience-sharing can be explored further to cover any potentially system-destabilising issues around guaranteed safe passage through chokepoints and port facilities for visiting extra-regional navies. The Indian Navy has emerged as a powerful force in the Indian Ocean, and can (and should) take a lead role in shaping the strategic discourse on its regional maritime order which is favourable to its national interests, and where it is, overwhelmingly, considered a benign and stabilising force, including by the US Navy. The latter is no doubt significant from a strategic point of view.

This discourse needs to be shaped carefully so that the tense fluidity of the situation in the South China Sea does not spill over into the Indian Ocean. Moreover, there are several member countries which are common to both IORA and ASEAN/East Asia Summit, thus bringing out the inter-connectedness of the two regions. Creating such an order in IOR would also help in strengthening the efforts for the growth of the Blue Economy, in terms of propagation as well as persuasion in both regions.

There is a renewed energy being brought into the creation of a Blue Economy for connecting the two regions (involving IORA as well) where India plays a leading role.[17] Both have significant capabilities, and Indian agencies, especially maritime, are fully engaged in the process. India's 'hard' and 'soft' capabilities can be leveraged to provide the strategic framework for Blue

Economy dynamics to develop between India and ASEAN where the current strategic turbulence is the trigger for significant steps towards maritime security as well as the Blue Economy. The existing structures in IOR can, with suitable upgradation, prevent the situation from getting strategically unstable.

The robust musculature for this skeletal strategic frame would need to be developed by greater engagement by other Indian maritime agencies. The involvement of the Indian Coast Guard in building capacities and sharing experience amongst the IOR littorals is important for the less developed countries especially in terms of creating a stable environment for the sinews of the Blue Economy to develop. We only need to remember the genesis of Somali piracy, to suppress which a huge international effort was required. Cooperation in the shipping sector, shipping infrastructure, and related skills development where India can contribute (and learn) has a huge potential. Coastal shipping remains undeveloped in India even in terms of India's shipping services to its proximate littoral neighbours, although these are no doubt well connected by smugglers' dinghies!

Critically important in the drive to develop a Blue Economy in the IOR as also in ASEAN countries is the Indian Ministry of Earth Sciences. Its role is not merely capacity building but also assisting the region, in collaboration with other countries and agencies, in monsoon and climate models, tsunami sciences, modelling and forecasting, and data-sharing arrangements regarding 24-hour accumulated rainfall. It's steadying strategic security and capacity bolster will channelise and shape the creative energies of the people unleashed by national, bilateral, and multilateral efforts to rejuvenate and modernise the Blue Economy in the two regions through cooperation. The Indian Ministry of Earth Sciences has lamented the nascent state of operational oceanography in the East, especially in African and Asian countries on the Indian Ocean littoral, pointing at enormous scope for cooperation in this sphere.[18]

IORA's website briefs both on 'maritime safety and security' and on 'disaster risk management' recognise substantial capacity limitations presently. The scope for cooperation between ASEAN and IORA was highlighted at a workshop on 'IORA and Strategic Stability in the Indian Ocean', where the ASEAN's example could be followed for IORA's own institution building.[19]

In all of these areas, enormous potential for a healthy dynamic of cooperation in 'blue economy' between India and ASEAN opens up. The various 'blue economy' agencies, identified in the numerous official documents, have a huge agenda to flesh out to develop the right synergies and leadership roles. It is also a vast field where there is scope for activities by government agencies from the national to the local level, non-governmental agencies, business and scientific community, civil society organisations, media and at the people-to-people level.

Conclusion

Managing the Blue Economy is a complex and challenging task, requiring sophistication of governance, micro-coordination with local communities, and sustainable business models. It is also a test of global/regional cooperation, and of trust levels needed for managing the global commons by sublimating narrow national interests and by finessing sectoral conflicts of interests. In this pursuit, both sides have established the basic roadmap for generating this dynamics, along with the supporting institutional mechanisms. However, they have a long road ahead.

It needs to be recognised that developing a virtuous Blue Economy dynamic is both an opportunity and an imperative necessity at this juncture in our two regions. This enterprise also demands a conducive geo-strategic environment at a time of aggravated global tensions. Hence, the failure to do so would trigger a vicious dynamic which could come about if the countries of the region lose clarity of vision and purpose.

NOTES

1. 'Summary of the first global integrated marine assessment', UNGA document (A/70/112 dated 22 July, 2015) under agenda item on Oceans and the law of the sea, daccess-dds-ny.un.org, p. 48, accessed 31 January 2016.
2. 'Blue Economy for Business in East Asia: Towards an Integrated Understanding of the Blue Economy', PEMSEA (Partnerships in Environmental Management for the Seas of East Asia) Report, November 2015, at pemsea.org, accessed 4 February 2016.
3. According to one study, every dollar invested in integrated coastal management (ICM) in Xiamen (China) has returned seven dollars in economic benefit to the city. See also, note no. 2, op. cit.
4. Stephen Harrison, 'Climate Change and Security,' in *Imagining Asia in 2030*, (eds.) Ajay Lele and Namrata Goswami, New Delhi: IDSA, 2011.
5. UNDP: 'Conserve and sustainably use the oceans, seas and marine resources', at undp.org, accessed on 2 February 2016.
6. Johnny Langenheim, 'Preventing Ecocide in the South China Sea', *The Guardian*, 15 July 2015, at theguardian.com, accessed on 2 February 2016.
7. James Borton, 'Why China's "Blue Economy" is one of the major environmental issues of

the 21st century', 28 September 2015, planetexperts.com, accessed on 3 February 2016.

8. Op cit., note 2.
9. World Resources Institute, 'Reefs at Risk in the Indian Ocean', February 2011, at www.wri.org/resources/maps/reefs-risks-indian-ocean, accessed 3 February 2016.
10. Wikipedia, 'Indian Ocean', at en.m.wikipedia.org, accessed 3 February 2016.
11. Carlyle Thayer, 'Beyond Territoriality: Managing the Maritime Commons in the South China Sea', 28th Asia-Pacific Round Table, 2-4 June, 2014, Kuala Lumpur, Malaysia, at isis.org, accessed 2 February 2016.
12. ASEAN website, at asean.org, accessed 2 February 2016. (EAS comprises ASEAN countries plus India, Australia, New Zealand, Japan, South Korea, China, US and Russia).
13. Declaration on the Conduct of Parties in the South China Sea between ASEAN and China, 2002.
14. Code of Conduct for the South China Sea between ASEAN and China, under negotiation.
15. IORA website, iora.net, accessed 11 February 2016.
16. Ibid.
17. The World Ocean Council aims to create a 'smart oceans' platform for multiple applications by developing improved, real-time availability of localised data such as currents, wave characteristics and water quality.
18. Draft Approach Paper for the 12th Five Year Plan, 2012-2017, Ministry of Earth Sciences, at http://www.moes.gov.in/Draft%20Approach12th%20FiVE%20YEAR%20PLAN.pdf., accessed 23 July 2014.
19. www.rsis.edu.sg/wp-content/uploads/2014/07/CR-2014-06-25-RSIS-IORA_WEB.pdf:, accessed 13 October 2014.

20

Beyond the Indian Ocean: India and its Blue Economy Partnerships in the South China Sea

Joefe B. Santarita

The oceans are a shared resource which require transboundary perspective and active partnerships of various stakeholders. Just like any bodies of water, the South China Sea (SCS) is an important 'development space' that needs utmost attention and collaboration. Unfortunately, this space is currently the source of contention between countries such as China, Vietnam and the Philippines among others. Nevertheless, the attempt to develop the blue economy in the SCS demands for new partnerships among the stakeholders within and across the area to include India. The latter's interest to get involve in the blue economy within the SCS zone, aside from its own Indian Ocean, is not surprising given its long history of interaction with Southeast Asian countries as manifested by its *Act East Policy* (rejuvenated Look East Policy).

This paper, therefore, will explore India's recent engagements with Southeast Asian countries to steer a sustainable blue-economy in the SCS. In particular, this paper will document collaborative programs and activities with countries (e.g. Philippines and Vietnam) such as food security, promotion of sustainable marine development and management as well as creation of wealth-generating opportunities based on inclusive, oceans-based economic growth. Lastly, it will also explore the role of Indian and ASEAN business and industrial sectors to complement government initiatives in effectively managing both fisheries and nonliving sea resources in the area.

Introduction

The oceans are a shared resource which require trans-boundary perspective and active partnerships of various stakeholders. Just like any bodies of water, the South China Sea (SCS) is an important 'development space' that needs utmost attention and collaboration. Unfortunately, this space is currently the source of contention between countries such as China, Vietnam and the Philippines among others. Nevertheless, the attempt to develop the blue economy in the SCS demands for new partnerships among the stakeholders within and across the area to include India. The latter's interest to get involved in the blue economy within the SCS zone, aside from its own Indian Ocean, is not surprising given its long history of interaction with Southeast Asian countries as manifested by its *Act East Policy* (rejuvenated Look East Policy). The SCS, located very close to the southern tip of the Andaman and Nicobar Islands, is very much a part of India's "extended neighborhood". It is of critical geopolitical, geo-economic and geostrategic importance and has a direct bearing on India's relations with a host of strategically relevant countries in the region.[1] The SCS covers an area of about 3.8 million square kilometres (km^2) in the western Pacific Ocean, including the Gulf of Thailand and Gulf of Tonkin. Its southern part lies on the Sunda Shelf and contains coral reefs in waters less than 200 metres (m) in depth, while further north there are basins with depths around 5,000 m. A semi-enclosed sea, the SCS includes over 200 islands and islets, and touches the coastlines of China, Hong Kong, Macau, Taiwan, the Philippines, Malaysia, Brunei, Indonesia, Singapore, Vietnam, Thailand, and Cambodia.[2]

The importance of SCS is reflected in various aspects. The area is one of the important waterways in the world. It facilitates inter-shipping of considerable volume of raw material and food accounting to more than 90 per cent of the total freight volume, among which petroleum and related products that account for 55 per cent and iron ore for 10 per cent. Statistics show that more than 40,000 vessels pass though the area annually.[3] The region, stretching from Singapore and the Strait of Malaca in the southwest to the Strait of Taiwan in the northeast, is considered as one the most significant trade routes in the world. It is home to rich resources and is of significant strategic and political importance.

Moreover, SCS according to U.S. Energy Information Administration has the potential as a rich source of hydrocarbons. The region has proven oil reserves of around 1.2 km^3 (7.7 billion barrels), with an estimate of 4.5 km^3 (28 billion barrels) in total. Natural gas reserves are estimated to total around 7,500 km^3 (266 trillion cubic feet). There are approximately 11 billion barrels of oil reserves and 190 trillion cubic feet of natural gas reserves[4]. As of 2011, the estimated oil production in the SCS reaches only to 1,255,000 barrels per day and around 3,400 billion cubic feet for natural gas. The major exploration and production areas include Baram Delta in Brunei Darussalam; Pearl River Mouth Basin, Qiongdongnan Basin in China; Natuna Basin in Indonesia; Sabah Sarawak Malay Basin (with Thailand); Palawan Basin in the Philippines; Gulf of Thailand Malaysia Basin (with Malaysia) in Thailand and Cuu Long Basin and Nam Con Son Basin in Vietnam. Such areas are either jointly or individually exploited by the respective countries' national oil companies and/ or leading foreign firms.[5]

The Chinese National Offshore Oil Company, however, in its report last November 2012 provided an estimate of the presence of around 125 billion barrels of oil and 500 trillion cubic feet of natural gas in undiscovered resources in the area. The report also said evidence reveals that most of these resources are likely located in the contested Reed Bank at the northeast end of the Spratlys, which are claimed by China, Taiwan, and Vietnam.[6]

In terms of fisheries and marine resources, the SCS is biologically diverse but knowledge of its marine fauna is relatively incomplete. The most comprehensive study was done in 2000 identifying at least 3,365 species in 263 families (Witter, et al 2015: 2). Reported fisheries landings in the SCS are around 10 million tons.[7]

In terms of tourism industry, only two countries (Vietnam and China) encourage cruising the area. The Vietnamese government particularly Ho Chi Minh City is offering a limited-time promotion for 180 Vietnamese to take a 6 day tour of the two reefs in the disputed Spratly Islands (Troung Sa) and partake in activities such as fishing, visiting a lighthouse and eating local seafood.[8] China too started in 2013 to introduce tourist cruises bound for the disputed Paracel islands in the SCS. The 4 day trip offered Chinese citizens a chance to see different smaller island sand reefs in the disputed waters.[9] In fact, Chinese tourist companies such as the Coconut Fragrance Princess Cruise was introduced in 2012 by the Hainan Strait Shipping Co. Ltd. (HSSC), to promote tourism in the Paracel Islands, especially to Quanfu Dao/All Wealth Island and Yagong Dao/Male Duck Island. Initially, the Princess Cruise made losses and was subsidized by the government. But its operational performance improved after Sanya became the departing port in September 2014 and Yinyu/ Observation Bank was added to the existing two destinations. Such tourism operations are inevitably linked to nationalism. Tour activities include flag-raising and oath-taking ceremonies. Over 10,000 Chinese tourists, touted to be patriots, have visited the Paracel Islands.[10]

Given the SCS' geo-political, geo-economic and geo-strategic importance, many countries are now interested to claim their stake in the area causing some irritants to the relations of these countries. Despite these issues, manifestations of collaboration are also observable among institutions, individuals and nation-states. This includes the cooperation of India and ASEAN countries in the SCS in recent times particularly in the field of blue economy.

India's Blue Economy Partnerships in SCS: A Survey

India's involvement in the blue economy has gone beyond its own domain, the Indian Ocean. In recent years, India has shown interests in its extended neighborhood by extending assistance and forging collaborative projects with its counterparts in the SCS area. A glimpse of the matrix covering the components of the ocean economy as provided by *The Economist* (2015) is imperative to give us an idea of the sectors that need utmost attention in the development of ocean economy.

Based on this matrix, India's engagements with countries in the SCS area in terms of blue economy remains limited. The lack or absence of these engagements in the abovementioned components should not be seen as weakness but rather as opportunities to work out in the near future.

In terms of harvesting of living resources, India since 1990s made several collaborative engagements with various countries in the SCS particularly on fisheries. It made cooperation with Indonesia through its MOU on Cooperation in Marine and Fisheries in 2011.[11] An MoU was also signed between National Fisheries Development Board, Hyderabad, Department of Animal Husbandry, Dairying and Fisheries, Ministry of Agriculture of the Republic of India and Directorate of Fisheries, Ministry of Agriculture and

Table 1: Components of the Ocean Economy

Type of activity	*Ocean service*	*Established industries*	*Emerging industries*	*New industries*
Harvesting of living resources	Seafood	Fisheries	Sustainable fisheries	
			Aquaculture	Multi-species aquaculture
	Marine bio-technology		Pharmaceuticals, chemicals	
Extraction of non-living resources, generation of new resources	Minerals	Seabed mining	Deep seabed mining	
	Energy	Oil and gas	Renewables	
	Fresh water		Desalination	
Commerce and trade in and around the ocean	Transport and trade	Shipping Port infrastructure and services		
	Tourism and recreation	Tourism		
		Coastal development		
			Eco-tourism	
Response to ocean health challenges	Ocean monitoring and surveillance		Technology and R&D	
	Carbon sequestration		Blue carbon (i.e. coastal vegetated habitats)	
	Coastal protection		Habitat protection, restoration	
	Waste disposal			Assimilation of nutrients, solid waste

Source: The Economist, 2015, p.6.

Rural Development, Government of the Socialist Republic of Vietnam on Cooperation in the Field of Setting up of Pangasius (catfish) Breeding and Farming in India last September 2014.[12]. In the latter development of the blue economy, there is the potential to look at the development of marine bio-technology particularly in the field of pharmaceuticals and chemical from the marine resources.

In terms of extraction of non-living resources, generation of new resources, India has sealed partnerships with Vietnam on seabed mining and oil and gas exploration. In October 2011, India's state-owned oil company ONGC Videsh Limited signed an agreement with Vietnam to expand and promote oil exploration in the South China Sea. Despite China's protestations that the exploration of Blocks 127 and 128 is in violation of its sovereignty, ONGC Videsh went ahead with the projects. More recently, during Vietnamese Prime Minister Dung's visit to India in October 2014, ONGC Videsh and PetroVietnam signed a mutual cooperation agreement on the exploration of several South China Sea oil blocks.[13]

In the Philippines, Energon, developer and owner of wind power assets in Asia with offices in Bangalore and Manila, has invested 110 MW of projects under construction in India and the Philippines. As of date, Energon has 27 wind mills in Pililla, Rizal in partnership with local government units of the province of Rizal.

In terms of commerce and trade in and around the ocean, India also contributed in the security of the area and in a way securing the safety of those cargo vessels passing the SCS. In the near future, it is also hoped that Indian government will assist the Philippines in the construction of its commercial ports in Palawan and even Kalayan Island in the West Philippine Sea. Similarly, it is also good to see India's lucid partnership with Vietnam and other countries in mainland Southeast Asian countries facing the SCS.

Brunei's main port, Muara—one of the main ports in Southeast Asia through which the bulk of the country's oil and gas exports to India take place—is in the South China Sea region and will become a major component of India's growing maritime partnership with Brunei.

In terms of response to ocean health challenges, India has limited participation in the ocean monitoring and surveillance, carbon sequestration and coastal protection in the SCS area. This is one of the components of blue economy which India could potentially explore in the near future. In particular, India too can assist the Philippines in hydrographical surveys as well as the mapping of the Ocean floor. India has recently embarked in the area of seabed mineral exploration research and the two countries can share their respective expertise.[14]

Role of Indian and ASEAN Business and Industrial Sectors

Investing in blue economy will make superior returns for the interested investors compared to business as usual. John Tobin opines that emerging industries showcase the potential of new technologies and approaches: aquaculture, the farming of aquatic organisms, is becoming increasingly productive and helps combat the problem of marine resource depletion. Tourism is economically important in many countries, particularly in coastal areas, and the growing ecotourism sector takes account of the need for preservation, while bringing in revenue. Moreover, investments in alternative energy technologies are increasing, and scientific research continuously improves our understanding of these complex ecosystems.[15]

As mentioned above, India and ASEAN countries in the SCS can potentially collaborate on the development and utilisation of ocean resources to advance marine bio-technology particularly in the field of pharmaceuticals and chemical given that India is known as one of the biggest producers and suppliers of affordable and high quality medicines in the world. The potentials of sea weeds and grasses thriving in the SCS area for drug materials will both benefit India and partner countries. In particular, the use of caragenaan as HIV antiretorvirals—a vaginal suppository made with seaweeds.[16] This will also translate to the efficient and effective delivery of health services of the governments of the day to their respective constituents. The case of **Botika sa Barangay** (medicines in the villages) program in the Philippines will greatly benefit from this possibility.

Another component that investors could possibly explore in the SCS is the blue economy initiative focused on the blue ecosystem called aquaponics, the combination of fish farming and vegetable farming. This sector represents the highest growth niche in the aqua culture business, which is now the world's fastest growing farming sector with an average worldwide growth rate of 6 to 8 per cent and a worldwide value of $86 billion in 2009 as cited in Pauli's case study.

Aquaponics produces cultured fish in a controlled environment. Hence, it does not deplete natural aquatic resources but only taps them for the initial stock. The leading producers of cultured fish are China, with 70 per cent of the market, India, Vietnam, Thailand, and Indonesia.[17]

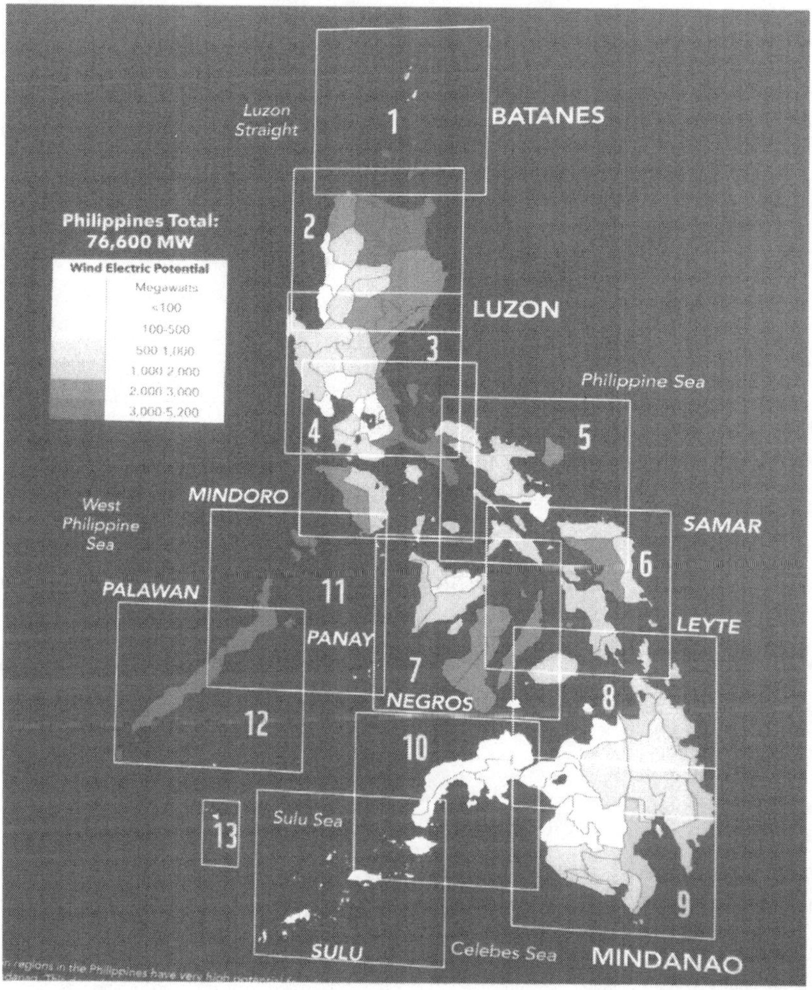

In terms of extraction of non-living resources, India and ASEAN countries can work on the development of the emerging industries such as renewable energy and fresh water production through desalination. Due to climate change, even countries that are currently enjoying fresh water supply will surely be affected by this condition particularly those coastal areas surrounding the SCS. Hence, it is imperative that countries in the region in partnership with India will contribute in addressing the freshwater shortages in the future.

Entrepreneurs both from India and Southeast Asia should also continue to harness the alternative energy such as wind farm in areas surrounding the

SCS. Despite the presence of windfarms established in the Philippines as stated above, there are more areas in the Philippines and Southeast Asia that have potential source of alternative energy. In the Philippines, regions such as 1, 2, 4, 11, 12, and 13 based on Wind Atlas are identified with regions 11 and 12 that have high wind electric potentials and have capabilities to produce 3,000-5,200 MW respectively. This is the sector in which India could possibly collaborate with the Philippines.

Indian investors along their counterparts in the area can work to develop the emerging industries such as partnership in the technology and R&D in ocean monitoring and surveillance. These institutions can also consider the academics and experts such as the Indian Institute of Technology, Jawaharlal Nehru University among others to collaborate with their counterparts in the University of the Philippines, Vietnam National University, National University of Singapore among others. Moreover, businessmen and non-governmental organisations can also work out in the growth in the coastal and ocean protection and conservation activities to include carbon sequestration—blue carbon (e.g. coastal vegetated habitats). Indian entrepreneurs through their company's corporate social responsibility program can also coordinate in the habitat protection and restoration to include waste disposal among others and perhaps recycle of this for other uses such as waste to fish food and others.

Conclusion

It is clear that India has vital maritime interests vested in the South China Sea. In pursuance of its Act East Policy, India's engagement with the South China Sea resident nations increased multifold and the economic ties flourished and lately engaging in the blue economy partnerships.

It is also important to note that in the process, a new direction has been shaped with blue economy as new paradigm for cooperation between India and the resident countries in the SCS region.

Another observation is that India's engagement in SCS is not just a pure government to government initiatives but also civil society organisations/non-governmental organisations and private institutions. Moreover, there is a realisation that even within the government to government purview, the engagement is not just between central governments but also local government units to include even the lowest/smallest political unit such as barangay or village officials—e.g. wind farms consortium. By doing so, the connection is binding and stakeholders in all levels have the sense of ownership and commitment to the engagements. Moreover, Innovative financing to direct investments into those economic activities that can enhance ocean health is also encouraged. Many public and private economic activities that could serve to restore ocean health will carry higher upfront costs and returns that will not immediately be accrued to investors. This suggests the need for new and innovative financing mechanisms, more capital than is currently being deployed, and for a greater degree of collaboration between the public and private sectors. Hence, a public private partnership is imperative to bolster the development of those "emerging" and "new" industries focused on restoring ocean health.[18]

Lastly, in order for the blue economy initiatives to work well, these should be complemented with the bold actions of all stakeholders to reform institutions governing the ocean economy to keep pace with accelerating economic activity. Good laws and regulations, strong institutions and inter-ministerial cooperation, inclusive decision making processes involving all stakeholders (including business), evidence-based support and credible arbitration mechanisms.[19] By doing so, India's experience in the Indian Ocean in terms of ocean governance will add value to the present and potential programs in the SCS. Subsequently, these initiatives will also reinforce India's presence in the area through its reinvigorated Act East policy.

NOTES

1. Shoikat Roy, 'Understanding India's Role in the South China Sea,' at http://takshashila.org.in
2. Alison Witter, et al., 'Taking Stock and Projecting the Future of South China Sea Fisheries,' Working Paper #2015-99. Fisheries Centre, The University of British Columbia. 2015.
3. 'Treasures in the South China Sea,' *China Economic Weekly*, 2012 as cited by Dr. Su Hao. Maritime Resources in the South China and China's Management in the International Legal Context, 7th Berlin Conference on Asian Security. 2013.
4. Lin Shu-yuan and Jaime Wang, 'U.S. report details rich resources in South China Sea,' *Focus Taiwan News Channel*, 2013, https://web.archive.org/web/20130213111846/http://focustaiwan.tw/ShowNews/WebNews_Detail.aspx?ID=201302090013&Type=aIPL.
5. US Energy Information Administration, South China Sea, 7 February 2013. https://www.eia.gov/beta/international/analysis_includes/regions_of_interest/South_China_Sea/south_china_sea.pdf.
6. Lin and Wang, n. 4.
7. Alison Witter, et al., Species that are harvested in the area include flying fishes, tunas, billfishes, mackerels, and sharks, snappers and soles, crabs, shrimps, squids, groupers, parrotfishes, rabbitfishes, and some herring, sardines and anchovies.

8. Michelle Florcruz, 'South China Sea Tourism?: Vietnam Sending Tourist Cruises to disputed Spratly islands,' *International Business Times*, 2015.
9. Florcruz 2015.
10. Xue Gong, 'Chinese Corporate Players in the South China Sea: Complicating the Disputes?,' RSIS Commentary, 14 September 2016, at https://www.rsis.edu.sg/wp-content/uploads/2016/09/CO16228.pdf
11. http://www.mea.gov.in/Portal/ForeignRelation/Indonesia_January_2014.pdf
12. http://pib.nic.in/newsite/PrintRelease.aspx?relid=109702
13. Danielle Rajendram, 'Lowy Institute Analysis,' 18 December 2014, at http://www.lowyinstitute.org/publications/indias-new-asia-pacific-strategy-modi-acts-east.
14. Pankaj Jha, 'Engaging Philippines under the Act East Policy,' Indian Council of World Affairs, at http://www.icwa.in/pdfs/PB/2014/EngagingPhilippinesPB06072015.pdf.
15. John Tobin, 'Global Head of Sustainability, The Future of the "Blue Economy",' 03 July 2015, at https://www.credit-suisse.com/ph/en/about-us/responsibility/news-stories/articles/news-and-expertise/2015/07/en/the-future-of-the-blue-economy.html.
16. Caregeenan is preferred ingredient due to its efficiency in removing the possibility of animal infections and is acceptable to vegetarians and is heat stable in tropical countries. Fiona Barry. Seaweed: the secret ingredient to HIV drug delivery? 09 September 2014, at http://www.in-pharmatechnologist.com/Drug-Delivery/Seaweed-the-secret-ingredient-to-HIV-drug-delivery
17. Cora Claudio, 'Mapping the Future: From green to blue economy,' Philippine Daily Inquirer, 23 June 2013, at http://business.inquirer.net/128587/from-green-to-blue-economy.
18. *The Economist*, p. 12
19. *The Economist*, pp. 11-12.

21

A Blue Economy Strategy for Indo-ASEAN Region

Girish Gujar and Hong Yan

Two novel but conflicting phenomenon emerged almost simultaneously in the United States of America in the latter half of the 20th century. The first idea was that of globalisation and free trade which was promoted and embraced with equal enthusiasm. The second was the phenomenon of Limits to Growth (LTG) and Sustainability which was widely recognised, and did find recognition in certain quarters but was not as aggressively promoted as the first phenomenon by policy makers—for obvious reasons.

Michael Porter has suggested that tempering unhealthy global trade competition is critical, and due recognition of both the above mentioned phenomenon will perforce lead to the mutation of sectors, regions, and countries to a higher, more evolved state of economic affairs. This evolved state of the economy is euphemistically termed as the Blue Economy. It signifies lower costs, reduced waste, greater efficiency as well as shared and added value in both manufacturing and services. It also means lesser production, reduced consumption, and near sourcing.

This essay attempts to outline a Blue Economy strategy for Indo-ASEAN countries in the face of the multifaceted challenges they are likely to face while attempting to suitably adapt to the brave new world.

The World in "The Box"

The world has experienced consistent economic and trade growth for over a decade. This has been largely due to the manipulation of supply side economic factors, greatly assisted by technological improvement, by almost all national governments in tandem. In the bargain, demand side factors and the potential impact of minorities were ignored. Hence, the world has entered an era of diminishing returns. However, the pace of technological change is increasing, and all these factors taken together are propelling the global economy into uncharted waters. In passing, it could be said that the exponential growth of the ocean transportation industry greatly assisted global economic growth.

Ever since the shipping of "fifty-eight aluminum truck bodies aboard an aging tanker ship moored in Newark, New Jersey", which "five days later [...] sailed into Houston, where fifty-eight trucks waited to take on the metal boxes and haul them to their destinations",[1] container shipping has become a global trade which involves containers standardized at 20 and 40 feet, with fixed dimensions and properties, to be shipped all over the world. The road towards this kind of standardization was not easy; but its eventual impact has been enormous, with substantial reductions in shipping costs over decades.

As supply chains became more global and more operations got outsourced and moved offshore, the impact of transportation on supply chain performance has increased. Nearly all the intercontinental transportation of goods has eventually begun to take place by sea, and an increasing share of this transport has become containerized. And yet, though containerization has been the main development of the maritime industry in the past fifty years, its full impact on the global economy has yet to be adequately assessed.

A wide variety of issues regarding transportation, with an immediate and direct impact on supply chain management, have recently begun receiving increased attention. These include tightened security, increased vulnerability, potential delays, additional requirements on information provisioning, restricted connectivity, and increased congestion. Some of these have resulted in increased duration and variability of travel time, heightened pressure on energy usage, and carbon emissions.

Since the early 1990s, world container traffic has been growing at almost three times world GDP growth,[2] while container port throughputs have increased even faster due to an increase in the number of containers being transshipped. In 2015, world container throughput at ports amounted to 650 million TEU—an increase of 4 per cent over the previous year—following multiple years of double-digit growth.[3] Despite the growth in throughput, there are many idle ships all over the world with unsustainably low freight rates, resulting in several shipping companies facing bankruptcies and closure.

A very important development took place in 2009. It was the birth of mega container carriers which drove a lot of decision making towards hub and spoke networks (Robinson, R., 2012).[4] Increasingly, larger containers ships (now up to 18,000 TEU) are now used to transport containers between large hubs such as Hong Kong, Shanghai, Shenzhen, and Rotterdam, while smaller feeder vessels are used to bring the containers to the hubs from smaller ports, and from downstream hubs to the port of destination. The main driver of this phenomenon has been the reduction in the average cost per container, which is lower for larger vessels due to economies of scale in construction, manpower, and energy usage.

Most of the important ports of the world today were constructed during the industrial revolution in the 19th century, which were incrementally expanded and modernised with the advent of containerization. Further capacity augmentation took place as a direct result of globalisation and the IT revolution. It also led to the deeper penetration of hinterlands, particularly in China, the USA, and Western Europe. However, the growth story took a downward turn with the financial crisis in 2008 which put sudden brakes on the high speed growth of port infrastructure. The globally orchestrated quantitative easing did delay the end for a couple of years; but the writing on the wall was clearly obvious to all concerned.

The current important trend of the outsourcing of manufacturing activities has had direct consequences on the type of merchandise shipped via ocean transportation. Traditionally, ocean transport was used predominantly for raw materials and agricultural products. This later shifted to consumer products, but is now dominated by intermediate products, i.e. products upon which additional value adding operations take place in the country of import. This suggests a further increasing importance from a supply chain perspective since now not only consumer products but also intermediates are shipped via ocean container transport, thus indicating even more than a single ocean link in the supply chain.[5] This trend depends heavily on improved process efficiencies. These will lead to the evolved state of the Blue Economy which demands a secure maritime domain to thrive and succeed.

However, this impressive growth in global trade has also led to the rise in amplitude of two major issues: sustainability and inequality. Though the issue of global warming has to a certain extent been addressed by improvements in green technology and the setting aside of financial resources for neutralising the impact of natural disasters by way of purchasing insurance, the impact of galloping inequality in the distribution of wealth has yet to be addressed. The impact of this phenomenon has been severely felt by policymakers in the recently conducted *Brexit* referendum. Perhaps the evolution of the Blue Economy could offer some solution by way of assisting in increasing the size of the global economic pie.

This would, however, necessitate the deployment of scarce financial and other resources to improve the skills required by the Blue Economy. The question that remains to be answered is: who would foot the bill? Unwilling corporate beneficiaries? Or, the slightly willing but pauperized national governments? In any case, it is quite obvious that current and prospective employees are both unable and unwilling to upgrade themselves to the required levels on their own.

The Evolution of Blue Economy

It should be remembered that since very recently we have begun to live in the era of the SMART (Specific, Measurable, Achievable, Relevant, Time-Oriented) economy where efficiency, adaptability, improvisation, innovation, and customer satisfaction matters much more than size, growth rate, or revenue generation. As such, the SMART global economic system could be defined as a sustainable, measurable, highly focused, self-assessing and correcting—that is, almost living creature.[6]. Moreover, the systems of tomorrow will also necessarily have to metamorphose themselves into SMART and adaptive and flexible entities that are forever willing to improve their service quality in an efficient manner in order to ensure increasing stakeholder satisfaction. They will have to consistently find innovative ways to cut costs, improve security, and eliminate waste. Eventually, value addition will be a mission rather than a process.[7]

Perhaps it was erroneous in the first place to expect perpetual linear growth in the global economy and trade without accounting for some negative side effects, such as global warming, poor security, and the unequal distribution of wealth. Hence, we are witnessing the evolution of a Blue Economy. The major players in this economy are in all industrial sectors (such as retail giants like Alibaba and Amazon) on one hand, and media/internet giants (such as Google and Facebook) have displayed growth of a different kind. Such commercial entities are nimble and SMART, and have also altered their business models accordingly. They have also managed to beat recession, and are back on the growth track. Those who have failed to do so find themselves on the slippery slopes of bankruptcy and destruction.

Establishing intelligent infrastructure is imperative to ensure smooth and efficient trade flows in the SMART system. Intelligent information technology—consisting of elements such as Bluetooth, hotspots or WLAN, cloud, mobile end devices, and more— are deployed to collect information in real time. An intermodal Traffic Centre will connect the various modes of transport, and make traffic flows on water, rail, and road more efficient. Such a centre will also process all traffic information collected in the smart port, and distribute it to all stakeholders. The stakeholders and decision makers will then be able to read relevant traffic information in real time, enabling them to choose the fastest and most favorable mode of transport to get their goods to their final destination.

The IT revolution has also facilitated deeper penetration, and hence economic growth has moved into hinterlands, particularly in China, USA, and Western Europe. However, the growth story took an interesting turn with the financial crisis in 2008 which put a sudden brake on the high speed port locomotive. The orchestrated quantitative easing by the G20 countries did delay the end for a couple of years, but the writing on the wall was clearly visible to all even then. The financial stimulus provided by respective national governments, in addition to creating excess capacities, also helped in providing research funding for developing innovative technology, helpful for cutting costs especially in the field of robotics, automation, and artificial intelligence.

The improvement in technology also gave a fillip for collecting and collating a vast quantity of information, aptly called 'big data', which helped to increase precision and eliminate waste as well as dramatically improve process efficiencies. As a result of this, companies and organisations have started to reduce their inventory. This has also resulted in the drastic shrinking of the shipping market, leading to a fall in freight rates.

Despite all this, the global economic system as a whole continues to face far greater risk due to the lack of cross board standardisation in several critical areas, some of which are enumerated below.

i. Ambiguous port and dry port logistics processes
ii. Low-speed hinterland connectivity
iii. Lack of adequate mechanisation/automation/robotics
iv. Non-transparent and inadequately integrated organisation structures
v. Inadequate investments in Wi-Fi and satellite based information systems
vi. Inappropriate capacity augmentation
vii. Unavailability of dedicated freight corridors
viii. Insufficient private sector participation and competition regulation
ix. Non-standardised environmental regulations
x. Ship and port security regulations

Having said this, the business models of the economic hubs of tomorrow will be far more extensive in scope. Some hubs have already invested in making steel, refining oil, generating electricity, processing food, operating tourist resorts, and retail distribution.[8] It goes without saying that technology will be playing a major role in the future growth and development of hubs not only in the physical movement of cargoes but, more importantly, in handling, storing and disseminating the information about the cargo handled by them. The value of such information cannot be overemphasised, as the information itself can be used in the economics of the supply chain of the entire range of cargoes. The corollary to this development would be the birth of virtual hubs which could be more productive and efficient than the physical entity.[9] How will such hub operating companies be governed and regulated? This question has yet to find a satisfactory answer.

Turbulence in the Indo-ASEAN Region

Presently the Indo-ASEAN region is viewed as a more "active" region than the Atlantic and Pacific Regions as it is hosting a spectrum of activities ranging from extensive trade, transportation as well as important energy transfers which are quantitatively as well as qualitatively much larger in scope and size than can be found in the other two regions. It is, perhaps, the only region through which SLOCs (Sea Lines of Communication) reach out to the entire world, be it those originating from the Persian Gulf with oil and gas laden ships, or those with other cargo or commodities from the littorals as well as transiting ships from the Far East. Significantly, some of the world's most important choke points and narrow passages provide access to the Ocean, and these can have associated vulnerabilities. Hence maritime security and the freedom of the seas in this region has become a pre-requisite for future global economic growth.

As such, the current accent on increasing globalisation in the economic field has brought attendant maritime security concerns to the fore for the littorals. Thus, with a rising trajectory of sea borne trade which compliments this accent, there seems to be a corresponding increase in asymmetric threats. Incidents of maritime transnational crimes (like modern piracy, terrorism, drug running, etc.) in their ever evolving manifestations have emerged as the bane of the sea farer. As these maritime security challenges are essentially asymmetric in nature, there have been strident calls for effective law enforcement as well as the maintenance of maritime order by all stakeholders.

At present, new concepts of common, comprehensive and cooperative security have been added to the old idea of collective security policies. Confusion was bound to follow as the term security is used to describe different things or conditions in different contexts. The question is less one of 'what exactly is security?' Rather, it is perhaps better phrased as 'what are the different ways in which to conceive of security; and what are the implications for economic policy development?'

The Indo-ASEAN region is a region that is alive to political turbulence as well as a complex jostle for power between emerging powers, rushing in to fill in the perceived erosion of US primacy or influence. While the erosion may be notional and debatable, the jostle for power is existent in that many participating major players are seeking to enhance their strategic influence in the emerging vacant niche, seeking primacy along with that of USA. The list of serious contenders includes India and China, with countries such as Australia, Japan, Indonesia and South Africa also in the fray, playing the role of king-makers.

The other reason for this jostle is geo-political. We are witnessing a near collapse of good order in the Middle East, with conditions of civil war in some states. The USA is pulling out its troops from the region as they cannot find any justification for their continuing presence in an endless conflict situation. The resulting vacuum will no doubt be filled with all and sundry warlords who will be unable to bring stability to this region. It will also have a negative impact on the surrounding countries, *including* India and China.

However, despite the strategic divergence and competitiveness on many issues in the region, both India and China are increasingly keen to assume the responsibilities of the global policing of the maritime commons which the USA has, so far, been discharging, especially after the exit of the British from the region in the late 1960s. This will necessarily mean clearly identifying and stating the common objectives as well as enumerating the areas of disagreement. The next step would be endeavoring to develop a short term as well as long term strategy and, finally, preparing a roadmap to implement it.

Given such a scenario, multinational forums in the region will necessarily have to come to the fore as they have an important role to play in this regard. Maritime initiatives like the Indian Ocean Naval Symposium (IONS) and those like IORA (Indian Ocean Rim Association) can also be used for the cooperation and development of policies related to overcoming issues deriving from such and similar issues. Similarly, the ARF (ASEAN Regional Forum), the ADMM Plus and its associated agencies (e.g., like the ASEAN Maritime Forum) could also play a significant role in encouraging cooperation.

Conclusion

Looking into the future, one can discern the blurred outlines of the Blue Economy of tomorrow. They will be highly integrated, with multi-roles and multi-national entities. It would also be logical to state that such entities would prefer to interact with similar entities in different regions in order to create synergies for the benefit of their customers, rather than with old inefficient behemoths. The present systems have only two choices: either to upgrade and connect to the new entity network, or shrivel and die.[10] The development of the Blue Economy network of the future will not only require large investments but, most importantly, a global vision on the part of policy makers and a missionary zeal on the part of the operators to mutate and evolve to a higher level of service provision. It goes without saying that revolutionary changes in the legal environment will also be necessary to dovetail into the technological change. Finally, it is critical to emphasise that the Blue Economy system is not any kind of science fiction of tomorrow but a fact of today on which the very survival of nations depends. The Darwinian message is clear: evolve or perish.

NOTES

1. M. Levinson, *The Box: how the Shipping Container made the World Smaller and the World Economy Bigger*, Princeton, NJ: Princeton University Press, 2006.
2. 'Regional shipping and port development strategies (container traffic forecast)', Report, ST/ESCAP/2398, UN-ESCAP (United Nations Economic and Social Commission for Asia and the Pacific), New York: United Nations, 2005.
3. Review of Maritime Transport, UNCTAD, 2013.
4. R. Robinson, 'Ports as elements in value-driven chain systems: the new paradigm', *Maritime Policy & Management*, 29(3), 2010, pp. 241–255.
5. X. Clark, Dollar, D., and Micco, A., 'Port Efficiency, Maritime Transport Costs, and Bilateral Trade', *Journal of Development Economics*, 2004, pp. 75, 417–450.
6. T. Notteboom, & Winkelmans W., 'Structural changes in logistics: How do port authorities face the challenge?,' *Maritime Policy and Management*, 28, 2011, pp. 71–89.
7. Port Reform Toolkit, World Bank, (n.d.), Retrieved from www.worldbank.org
8. P. Cariou, 'Dedicated terminals in container ports: A cost-benefit analysis', Research seminar: Maritime transport, globalisation, regional integration, and territorial development, 2013.
9. 'Global container terminals: Profit, performance and prospects', Drewry Shipping Consultants, London: Drewry, 2013.
10. G. Akerlof, 'The Market for Lemons: Quality, Uncertainty and the Market Mechanism', *Quarterly Journal of Economics,* 2010, pp. 84, 488–500.

22

Protecting and Preserving a Shared Cultural Heritage

Himanshu Prabha Ray

The traditionally accepted image of relations between ASEAN and India revolves around the spread of religions such as Buddhism and Hinduism, and the sharing of knowledge systems—for example, the Sanskrit language. In addition to these, two other staples may be added—the *Ramayana* and its influence across Asia; and trade in Indian textiles across the Indian Ocean. More recently, attention has shifted to historical developments in the region in the nineteenth and early twentieth century, as these have a direct bearing on present concerns.[1]

A somewhat under-researched theme continues to be the development of new disciplines such as archaeology and art history, which evolved from a European intellectual milieu and was transposed on to countries of Asia under colonial rule.[2] By the beginning of the twentieth century, state institutions had been firmly established in several regions of Asia for the practice of archaeology, which was largely concerned at this time with conservation work and reclaiming the heritage of the colonies, as also displaying it through exhibitions in Europe. Thus, the nineteenth and twentieth century marked major transformations in an understanding of the past, but more importantly brought it into the public domain. It is important that these changes be documented and understood as we engage with our neighbours across the seas. More importantly, common solutions need to be found to problems of preservation and sustainable development, as cities expand and steam roll heritage structures from the past.

In several earlier meetings, such as Delhi Dialogue VII held in March 2015, participants emphasised the urgent need for the effective implementation of efforts in deepening cultural exchanges and reconnecting the civilisational links that ASEAN countries and India share. Speakers underscored the need to put in place resources for historical research and education, as also in restoration works in the development of heritage sites that could help rekindle historical ties across the region and forge new avenues for research collaboration and scholar exchange.

The author is Chairperson, Academic Committee, Project Mausam, and was Former Chairperson, National Monuments Authority. These issues were reiterated at the 'International Conference on ASEAN-India Cultural Links':

> Historical and Contemporary Dimensions' hosted by RIS and MEA in July 2015. Eminent participants stressed the need to shift the focus from traditional national histories towards researching multi-religious and plural cultural landscapes across maritime boundaries and present political units.

There is, thus, an urgent need not only for regular meetings and sharing of knowledge, but also, more importantly, for an institutional base where both senior and younger scholars could interact in joint teaching and research programmes. Support for institutional frameworks needs to be created, and collaborative research projects identified in which archaeological conservation, community development, cultural awareness and economic empowerment are integral and complementary components. This essay presents an overview of the existing support networks within UNESCO's global framework, and suggests steps that could provide a way forward in institutionalising this important phase of world history from the ASEAN-India perspective. The essay begins with tracing the history of dialogue across Asia as several nations threw off the colonial yoke in the middle of the twentieth century, achieved independence, and were faced with challenges relating to the future identity and culture of Asia.

Evolving Partnerships: Memory, Monuments, and History

The importance accorded to civilisational links across Asia and the building of partnerships for the present and the future is evident from the fact that the first ever Asian Relations Conference was held in Delhi from 23rd March to 2nd April 1947—that is, even prior to Indian independence on 15th August

1947. It was attended by approximately two hundred and fifty delegates from some thirty-two countries, observers from across the globe, and about 2000 local visitors.[3]

The conference venue was the 16th century historic fort of Purana Qila, built by the second Mughal Emperor Humayun (1508–1556), but subsequently captured by the Afghan Sher Shah Suri (1486–1545) who ruled Delhi briefly in the mid-sixteenth century, before ceding it back to the Mughals. However, the Purana Qila is much more than merely a medieval structure. Archaeological excavations conducted within its ramparts by the Archaeological Survey of India from 1950 onwards confirm that it represents the site of Delhi's earliest settlement, dating to the first millennium BCE. It represents both continuity of habitation at the site and also the essence of the city. "A Mughal chronicler from the time mentions that Humayun's fort was built on the hallowed site of Indraprastha, a story that sits in the shimmering realm between myth and history,"[4] or between historical memory as enshrined in the Epics—in this case, the Sanskrit epic, the *Mahabharata* and its constant restructuring by subsequent rulers.

In 1911, the capital of colonial India shifted from Calcutta to Delhi and, in laying the foundations of the new city of Delhi, Edwin Lutyens took care to align it to the ancient Purana Qila. The venue of the first Asian Relations Conference is, thus, a potent marker of Delhi's urban history, a reminder not only of the first attempt at building partnerships between Asian countries and India, but also a grim reminder of the increasing distance between the fast depleting heritage and ever expanding cities across the region. This, then, raises the critical issue of preserving the remnants of the past for future generations, as also of sustainable community development around monuments and heritage structures.

At the 12th ASEAN-India Summit held in Myanmar, in November 2014, world leaders identified challenges of the future, as among others, the following.[5]

- How to address the so-called cultural loss in ASEAN countries?
- How to achieve an orchestrated preservation of cultural heritage?
- How to protect cultural heritage, as also indigenous people's rights?

These challenges continue to remain daunting, and need to be tackled at the earliest. The Indian Ocean was mentioned in the concluding session of Delhi

Dialogue VII as the ocean of the coming decades in terms of Maritime Security. However, here I would like to underscore its importance in facilitating partnerships relating to culture and heritage. In the next section of this essay, a brief overview of the heritage that connects the ASEAN-India region is discussed. This by no means implies that other issues are less important; this has been done only to highlight an under-researched theme which needs to be worked upon.

Coastal Monuments: Visual Ordering of the Sailing World in the Pre-modern Period

Increasingly, maritime historians are agreed that the history of the seas that unite the ASEAN-India region should be discussed as 'connected history' across porous borders, linked through boat-building traditions, community networks, and cultural practices. While the history of maritime trade, trading commodities, and ports has received attention, and there is a rich secondary literature available on these themes, this is not the case with subjects such as coastal architecture, heritage practices, and boat-building traditions.

The ASEAN-India region presented a unique environment to the sailor in antiquity. This was different both from that in Egypt or the Mediterranean. To sail in this region, ships had to be 'good weatherly sailers, fast, good carriers, deep-drafted, and able to go to windward as well. In short, they had to be *real* sailing ships'.[6] It is significant that, before the construction of coastal facilities such as docks and ports, sailing ships anchored at some distance from the coast, and small boats were used to ferry passengers and cargo to the shore. At the same time, the region also presented special problems for the historian and the archaeologist. On the one hand, it provides a profusion of ethnographic data on local traditions of fishing and boat-building; on the other hand, actual remains of wrecks are rare.

The oldest shipwreck in the region dates to first century BCE/first century CE, and lies off the fishing village of Godavaya on the south coast of Sri Lanka. The ship was transporting a cargo of raw materials, including what appears to be ingots of iron and others of glass, as well as finished stone querns (hand-operated mills) and ceramic bowls, when it sank some time before the first century CE.[7] Further, across the Indian Ocean, a somewhat later ninth century shipwreck of a vessel of possible Indian or Arab origin was found in Indonesian waters. The wreck was located just north of the main town and port of Belitung

Island, Tanjung Pandan. A large number of seventh century Chinese coins and ceramics were recovered from the site, indicating that the ship was travelling on the route from the Persian Gulf to China.[8] Thus, the data from shipwrecks is gradually adding to our understanding of the cultural milieu of maritime activity in the region.

Other indicators of the deep engagement with the sea include archaeological artefacts, as evidence of ancient settlements and routes and architectural edifices and their networks of interaction. The larger issue addressed here relates to perspectives through which monuments, especially those located on the coast, are to be understood and made meaningful to contemporary societies, both for an appreciation of their aesthetic value as also to aid in their preservation for posterity. This essay attempts to articulate the complex connections built through the mediation of the sea, both spatially and chronologically, by an examination of coastal architecture. Recent archaeological research has brought to light several Buddhist sites in coastal Odisha, though the major expansion occurred from the fifth to thirteenth centuries CE, when more than one hundred Buddhist sites are known in the region. Nearly 140 Buddhist sites are listed along the Andhra region, dating from the second century BCE onwards, and the distribution along the coast from Srikakulam in the north to Ramatirtham and Nandalur in the south is quite striking. Of these, thirty Buddhist sites have yielded stone inscriptions recording donations made by a cross-section of the populace to the Buddhist Sangha or community of monks.

Some issues that require consideration relate to the extent and vigour of the trading network linking eastern India with the Bay of Bengal, and to evidence for the spread of Buddhism across the Ocean. A cluster of fifth century inscriptions of unequivocal Buddhist affiliation was found in Kedah, on the west coast of the Malay Peninsula. Three of these inscriptions are made of local stone, and bear similar illustrations of Buddhist stupas. Texts very similar to these inscriptions have been found on the island of Borneo and on the coast of Brunei.[9] The most interesting of these inscriptions is in Sanskrit, and refers to the setting up of the stone by the mariner Buddhagupta, resident of Raktamrttika, identified with Rajbadidanga in Bengal, on the successful completion of his voyage.[10]

There was a shift in maritime networks around the middle of the first millennium CE, and pilgrims visiting sites associated with the life of the

Buddha formed a major category of travellers. The Chinese pilgrim Faxian arrived overland in India in CE 399, and returned by sea to China in 413–414 CE from Sri Lanka, heading towards the northwest tip of Sumatra. The ship was wrecked on the way, and perhaps landed in the Andamans. The next phase took Faxian to the northwest of Borneo, where he arrived in 414 CE after 90 days at sea. The pilgrim remained in Borneo for five months and then left for China in mid-414 CE heading towards Canton.

Perhaps the most relevant example for this paper is the Buddhist monastery at Nagapattinam, which was a major landmark on the Tamil coast from the seventh to the nineteenth centuries CE. A Buddhist temple was erected at Nagapattinam specifically for Chinese Buddhists at the instance of a Chinese ruler during the reign of the Pallava ruler Narasimhavarman II (*c.* CE 695–722). The Chinese monk Wu-hing visited the site on his way to Sri Lanka (Ramachandran 1954: 14). One of the later Srivijayan kings, perhaps from the island of Sumatra, Maravijayottungavarman, is known to have provided for the construction of the temple. Revenues of a large village Anaimangalam were granted for its upkeep in 1006 CE by the ruler of the Chola dynasty of south India, King Rajaraja I.[11]

Sir Walter Elliot (1803–1887), a Scottish civil servant in India, visited the Chinese Pagoda, as the site was then known, in 1846 on board the government steamer *Hugh Lindsay*, which travelled down the coast. Elliot described the structure at Nagapattinam as a 'four-sided tower of three stories constructed of bricks closely fitted together without cement'.[12] There was a fort in its vicinity and,

> about 11/3 miles NNW from the fort stands the old Black Pagoda, which is one of the most conspicuous objects in approaching this part of the coast, the whole of which has a low, drowned aspect when first seen from the offing, consisting as it does of a sandy barren soil planted with coconut trees.

It may be mentioned that Nagapattinam was also the terminus of the great south Indian railway, and an important landmark for the large numbers of ships and steamers travelling to the roadstead.

This interrelationship between coastal shrines and travelling groups was by no means restricted to Buddhism. From the ninth to the mid-fourteenth centuries, two of the merchant guilds that dominated economic transactions in south India were the Manigramam and the Ayyavole. Associated with these two merchant guilds were associations of craftsmen such as weavers, basket-makers, potters, leather-workers, and so on. As late as the 17th century, the Ayyavole seemed to be concentrated in the cotton producing areas of coastal Andhra. Though these two guilds originated independently of each other, from the mid-thirteenth century onward, the Ayyavole association became so powerful that the Manigramam functioned in a subordinate capacity to it. Not only did these merchant associations develop powerful economic networks, but also employed private armies.[13] The range of their operations extended well beyond the boundaries of the Indian subcontinent into Southeast Asia.

In the tenth century, local versions of these merchant guilds (termed the *banigrama*) appeared in the north coast ports of both Java and Bali, especially at Julah on the Balinese coast. There are seven Javanese inscriptions dating from 902 to 1053 CE that refer to merchant associations called *banigrama* and to the various tax concessions granted to them. While some foreign merchants may have been included in these groups, these appear largely as indigenous organisations associated with the local economic networks as tax-farmers.[14]

Several clusters of Tamil inscriptions have been found on the eastern fringes of the Indian Ocean from Burma to Sumatra. Of the seven mid-ninth to late thirteenth century Tamil or part-Tamil language inscriptions so far found in Southeast Asia, one has been found near Pagan in Burma, two just south of the Isthmus of Kra in the Malay peninsula, and four in north and west Java. Perhaps the easternmost record is the bilingual Tamil and Chinese language inscription found associated with the remains of one of the two Siva temples at Quanzhou. These inscriptions connect merchants associations operating out of south India with the founding (or the endowing) of temples or other structures for the use of the resident Indian merchant community.

Another important area is Vietnam and the Kingdom of Champa, which was situated on the great maritime routes connecting the two major Asian civilisations: India and China.[15] The Kingdom's economy was based on maritime trade, which was facilitated by a network of wells that provided fresh water to Cham and foreign ships along the coast of Champa, and the islands of Cu Lao Cham and Ly Son.

Between the 4th and 19th centuries, a unique culture which owed its spiritual origins to Indian Hinduism developed on the coast of contemporary Viet Nam. This is graphically illustrated by the remains of a series of impressive tower-temples located in a dramatic site that was the religious and political capital of the Champa Kingdom for most of its existence.

This is the description given on the UNESCO World Heritage site for the sanctuary of My Sõn inscribed in 1999. My Sõn was one of the longest surviving historic sites in the whole region. It shows constant development of the architectural temple-towers from the late 4th to 19th centuries, and this makes the sanctuary historically and archaeologically unique and significant for investigating within the framework of ASEAN-India cultural contacts, both for its architectural grandeur, but more so through its participation in the maritime networks of the South China Sea and the Indian Ocean.[16]

In the 17th and 18th century, major transformations are evident along the Indian coast, with the development of fortified factories of the European Trading Companies, such as the East India Company. These commercial stations, with facilities for storage in warehouses and residences for merchants, were established at pre-existing coastal centres. It was only in the 1860s that regular cargo services entered the ocean with the establishment of the liner companies. The all-weather steam vessel was larger, faster, safer, and more reliable than indigenous craft on long-haul coastal and trans-oceanic voyages, and brought with it radical alteration in the relationship of the sea and the land. An indicator of this changed environment is the lighthouse, which emerged as an aid to navigation at the turn of the 18th century. It was able to beam light over great distances cheaply through the use of Fresnel lenses. Most were built during British rule, and are a motley collection—some painted with traditional red and white candy stripes; some modern and imposing; and some built in the vicinity of ancient temples, as at Mahabalipuram.

In addition to coastal temples and lighthouses, forts were other important structures that played a major role in the demarcation of the visual topography of the region from the beginnings of the Common Era onwards, though few survive from that early period. One of the characteristic features of maritime trade from the ninth and tenth century onwards was the location of markets in fortified settlements along the Indian Ocean littoral. Rules governing the payment of taxes and regulating the functioning of the markets were often inscribed on copper plates, and provide useful insights into the organisation of the trade network. Unfortunately, there is very little that remains of these earlier fortified settlements, and a majority of the present forts date from the thirteenth century onwards, though most of these are at present in a poor state of preservation.

This brief overview has highlighted the diverse nature and importance of coastal architecture that circumscribed the traditional sailing world in the ASEAN-India region, as also the maritime communities that travelled across the seas. It is evident that this ancient heritage needs to be preserved and protected for future generations. At present, efforts being made to protect and manage maritime heritage are structured within national interests and draw from national concerns. For example, in India, there are about 3700 nationally protected monuments notified by the Archaeological Survey of India all over the country. However, coastal structures are not identified as a separate category; nor are there attempts being made to mitigate ecological and environment concerns such as weathering due to salt (and salt-spray) action, soil erosion, corrosive effects on building materials, and natural calamities such as cyclonic storms, sea surges and tsunamis.

The biggest threat to maritime heritage in the twenty-first century is from unregulated urban growth and vandalism, even though all spatial development planning laws now recognise conservation as a key component of development. Research in several parts of the Indian Ocean has shown a loss of bio-diversity as well as coastal degradation. Unplanned urban expansion along the coasts has meant the marginalisation of local communities, including those involved in fishing and the utilisation of marine resources.

Building Bridges across the Seas

In this final section, I would like to suggest possibilities within available global practices for protecting and preserving the maritime heritage of the ASEAN-India region. The General Conference of the UNESCO in 1972 adopted a Convention concerning the Protection of World Cultural and Natural Heritage. The Convention sought to encourage the identification, protection, and preservation of cultural and natural heritage around the world considered to be of outstanding value to humanity. Since then, several monuments and archaeological sites in the ASEAN-India region have been inscribed on the World Heritage list, with the exception of Brunei. Categories of heritage within the framework of the World Heritage Convention have been broadened over the decades to include cultural landscapes, industrial remains, and heritage routes, which are all now valued as part of our cultural heritage.

The UNESCO Universal Declaration of Cultural Diversity, adopted in November 2001, states

> Culture takes diverse forms across time and space. This diversity is embodied in the uniqueness and plurality of the identities of the groups and societies making up humankind. As a source of exchange, innovation and creativity, cultural diversity is as necessary for humankind as biodiversity is for nature.

Within this framework, the countries of the ASEAN-India region have nominated and inscribed archaeological sites and monuments on the World Heritage list that have been identified nationally for their unique universal values. It is significant that many of the World Heritage sites in the ASEAN-India region are in coastal areas (or river valleys) that provide communication between the coast and the interior, and are known to have participated in the maritime networks historically. It is time to underscore their connectedness within the larger oceanic system, and to bring these sites into dialogue with each other as also those across political boundaries.

For example, one of the earliest sites in the region is the Ban Chiang Archaeological Site in Udon Thani Province of northeast Thailand, within the watershed of the Mekong River. Archaeological excavations and research have revealed that the site dates from 1495 to 900 BCE, and contains early evidence for settled agrarian occupation in Southeast Asia, along with evidence of wet rice agriculture, an associated technological complex of domesticated farm animals, ceramic manufacture, and bronze tool-making technology. The location of Ban Chiang in the watershed of the Mekong River is significant as the Mekong provided an outlet to the sea, as is evident from an analysis of one of the important trade goods of prehistory—that is, beads. These linkages were by no means restricted to the major river valleys but extended across the ocean to the Indian subcontinent.[17] Early states developed from 500 BCE to 500 CE in the delta areas, and this process is especially marked in the Mekong delta (now southern Cambodia and southern Vietnam), which then led to the emergence of the stupendous Angkor civilisation.

The Angkor Archaeological Park in Cambodia (extending over 400 square kilometres) contains the magnificent remains of the different capitals of the

Khmer Empire, from the ninth to the fifteenth century. Khmer architecture evolved largely from that of the Indian sub-continent, from which it soon became clearly distinct as it developed its own special characteristics; some evolved independently, and others acquired from neighbouring cultural traditions. The result was a new artistic horizon in oriental art and architecture. Related to the Khmer Empire is the Temple Complex of Vat Phou in Laos which represents a development ranging from the fifth to the fifteenth centuries.

While Angkor as the pinnacle of Khmer art and architecture has found its rightful place, it is perhaps time to place this extraordinary development within the context of wider networks of coastal sites such as Oc-Eo, located within a network of ancient canals in the Mekong delta. Oc-Eo is one of a cluster of several archaeological sites in southern Vietnam, and especially in the Mekong delta. Findings from archaeological work suggest that large populations lived, constructed stone statuary and brick monuments, and inscribed stelae during the first millennium CE.[18] There is need today to protect, preserve, and research not only monumental specimens of architecture, but also smaller sites which are fast disappearing.

Analogous development is also evident further north in Vietnam. During the 4th to the 13th centuries, there was a unique culture on the coast of contemporary Vietnam; this is graphically illustrated by the remains of a series of impressive tower temples in a dramatic site that was the religious and political capital of the Champa Kingdom for most of its existence—that is, the site of My Son. The source of the Thu Bon River is here, and it flows past the monuments, out of the basin, and through the historic heartland of the Champa Kingdom, draining into the South China Sea at its mouth near the ancient port city of Hoi An. The ancient town of Hoi An is located in Viet Nam's central Quang Nam Province, on the north bank near the mouth of the Thu Bon River. It is an exceptionally well-preserved example of a small-scale trading port, active in the 15th to 19th centuries, which traded widely both with the countries of Southeast and East Asia, and with the rest of the world. This exercise of tracing interconnectedness of many of the World Heritage sites in the ASEAN region may be repeated for sites such as the Pyu Ancient Cities in Myanmar, which include the remains of three brick, walled, and moated cities of Halin, Beikthano, and Sri Ksetra, located in vast irrigated landscapes in the dry zone of the Ayeyarwady (Irrawaddy) River basin. They reflect the Pyu Kingdoms that flourished for over 1,000 years, between 200 BCE and CE 900. The point, however, has already been made of the linkages of the major river valley of mainland Southeast Asia that lead to the sea.

The Borobudur Temple Compound in Indonesia is one of the greatest Buddhist monuments in the world, and was built in the 8th and 9th centuries CE, during the reign of the Shailendra Dynasty. The monument is located in the Kedu Valley, in the southern part of Central Java, at the centre of the island of Java, Indonesia. It is seldom appreciated that the beautifully sculpted panels of the monument propagate the acquisition of knowledge through travel and pilgrimage. The *Gandavyuha*, part of the *Avatamsakasutra*, is an important text for the study of travel in early Buddhism. It dates back, in all probability, to the early centuries of the Common Era, and describes the attainment of enlightenment through pilgrimage. The somewhat slender narrative provided by the text of the *Gandavyuha* has been profusely sculpted on the eighth century Buddhist monument at Borobudur in central Java, though there are a number of variations between the sculpted panels and the textual data, and there is 'no clear correlation between the iconography and the location of the narrative scenes and the corresponding passages in the text.'[19] The travel to Buddhist imaginaries no doubt helped breakdown the temporal and spatial barriers between the universal *dhamma* and local practices followed by lineages of Buddhist teachers.

The historic cities of Sukhothai and Ayutthaya were the political and administrative capitals of the first Kingdom of Siam in the 13th and 15th centuries. Si Satchanalai was the spiritual centre of the kingdom, and the site of numerous temples and Buddhist monasteries. Si Satchanalai was also the centre of the all-important ceramic export industry. The third town, Kamphaeng Phet, was located at the kingdom's southern frontier, and had important military functions in protecting the kingdom from foreign intruders as well as providing security for the kingdom's extensive trading network. The historic city of Ayutthaya, founded in 1350, was the second capital of the Siamese Kingdom. It flourished from the 14th to the 18th centuries, during which time it grew to be one of the world's largest and most cosmopolitan urban areas as well as a centre of global diplomacy and commerce.

The last two examples come from Malaysia and the Philippines. Melaka and George Town represent exceptional examples of multi-cultural trading towns in East and Southeast Asia, forged from the mercantile and exchanges of Malay, Chinese, and Indian cultures, and three successive European colonial powers for almost 500 years, each leaving its imprints on the architecture and urban form, technology and monumental art. In the Philippines, the four Baroque churches, the first of which was built by the Spanish in the late 16th century, are located in Manila, Santa Maria, Paoay and Miag-ao. Their unique architectural style is a reinterpretation of European Baroque by Chinese and Philippine craftsmen.

These stupendous monuments are no doubt extraordinary. But, what is often neglected is the amazing density of archaeological structures in the ASEAN-India region. Over four thousand temples of Pagan (Myanmar), over two thousand Khmer archaeological sites in mainland Southeast Asia, some two hundred brick temples still standing on the sea coast of Vietnam working as light-houses for ships navigating the Indian Ocean are historic reminders of the interactions across the seas. Most of these modest structures are in a state of neglect and decay. Many of them have disappeared. The remaining ones will disappear in the course of the twenty first century, and with them will disappear all the records of our past relationships. The villages, which shelter archaeological sites should, ideally, be partners in conserving the sites and in pioneering rural development through the promotion of cultural assets.[20] It is time to redress this situation through public outreach, collaborative research, and joint programmes of heritage management.

In conclusion, I would like to stress the need to promote research on themes related to the study of Maritime Cultural Routes that connect the ASEAN-India region through scientific seminars and meetings, and by adopting a multidisciplinary approach. It will encourage the production of specialised works as well as publications for the general public with an attempt at promoting a broader understanding of the concept of a shared heritage and multiple identities.

NOTES

1. Anjana Sharma (ed.), *Civilizational Dialogue: Asian Inter-connections and Cross-cultural Exchanges*, New Delhi: Manohar, 2013.
2. Himanshu Prabha Ray, 'Archaeology and Empire: Buddhist Monuments in Monsoon Asia', *The Indian Economic and Social History Review*, 45, 3, 2008, pp. 417–449.
3. *Asian Relations: Report of the Proceedings and Documentation of the First Asian Relations Conference*, New Delhi, March-April 1947, New Delhi: Asian Relations Organization, 1948.
4. Please see, http://www.theguardian.com/cities/2015/mar/26/delhi-purana-qila-fort-history-cities-buildings accessed 5 February 2016.

5. Julito D. Vitriolo, 'A View on a Post-2015 Agenda in Education, Skill Development, and Mutual Recognition, Cultural Linkages and People-to-People Contact: Strengthening the Context of ASEAN-India Partnership', in Rumel Dahiya and Udai Bhanu Singh (eds.), *Delhi Dialogue VII: ASEAN–India, Shaping the Post 2015 Agenda*, IDSA, New Delhi, 2015, p. 102.
6. A. Villiers, *Monsoon Seas: The Story of the Indian Ocean*, New York: McGraw Hill Book Co., 1952, pp. 56–7.
7. Deborah N. Carlson and Ken Trethewey, 'Exploring the Oldest Shipwreck in the Indian Ocean', *Institute of Nautical Archaeology Quarterly*, Vol. 40, No. 1, Spring 2013, 9–14.
8. Michael Flecker, 'A 9th-century Arab or Indian Shipwreck in Indonesian Waters', *The International Journal of Nautical Archaeology*, 2000, 29(2), pp. 199–217.
9. J. W. Christie, 'State Formation in Early Maritime Southeast Asia: A Consideration of the Theories and the Data', *Bijdragen tot de Taal-, Land- en Volkenkunde*, 151(2), 1995, pp. 235–88.
10. B. Ch. Chhabra, *Expansion of the Indo-Aryan Culture during Pallava Rule*, Delhi: Munshiram Manoharlal, 1965, pp. 23–4.
11. Himanshu Prabha Ray, 'A "Chinese" Pagoda At Nagapattinam On The Tamil Coast: Revisiting India's Early Maritime Networks', *India International Centre Occasional Publication*, 66, New Delhi: 2015.
12. Sir Walter Elliot, 'The Edifice Formerly Known as the Chinese or Jaina Pagoda at Negapatam', *The Indian Antiquary*, Vol. 7, 1878, pp. 224–7.
13. Meera Abraham, *Two Medieval Merchant Guilds of South India*, New Delhi: Manohar, 1988.
14. Jan Wisseman Christie, 'Asian Sea Trade between the Tenth and Thirteenth Centuries and its Impact on the States of Java and Bali', Himanshu Prabha Ray (ed.), *Archaeology of Seafaring: The Indian Ocean in the Ancient Period*, Indian Council for Historical Research, Monograph I, New Delhi, 1999, pp. 242–5.
15. 'Tran Ky Phuong and Vu Huu Minh, ua Dai Chiem (Port of Great Champa) in the 4th-15th centuries', *Vietnamese Studies*, 2, 30, 1991, pp. 17–24
16. Tran Ky Phuong, 'The Coastal Temples Of Vietnam: Sanctuaries Of International Maritime Pilgrims On "The Silk Road of the Sea",' Himanshu Prabha Ray (ed.), *Mausam: Maritime Cultural Landscapes across the Indian Ocean*, National Monuments Authority & Aryan Books International, New Delhi: 2014.
17. Himanshu Prabha Ray, *The Archaeology of Seafaring in Ancient South Asia*, Cambridge University Press, 2003.
18. Pierre-Yves Manguin, 'The Archaeology of Early Maritime Polities of Southeast Asia', Ian Glover and Peter Bellwood (eds.), *Southeast Asia: From Prehistory to History*, Routledge Curzon, London and New York: 2004, pp. 282–313.
19. J. Fontein, *The Pilgrimage of Sudhana: A study of Gandavyûha Illustrations in China, Japan and Java*, Mouton, The Hague: 1967, p. 125.
20. S. Sahai, 'Archaeology as Soft Power or Power of Plurality in ASEAN-India Cultural Contexts', *ASEAN-India Cultural Links: Historical and Contemporary Dimensions*, RIS-AIC, New Delhi, 2015, pp. 220–9.

REFERENCES

Abraham, Meera, *Two Medieval Merchant Guilds of South India*, Manohar, New Delhi, 1988.

Asian Relations: Report of the Proceedings and Documentation of the First Asian Relations Conference, New Delhi, March-April 1947, New Delhi: Asian Relations Organization, 1948.

Carlson, Deborah N. and Ken Trethewey, "Exploring the Oldest Shipwreck in the Indian Ocean", *Institute of Nautical Archaeology Quarterly*, volume 40, number 1, Spring, 2013, pp. 9–14.

Chhabra, B. Ch., *Expansion of the Indo-Aryan Culture during Pallava Rule*, Delhi: Munshiram Manoharlal, 1965.

Christie, Jan Wisseman, "State Formation in Early Maritime Southeast Asia: A Consideration of the Theories and the Data", *Bijdragen tot de Taal-, Land- en Volkenkunde*, 151, 2, 1995, pp. 235-88.

Christie, Jan Wisseman, "Asian Sea Trade between the Tenth and Thirteenth Centuries and its Impact on the States of Java and Bali", Himanshu Prabha Ray (ed.), *Archaeology of Seafaring: The Indian Ocean in the Ancient Period*, New Delhi: Indian Council for Historical Research Monograph I, 1999.

Elliot, Sir Walter, "The Edifice Formerly Known as the Chinese or Jaina Pagoda at Negapatam", *The Indian Antiquary*, vol. 7, 1878: 224–7.

Flecker, Michael, "A 9th-century Arab or Indian Shipwreck in Indonesian Waters", *The International Journal of Nautical Archaeology*, 2000, 29. 2, pp. 199–217.

Fontein, J. *The pilgrimage of Sudhana: A study of Gandavyûha illustrations in China, Japan and Java*, Mouton, The Hague: 1967, p. 125.

Manguin, Pierre-Yves, "The Archaeology of Early Maritime Polities of Southeast Asia", Ian Glover and Peter Bellwood (ed.), *Southeast Asia: From Prehistory to History*, London and New York: Routledge Curzon, 2004, pp. 282–313.

Ray, Himanshu Prabha, *The Archaeology of Seafaring in Ancient South Asia*, Cambridge University Press, 2003.

Ray, Himanshu Prabha, "Archaeology and Empire: Buddhist Monuments in Monsoon Asia", *The Indian Economic and Social History Review*, 45, 3, 2008, pp. 417–449.

Ray, Himanshu Prabha, "A 'Chinese' Pagoda At Nagapattinam On The Tamil Coast: Revisiting India's Early Maritime Networks", *India International Centre Occasional Publication*, 66, New Delhi: 2015.

Sahai, S., "Archaeology as Soft Power or Power of Plurality in ASEAN-India Cultural Contexts," *ASEAN-India Cultural Links: Historical and Contemporary Dimensions*, RIS-AIC, New Delhi: 2015, pp. 220–9.

Sharma, Anjana, (ed.) *Civilizational Dialogue: Asian Inter-connections and Cross-cultural Exchanges*, New Delhi: Manohar, 2013.

Tran, Ky Phuong and Vu Huu Minh, "ua Dai Chiem (Port of Great Champa) in the 4th-15th centuries," *Vietnamese Studies*, 2, 30, 1991: 17-24.

Tran, Ky Phuong, "The Coastal Temples Of Vietnam: Sanctuaries Of International Maritime Pilgrims On The Silk Road Of The Sea," Himanshu Prabha Ray (ed.), *Mausam: Maritime Cultural Landscapes across the Indian Ocean*, National Monuments Authority & Aryan Books International, New Delhi: 2014.

Villiers, A., *Monsoon Seas: The Story of the Indian Ocean*, New York: McGraw Hill Book Co., 1952.

Vitriolo, Julito D., "A View on a Post-2015 Agenda in Education, Skill Development, and Mutual Recognition, Cultural Linkages and People-to-People Contact: Strengthening the Context of ASEAN-India Partnership", in Rumel Dahiya and Udai Bhanu Singh (eds.), *Delhi Dialogue VII: ASEAN-India, Shaping the Post 2015 Agenda*, IDSA, New Delhi: 2015.

23

India-Southeast Asia Civilisational Linkages

Eddin Khoo

We in South East Asia I suppose like the rest of the world are beginning to have major problems grappling with history and that most confounding of words, 'identity'. I think most of us go through the press today and through 24 hours news falling back on what was perhaps one of the great phantasmagoric poems written at the turn of the last century by an Irish man, that book was called Ulysses and the author is James Joyce, who said history is a nightmare from which I am trying to awake and that could not be more true than it is today.

We started off this conference inevitably talking about the dangers of terrorism and the threat posed by ISIS and all the various strategies and pragmatic plans we should put into action to ensure that this scourge does not encroach upon our lives and literally blow up in our face. I am always amazed that nobody ever talks about these wars essentially as cultural wars and wars that are conducted on a subliminal level and really dealing with psychology. I met by chance yesterday someone from the Russian Embassy who had a very traditional sociological point of view that if your rate of development was just about that high and if your economic standards were that high, people will not be drawn into terrorism without being reminded that the pilots who drove the planes into the Twin Towers were mostly PhD holders. So, we enter really a realm that is very very abstruse, opaque and surreal almost. Really the things that charge such sensibility and such disposition today is a cultural one. The past is really not something quaint or romantic or nostalgic and this is a particular problem when South East Asians and Indians get together, they tend to get very nostalgic and they bring out that ledger of debt and claim of we owe you this and we should remember this when actually it is the entire organic nature, the syncretic nature of the relationship between South East Asia and the Indian subcontinent that is huge crucial, one that has never ended from times of early maritime trade and the bequest of statecraft and religion as you put it very well into the stirrings of nationalism in the 1930s. Remember that Subash Chandra Bose based the Indian National Army in Singapore in which at least half of my family served in the Queen of Jhansi regiment and of course this imagining of many Indian artists beginning with Tagore and of course one of the great works that Uday Shankar wanted to produce but failed to do so was set in Bali.

We also remember when we try to figure out why this relationship between India and South East Asia has not been fully realised, of course there is the hangover of the Cold War and for the long time we in Malaysia anyway were raised with the notion that the Indians had a close relationship towards the Soviet Union while we maintained other kinds of loyalties. These are hangovers that I think we need to grapple with and history and culture is of course a major foothold in our engagement of issues that will remain increasingly more complex and more weblike.

Let me refer to a very interesting incident that happened just a few months ago. I have organised a regional South East Asian cultural conversation series where we bring about 10 artists from various South East Asian countries to sit and talk about the nature of South East Asia. Of course South East Asia is as illusive a term as you can get and one of the main questions that is asked of South East Asians as we enter ASEAN integration and so on is does such a region actually exist. We know at least half of it was a concoction of the State Department during the time of the Vietnam war and one of the very interesting characteristics was that when it came to discussing history, history as the spawn of borders and nation States, every single one of these liberal, open-minded cosmopolitan artists began to get very dismissive if not argumentative about their own territorial concerns and considerations. That was the first day. On the second day we spoke of myth. When we spoke of myth, what I think is the binding factor in the South East Asian psychology, there seem to be a flawless confluence between people who are just arguing and kind of debating very heatedly the day before. So, if we begin to ask questions about proximity, about bringing these two regions together again, I think there is a need to really relook how we approach metaphysically and existentially questions of history and myth, one that allows for a great deal of more confluence between the concepts of such things as factual and empirical history and the history of the imagination which so much informs really our sustained relationship.

The question has been asked for a very long time, one of my great literary teachers, the poet and scholar, AK Ramanujam, had spent a great deal of his time and a lot of effort in studying of course the web of Ramayanas that flow through not just India alone but in other parts venturing into South East Asia. I also refer to a very interesting book that I found very intriguing but was largely ignored, by a former High Commissioner of India to Malaysia whose name is Veena Sikri and she wrote a very provocative book on Malaysia-India relations and part of the entire book was her frustration as to why policymakers could not get together and forge a relationship that was far more binding and deep set. But what was also of very deep interest to me was that at least a third of that book was a very close cultural examination of the kind of exchange and interchange that had taken place throughout the years and as I have said, it is sustained and consistent, it began with religion, it began with trade, it began with statecraft, the bequest of statecraft and of course in modern times the story of labour which is incredibly important to the really flourishing of South East Asia and my country, Malaysia in particular. My father is a historian and one of the great battles we have in Malaysia is a value based approach to history in a diverse and multiracial society that can be extremely dangerous. Who contributed more to what and I think it is one of the great achievements of my father, if I may be so immodest, as to make an empirical stand to say that in history we don't talk of contributions, we talk of roles and of course the role of Indian labour has been incredible, 40 per cent of the beginnings of the foundations of Malaya Railways and rubber were attributed to Indian indentured labour. That has not been properly acknowledged I think in history in my country whereas on the other side of the border it is somehow romanticized. So, a distinct empirical approach is still a major problem especially with modern history.

But really what is the great challenge? This is not my first time to Delhi, I was here last November and this is one of the very interesting things we need to address when we talk about institutional relations because some of the best work in culture is not done by institutions, it is done by independent bohemian people on the ground and I happen to be one of them and there seems to be not enough of an effort to embrace these attitudes which sometimes may be radical and sometimes may even be subversive but on the whole are very commonsensical and tell you a great deal about what is actually happening on the ground of culture in South East Asia. But as I said I have been working with two very interesting individuals, an Indian cultural critic by the name of Rustom Bharucha and an American scholar by the name of Paula Richman studying the Ramayana. So, I have been to India every year talking about the Ramayanic web and fabric around the world. So, these engagements are actually happening on a very very regular basis.

One of the problems of course I find when I do engage with my Indian counterparts is the weight of Indian history in the sense that genealogies of Hanuman for example can be so incredibly complicated, he is married to who, she ran away with him and she had this son, so there is an incredible map and fabric. Of course South East Asia we are a culture of dastardly, a marginal culture that thrives essentially on a great deal of improvisation. One of the challenges is always to find equal ground because on the one hand there is one aspect of South East Asian culture that likes to fiddle and jig and then there is a weight of greater India that drops on you. These are territories that are very interesting to work out.

But, let me just state what I think the principal problem is. The principal problem of course is politics, I believe and one of the major issues that are constantly dealt with when it comes to culture, when it comes to history, when it comes to myth is reimagining, reconstruction and reinvention of history. There are two major cultural battles being fought in South East Asia. One is in island South East Asia where the infection of Wahabism, let us not call it Islamic fundamentalism, let us not even use the word Islam because Islam is a religion and is abstract, this is the infection of Wahabism, a particular puritanism that is spreading through and one of the very interesting things that is happening now is that very local groups, not so much the liberal Islam who are seen to be highly westernised and really quite marginal I think in the greater scheme of the Indonesian politics but the move by traditionalist groups like the Nahldlatul Ulama to fall back again on a cultural rhetoric. One of their major statements now is that just because we are Muslims we don't need to be Arabs. That is a major statement/remark that is being made by them. We also remember President Gusdor or President Abdurrahman Wahid who constantly battled fundamentalists or puritans with the phrase, God does not need to be defended. But on the other hand the puritanism of the greater culture, of the greater Ramayanic motherland and so on is also a contentious one. So, these are issues that need to be deliberated upon and also grappled with in a seriously fundamental way and on a consistent basis.

So, I think at the end, like everything else in this world, at present what is really needed is political will.

Thank you.

24

Popular Diplomacy: Reinvigorating the Civilisational Connect

Baladas Ghoshal

The objective of this paper is to look back into India's civilisational and historical links with Southeast Asia and how they can be of contemporary relevance in popular diplomacy to widen and deepen our engagement with ASEAN. While economic, political, and strategic interactions between countries are major determinants in strengthening both bilateral and multilateral relations, culture can bring people emotionally closer to each other. Culture creates a sense of commonness, and allows people to relate to each other. It builds bonds based on common religious, linguistic, and ethnic beliefs which, when used creatively, can become enduring links between people of different countries and even different cultures. 'Culture' refers to a group or community with which we share common experiences that shape the way we understand the world. It includes groups that we are born into, such as gender, race, national origin, class, or religion. It can also include groups we join or become part of. For example, we can acquire a new culture by moving to a new region, by a change in our economic status, or by becoming disabled. When we think of culture in this broad way, we realise we all belong to many cultures at the same time.

India and the Southeast Asian nations had a vibrant relationship which can be traced as far back as the 1st century BC, mainly through trade and socio-cultural links that also saw the influence and spread of Sanskrit and Indian art forms in those countries. The ancient Javanese script has many Sanskrit words—like 'kshatriya' and 'dharmaputra'—while shards of Indian pottery with the ancient Kharoshti script once prevalent in India have been found in Bali. The spread of the Sanskrit script helped the countries in the region communicate over vast regions. According to experts, the Chinese script 'did not have grammar as such,' and Sanskrit was used to separate the consonants from the vowels, and provided a base for the use of local languages as official language. Likewise ships, horses, temples, sculptures, and the performing arts were important facets linking the countries of Southeast Asia to ancient India. Indian pottery was found in Sembiran, Indonesia, inscribed with the ancient Kharoshti script.

In Sembiran and Pacung on the northern coast of Bali, some coarse Indian dishes were popular. The influence of Sanskrit is seen in old Javanese script, with wide use of Sanskrit words in ancient texts like the *Bhisma Parwa*. Excavations of the Pyu settlements in present day Myanmar show evidence of the earliest South East Asian contacts with India. One of the sites is called Beikthano, meaning the 'City of Vishnu'. Indian influence is evident in Pyu architecture, coinage, statues of Hindu deities, and the Buddha as well as other early forms of epigraphy. Pyu coins have been unearthed as far as the Mekong Delta, indicating that trade and culture followed the same route. The interactions between India and Southeast Asia not only created widespread religious and political affinities with the Indian sub-continent, but also with Indian statecraft, particularly under the Gupta dynasty which

> provided an attractive coherent model of political, social and religious integration for rulers of South East Asia, and its success was emulated in South East Asia, where Indian constructs such as iconography, the Sanskrit language and religious practices were utilized, often for political ends. Importantly, these constructs spread, not through conquest but essentially through non-political agents such as merchants and religious men, and were an indicator of the 'soft power' that India enjoyed in its extended neighbourhood.[1]

Buddhism also travelled from India mainly through monks sent by Indian kings, particularly Emperor Ashoka who sent Buddhist emissaries to Myanmar, Thailand, Cambodia, Vietnam as well as the Malay Peninsula. Along with religion also went linguistic, architectural and literary influences. The spread of Buddhism to South East Asia 'went beyond the linear path'. 'Contrary to what is traditionally traced from India towards the East, Buddhism instead, once transmitted from India to the East, was localised, re-created and diffused again, through different parts of Asia, including India.'[2] However, one has to take note of the fact that this flow of cultural influences was neither one-way traffic nor was it an imposition on the people of Southeast Asia. An element of choice was exercised by them. They received only that part which suited their local traditions and culture, and sometimes improvised elements from them according to their needs.

What do all these cultural interactions mean in today's context as well as for foreign policy and inter-state relations? Common cultural traditions promote a convivial atmosphere and create conditions for cementing bond between countries, which is one of the main objectives of the foreign policy of a country. While geo-politics and geo-economics also shape objective conditions for the convergence of interests and the improvement of relations between countries, they can also be contentious under different conditions, and can lead to conflicts. Geo-civilisational contacts often shape a common world worldview.

Among other civilisational links and the contribution of India, three stand out quite clearly: statecraft and state-building; diffusion of knowledge; and a secular and a composite culture marked by a confluence of religions and diversity. The Indian concept of 'Divine King' (Devaraja) had a profound effect on Southeast Asian ancient tribal societies by lending legitimacy to the state practices and state-building. It enabled the monarch to claim divine authority which was then used to ensure political legitimacy, the management of social order as well as the economic and religious aspects of the state. Thus, the promotion of India's strategic objectives need not be through only the projection of its hard military power as the 'Realist' school would have us believe.

This promotion could, perhaps, be more effective through the exercise of its 'soft' power, in terms of education, culture and democracy. The liberal institutional approach emphasises soft power aspects, with cultural attraction, ideology, as well as international institutions being the main resource. Soft power strategies rely more on common political values, peaceful means for conflict management, and economic cooperation in order to achieve common solutions. India's ability to play a major role in Asia lies not so much in the area of trade and investment (wherein China has overwhelming presence), but in its human resources, democracy, and culture in which it has a distinct advantage over other Asian countries. It is in the area of creating and maintaining capabilities that India has a competitive advantage vis-à-vis China. Its basic feature is the widespread working knowledge of the English language, and a large education and skills infrastructure.

In the present day context, India's experience of nation-building through a democratic and a decentralised polity is something that can be shared with ASEAN countries to promote popular participation in the political process, and the democratisation of their polities and societies. India's democracy may be messy; but it has shown a lot of creativity in managing a multiracial and multicultural society, and in the processes of people's empowerment. It is here that India can make an abiding contribution to the process of democratisation and nation-building in the region by helping ASEAN countries in human resource development and democratic capacity building. Southeast Asian countries are multiracial and multicultural, with some of them also being in the process of democratic transformation. The Western model of democracy may not be of much relevance to these countries, as their societal and historical circumstances are quite different. India's experience in nation-building and democracy—which grew and evolved out of its own social and cultural base and created its own resilience—could be much more relevant to them. Helping the countries of Southeast Asia in their journey toward democratisation of their polities and societies can not only help in fostering greater bonds between India and the countries of ASEAN but also further India's interests in Southeast Asia. Organising elections for a potential constituency of 670 million voters is an incredible undertaking that India can be proud of. Countries like Indonesia, Thailand, Cambodia (where elections are now taking place periodically), and now Myanmar, (which has started its difficult journey towards democratisation facing multiple challenges emanating from ethnic conflicts and a general lack of capacity) could learn much from the speed and transparency with which Indian votes are tallied, and the extensive powers accorded to the Indian Election Commission (EC). Thailand is currently passing through political uncertainty, and is now under an interim government which professes to return the country to democracy once it is able to sort out the mess and carry out institutional reforms. An offer from India to share its experiences in building an independent and transparent Election Commission should be welcome.

Many Indonesians—like former Presidents Abdurrahman Wahid and

Susilo Bambang Yudhoyono—had great respect for India's ability to practice democracy despite its many shortcomings. While the central government in Indonesia has already implemented the devolution of power hoping that a fairer distribution of national wealth will reduce separatist sentiments and regional violence, there is a lack of institutions at the local level to absorb such autonomy. This is where India can help through its ITEC (technical cooperation) programme, which can impart training in local self-government and institution-building at the grassroots level.

Myanmar is another example wherein India can help in building capacity for the promotion of democracy, particularly in the sphere of human resource development. More than five decades of military rule in Myanmar had transformed the nature of administration in the country in which civilians were replaced with military personnel, even at the village level. The return of true democracy to the country will require replacing military personnel with civilian ones, along with changes in norms, values, and practices. Myanmar currently does not have either the base or the training facilities to create a pool of civilian administrators on their own. Similarly with its parliamentarians who are still quite new in the game parliamentary politics and practices. India has both training facilities for civilian administrators as well as parliamentary experience to pass on to the fellow parliamentarians in Myanmar. With little investment, India can reap rich dividends in terms of both the promotion of democracy in a vitally important neighbouring country as well as foster goodwill in the Myanmar leadership and the people.

Second, India's contribution to philosophy, logic, and theology is well-known. The old Nalanda University was an example of pan-Asian cooperation. At its peak, the university attracted scholars and students from Korea, Japan, China, Tibet, Indonesia, Turkey, Greece, and Persia. The subjects taught included Religion, History, Law, Linguistics, Medicine, Public Health, Architecture, Metallurgy, Pharmacology, Sculpture and Astronomy. There was a network of educational institutions spread across Asia which had links with Nalanda. Chinese scholars learnt Sanskrit in what was then called Srivijaya (which is now mainly in Sumatra) on their way to Nalanda in India by the sea route. Chinese sources record 162 visits to India of Chinese of Buddhist monks from the 5th to the 8th century AD. Many more may have travelled without having left a trace in such official records. This was, no doubt, an amazing international scholarly exchange programme for that day and age. There is already a functioning Nalanda-Srivijaya Centre in Singapore, and proposals for cooperation with universities in China, Korea, Japan, Thailand and elsewhere are being explored.

Rabindranath Tagore was the first Asian to talk about Asian solidarity based on intellectual and cultural cross-fertilisation between the people of Asia. This found expression in his writings as well as in his effort to bring in to India some of the best minds and scholars from China, Japan, Indonesia, and other parts of Asia. The Taman Siswa movement started by Ki Hadjar Dewantoro, one of the leading educationists of Indonesia, in the first part of the 20th century was patterned on Tagore's Shanti Niketan. In recognition of Tagore's contribution as a cultural bridge-builder and a pioneer in the cultural and educational cooperation he initiated in Shantiniketan, his bust was installed at the Borobudur temple in Yogyakarta on 26 November 2012. Taking a cue from such a past, cooperation and joint action is possible in the sphere of education and research involving all countries of ASEAN.

Third, India's religious diversity and composite culture as well as its attempt to build a secular state and society is another area where experiences can be shared with the countries of ASEAN. India and most countries of Southeast Asia are all plural societies, and home to many religious and ethnic groups. Under the pressure of globalisation, as well as developments both national and international, all these countries are experiencing some form of extremism and fundamentalism that are posing a challenge to social harmony in each of these countries as also to the peace and stability of the region. Cooperation on combating radicalism and terrorism already exists between India and the ASEAN. This was further strengthened in the last India-ASEAN summit in Laos wherein the delegates drew attention to terrorism as a significant threat to peace and stability in the region, and made a strong commitment to combat terrorism in all its forms and manifestations. 'We express our determination to take concrete measures to step up cooperation and coordination among our law enforcement and security agencies,' said the Declaration at the end of the 14th ASEAN-India summit in Laos, stressing that there can be no justification for acts of terror on any grounds. Prime Minister Narendra Modi told the leaders attending the summit that 'In the face of growing traditional and non-traditional challenges, political security cooperation is a key emerging feeler of our relationships.' The rising export of terror, growing radicalisation through the ideology of hatred, and the spread of extreme violence defines the landscape of common security threats to our societies, he said. 'The threat is local, regional and transitional at the same time. Our partnership with ASEAN seeks to craft a response that relies on coordination and cooperation at multiple levels,' he noted. The countries recognised the need to counter and prevent the spread of violent extremism and radicalism that leads to acts of terrorism. ASEAN and India also supported the early adoption of the Comprehensive Convention on International Terrorism, currently under negotiation at the United Nations. 'We agreed to cooperate towards addressing traditional and non-traditional security challenges, including in areas of de-radicalisation and prevention of violent extremism,' the Declaration added.

While the hardware of radicalisation can be fought through intelligence-sharing and military means, its software—that is, the jihadi Salafi and Wahhabi ideology or its more extreme form manifested in the ISIS—can only be fought at the level of hearts and minds. Thus, there is need for a civilisational dialogue among religious scholars and leaders as well as among leaders of ethnic groups from both India and ASEAN to deal with this challenge. India and ASEAN can establish an institutional mechanism (like many other mechanisms it has set up to deal with other issues) within which such dialogues can take place on a periodic basis. This is one more area where India-ASEAN cooperation can be widened and deepened.

Another area India can make an impact is in the field of higher education. During his visit to Indonesia in April 2005, while commemorating the Bandung Conference, Prime Minister Manmohan Singh declared that India intended to stay engaged by sharing experiences 'gained from our own development process—with nations in Asia. He also added the following:

> Human resource development holds the key to employment and wealth creation, particularly in this age of globalization. This has been our strategy and we have laid particular emphasis on training and skills development as we globalize. We have extended technical assistance valued at about US$1 billion. We stand ready to do more.

Undoubtedly, Indonesia has been one of the prominent beneficiaries of Indian technical cooperation programmes meant for fellow developing countries. Around 1,000 Indonesian experts as well as officials received training in India under the ITEC programme, and India offered more than 1,100 scholarships to Indonesian students to study at Indian universities. In May 2006, India opened a US$ 750,000 Vocational Training Centre in the country, and another in Aceh in 2010. During the State visit of President Yudhoyono to India in January 2011, a MoU for Cooperation in the field of Education was signed between the two sides. Pursuant to the MoU, the second meeting of the Joint Working group took place in Yogyakarta in July 2012. Indonesia is a major recipient of ITEC (75 slots) & TCS of the Colombo Plan (35 slots) scholarships. The Indian Council for Cultural Relations (ICCR) offers 20 scholarships every year to Indonesian students for pursuing higher studies at under-graduate, post-graduate, doctoral, and post-doctoral levels in 181 participating Universities and educational institutions all over India. An IT Lab was set up in Magelang in West Java, and handed over to the Indonesian Military Academy in May 2011.

It is not only with Indonesia that India has educational exchanges. About 2000 Indian students are studying in Malaysia, while an estimated 3000 Malaysian students are studying in India. New Delhi has an MOU on Higher Education with Kuala Lumpur under which India offers about 25 slots under the ITEC programme and 5 under the Colombo Plan. India also offers nearly 30 scholarships for studies in graduate, post-graduate, and research programmes in universities in India. Thai students are recipients of 130 scholarships under the ITEC and ICCR sponsored schemes. The Ministry of Human Resource Development provides for the secondment of 8 professors every semester for the Asian Institute of Technology (AIT), Bangkok. India has contributed Rs 1.25 crores to the Sanskrit Studies Centre at Silpakorn University in Bangkok, and has deputed a Sanskrit professor there. An India Studies Centre is functioning at the Thammasat University of Bangkok since April 1993. In 2008, the Mahidol University of Bangkok started a Masters of Arts course on Indian studies. The ICCR has a Chair in the Chulalongkorn University's India Study Centre which was inaugurated by HRH Princess Maha Chakri Sirindhron in March 2012.

India has also been contributing to capacity building in Cambodia, and has set up a Cambodia-India Entrepreneurship Development Centre (CIEDC) in Phnom Penh in February, 2006, and Cambodia-India Centre for English Language Training (CICELT) in August 2007. Cambodia is a major recipient of India's ITEC programme, and has utilised around 1000 civilian training slots and about 100 defence training slots till date. Taking note of increasing demand for civilian training courses, slots for Cambodia under the ITEC programme have been enhanced to 100 between 2011-12. Separately, 15 education scholarships are offered every year, 10 under MGC and 5 under GCSS. Work on establishing an India-Cambodia Centre of Excellence & Talent Development (ICCETD) has begun. These Centres will be established at Phnom Penh, Siem Reap, and Sihanoukville. Under human resource development, the Government of India has been providing over 150 scholarships to Lao nationals through the Indian Technical and Economic Cooperation [100 slots], the TCS Colombo Plan [30 slots], the Mekong-Ganga Cooperation Scholarship Scheme [12 slots] and the General Cultural Scholarship Scheme [8 slots for higher studies]. So far, under ITEC, GOI has trained about 1300 Lao nationals. The LICELT [Lao India Centre for English Language Training] was set up in Vientiane on 12 June 2007 under the India-ASEAN Cooperation framework. The LICELT is one of India's assistance projects in human resource development. The effort is in the direction of the capacity-building and self-sustaining capability of Laos. India set up an IT centre in Vientiane in November 2004, as well as a National Data Centre in May 2006.

The Philippines is another country that has benefitted from programmes under ITEC and Colombo Plan. In 2014-15, 40 slots under ITEC and 15 slots under the Colombo Plan were allocated to the Philippines. Significant effort is also being exerted to further deepen the people-to-people cooperation between India and the Philippines. Under the ASEAN-India rubric, journalists from the Philippines have been regularly visiting India, the latest being in August, when Indian journalists visited the Philippines, and March 2015 when journalists from Philippines visited India. In addition, every year, 25 Philippine students in the 17-28 age group visit India (the latest being in November 2015) under the ASEAN-India Students Exchange Programme; and 3 school children visit India to participate in the National Children Science Congress. So far, almost a thousand Filipino nationals have benefited under these schemes, covering a wide range of technical courses, such as rural development, agriculture, renewable energy, small scale industries, banking, finance and management, quality control and marketing, planning and public administration, textiles, parliamentary studies and legislative practices, computer software, water resources management, defence, etc. The Philippines is also beginning to emerge as a destination for Indian students. There are more than 4000 Indian students pursuing medical courses in various universities in the Philippines. Currently nearly, 50 per cent of the students at the prestigious Asian Institute of Management in Manila are from India. Flying schools are also attractive to Indian learners as instructions are in English, and Indian students do not have to learn the local language. Several universities in the Philippines—such as the University of Santo Tomas, the University of the Philippines, the University of the Visayas, Adamson University, the University of Mindanao and others—have opened special 'India chapters' in their prestigious libraries, which house collections of books on India.

Myanmar has also benefitted from training programmes under different schemes—such as Indian Technical & Economic Cooperation (ITEC) Programme, Technical Cooperation Scheme (TCS) of the Colombo Plan. Also, there are various scholarships offered by the Indian Council for Cultural Relations (ICCR)—like the General Cultural Scholarship Scheme (GCSS), Mekong Ganga Cultural Scholarship Scheme (MGCSS), the Ayush Scholarship—to BIMSTEC member countries. The training slots under ITEC/TCS were enhanced to 525 for the year 2013-14 because of the enthusiastic response from Myanmar. The specialised training programme for Parliamentarians and Parliamentary staff were also organised wherein 42 MPs and 30 staff attended the training course. Myanmar diplomats have also been attending training courses at the Foreign Service Institute of India, along with other foreign diplomats. This is only miniscule compared to what Myanmar needs in terms of building its capabilities, and India needs to make large investments in building these capabilities within India's boundaries. This is so especially in the Northeast where there is the added advantage of a large school base, with a pre-existing and widespread competence in English. India can possibly increase the number of seats available to Myanmar students that can help them to acquire capabilities in engineering, skilled technical trades, medicine, pharmacy, nursing, construction, law, management, and commercial skills.

While a lot has been done between India and the ASEAN countries in the field of educational cooperation, there is still greater potential for further cooperation in education which will benefit both countries. Everywhere in Asia, there is greater demand among the younger generation to learn English, the language of globalisation. Myanmar and the two least developed countries of Indochina—Cambodia and Laos—can benefit from India's abundant English language teachers who could help these countries at much less expense than British or Australian teachers. One of the important reasons for the Asian economic crisis of the late 1990s was that while there had been a shift in the production line, there was no commensurate development in higher education in most of the Asian NICs to keep pace with such a shift. India has a lead in information technology, and Indian IITs and IIMs have a very high reputation in these countries. Many Southeast Asians have expressed their interest not only to come and study in these institutions but also to have these institutions open their campuses in their countries, particularly in Malaysia Indonesia. There are businessmen of Indian origin who would be only too glad to raise the money for opening these campuses and support the faculty. What they want is the brand name, and some experienced backup faculty from India. Again, the dividends that India will get will be rich and unmatched.

Yet another area that can promote India's soft power in Southeast Asia in general is its culture. Indian culture is an inseparable part of the customs, values, and practices of many countries in Southeast Asia, bearing in mind the history of the civilisational contacts between India and the countries of Southeast Asia over 2000 years. If carefully pursued, Indian cultural diplomacy can further cement the bond between the two regions. These can be based on pluralist traditions and the need for maintaining 'unity in diversity.' While India has cultural exchanges with the countries of Southeast Asia, these are mostly restricted to the performing arts, the promotion of the Hindi language, and training in Yoga. However, culture needs to be understood in a broader way which reflects a world view and a way of life that requires not only cooperation in the performing arts, but also the sharing of experiences in terms of tackling the problems of diversity and nation-building. The promotion of tourism as a means of people-to people contact can be an important instrument of Indian cultural diplomacy. For example, Indonesia happens to be the largest Muslim country in the world; yet its cultural heritage is essentially Hindu-Buddhist in origin, and is manifested in the temple architecture of Prambanan and Borobudur in Central Java as well as in the innumerable Candis scattered all along the nation. While their origin might have been from India,

Indonesians themselves have contributed significantly in improvising and enriching that culture. Indian tourists could be encouraged to travel in larger numbers to these sites to discover the inherent genius of the Indonesian people in preserving such culture and values and, in the process, build a common bond between the two countries.

Similarly, Islamic cultural heritage and monuments are part of the composite Indian civilisation. These need to be presented before the Muslims of Indonesia and Malaysia. The Taj Mahal, Fatehpur Sikri, Ajmer, Delhi, Hyderabad, the abode of Tipu Sultan in Mysore, as well as the innumerable Islamic cultural sites and Sufi shrines in India could be a spiritual feast for tourists from these countries. No doubt Muslims all over the world will surely go to Mecca (the birthplace of Prophet Mohammed) for pilgrimage; but for spiritual experiences, they need to be exposed to India. Here they can discover pluralism and multiculturalism at its best.

Similar things can be done with the Buddhist heritage in India. Nalanda is one of the oldest universities in the world, whose revival with the help of countries like Singapore, Japan, South Korea, and China has heralded a major transformation in regional cooperation. Bodh Gaya, Sarnath and Nalanda could be developed as places of pilgrimage for Buddhists in Southeast Asia, and an annual event on the birthday of Buddha could be organised to attract Buddhists from all over the world as a pilgrimage destination—much like Muslims going to Mecca for their Haj. Past mentors like Amartya Sen have envisaged the Nalanda project like an international university recalling the glorious past of the 5th century, and making it an 'icon of Asian renaissance' and a 'centre of civilisational dialogue and inter-faith understanding.' The vision for setting up such an institution was first spelt out by Indian President A.P.J. Abdul Kalam. Durable and abiding relationships are based not on intergovernmental contacts but on people-to-people contacts. Culture is the best bond between people, and Nalanda can be the bridge between the peoples of Asia.

Even though tourism is an important item of the Indian dialogue with ASEAN, not much has been done to develop this area to promote people-to-people contact. So far, tourism has been moving in only one direction—Indians going to Southeast Asia. However, the reverse is not the case. Imaginative packages need to be evolved, and sufficient incentives offered to attract tourists from countries in Southeast Asia, and from Indonesia in particular. This will not only bring revenues to India but will also cement civil society interactions—an important component of mature and enduring state-to-state relations. Let India initiate an innovative political and cultural charm offensive to give more substance to India's Act East Policy.

In conclusion, it can be said that while India can and must do still more to give meaning to its civilisational links by building educational, cultural, and other links, there is not much effort from the Southeast Asian countries to reciprocate India's earnest efforts and its limited resources. While India has established Chairs in many countries of ASEAN to promote Indian studies programmes, there is no similar effort on the part of the Southeast countries to help in developing Southeast Asian studies programme in India. Southeast Asia programme in Indian universities suffer from the lack of teachers in Southeast Asian languages, books, and other research material on those countries. ASEAN countries can, at least, support Indian universities in providing language teachers and research materials to help Indian students who cannot afford field-research in those countries. Except in the case of Singapore (which has very strong Indian studies programme and which offers a large number of scholarships to Indian students to study in Singapore) and now Vietnam (which has recently launched an Indian studies programme), other countries in ASEAN have not done much to promote Indian studies. Hopefully, ASEAN countries will take note of this fact and take some important steps in reciprocating the forging of civilisational links.

NOTES

1. Keynote address by Secretary (East) at the Inaugural Session of the International Conference on 'ASEAN-India Cultural Links: Historical and Contemporary Dimensions' held at New Delhi (July 23, 2015).
2. Ibid.

25

The Forgotten Saka Linkage between India and Southeast Asia

Sachchidanand Sahai

> Indeed, upon no subject that I know of are there greater discrepancies among writers, from the circumstances, I suppose, of these nations (Saka) being so extremely numerous, and of such migratory habits.
>
> —Pliny the Elder, *Natural History*, Book 6, Chapter 19

The present paper attempts to pinpoint missing civilisational links between India and seventh century mainland Southeast Asia, taking into account the least known presence of the Saka in the kingdom of Ishanapura (Sambor Prei Kuk) in present day central Cambodia. As we trace their successive movements, the nomadic groups of Saka appear to connect Iran, Central Asia, India and Southeast Asia.

The term śaka represents an ethnic group of Eastern Iranian origin, mentioned as Sakā in Old Persian, Sakai in Greek, Sacae in Latin, and Sāi in Chinese. Their arrival via India to Funan, then to Ishanapura (Sambor Prei Kuk) and, finally, to Angkor in mainland Southeast Asia provides an insight into the pan-Asian network of relationships. Durgasvami, the son-in-law of Ishanavarman, was a śaka according to a Sanskrit inscription of Sambor Prei Kuk (K 438), inscribed on the doorjamb of a temple (N 16) now completely destroyed.

The Saka-Scythian Ambivalence

If one subscribes to the view that the Saka and Scythians formed a single cultural group with regional variations, Ishanapura assumes the role of a cultural hub of great consequence. In fact, the fifth century BC Greek historian Herodotus (7.64) says "the Persians called them Sacae, since that is the name which they give to all Scythians" (Kuz'mina 2007).

This ambivalence stems from the similarity of culture and way of life of all the Iranian speaking nomads (Abetekov and Yusupov 1999). However, it has been argued recently that the Saka were not Scythians, nor any variation thereof. The Scythia of Greek texts was a fairly small country that consisted of the grasslands of today's Moldova, Ukraine, and Crimea. The original homeland of the Saka extended from the Fergana Valley in Tajikistan to Tashkent in Uzbekistan.[1]

The 2,500 years old Royal Scythian frozen burial mounds (kurgans) in the Altai Mountains, represent a common Saka-Scythian heritage over a vast area, including the Russian steppe, China, Persia (Iran), and Greece—that is, extending from the Yellow River to the Black Sea. This includes the sharing of common items of dress (tunics, trousers and tall pointed caps). In fact, the Altai, "the ancient crown of Asia", is now the meeting place of four modern states: the Russian Federation, China, Kazakhstan, and Mongolia.

The Meaning of Saka

The term Sakā is universally accepted to be of Iranian origin, used for the first time in Iranian inscriptions. However, a definitive explanation of the term is still a challenge for linguists. The term is variously equated with spaka (dog), with aspa (horse), or with the stem sak, meaning to roam as a 'nomad' (mirfendereski). In Sanskrit, śaka could be derived from the stem śak, meaning to be able. The inscription of Durgasvami at Sambor Prei Kuk, says "though he was śaka (able), he was ashamed..." The expression remains enigmatic due to the lacunae in the text; but it is clear that many efforts were made to define the word śaka.

The Saka Language

The Saka language belongs to the eastern branch of the Iranian languages, which was one of the most widespread of the Indo-European family of languages, spoken in most of Europe, Iran, India, and other parts of Asia. It shared a common origin in the steppe region during the Bronze Age, perhaps about 2500 BC (Mallory 2010).

The Khotanese Saka language is attested from over 2,300 texts from Dunhuang, written in modified Brahmi script on wood and paper, dating from the fourth to the eleventh centuries. The language became extinct after the Turkic Muslims conquered Khotan (in modern Xinjiang, China) in AD 1006 (Bailey 1970).

Iranian Antecedents

Around the seventh century BC, the Achaemenid Empire of Iran established the Syr Darya (the Jaxartes River) as its northern frontier against the nomadic Saka. In his Naqsh-i Rustam inscription, Darius I (552–486 BC) lists three groups of these nomads: (i) the Saka taking a trance-inducing drink (haumvarga), (ii) the Saka wearing pointed hats, and (iii) the Sakā living across the sea/river) or the European Saka/Scythian of the Black sea in the Danube region.

The Tall Cap-Wearing Iranian Saka

The men and women wearing tall caps on the temple walls of Ishanapura gain special meaning in the context of the tall cap wearing Iranian Saka, depicted in the bas-relief on Mount Behistun as one of the nine rebels against the Iranian King Darius I. He is named as Skunkha, the Saka. The tall pointed shape of the headwear indicated status. He who wore it could be distinguished from the rest of the tribe. In the procession of captive kings, as represented before Darius I at Behistun, the Saka captive king with his tall hood has been placed at a slightly lower level. This way, the vanquished Saka appears shorter than Darius. In the representation of the Saka throne bearers at Persepolis, the pointed part of the cap was bent into an arc in order to avoid asymmetry that the tall pointed tip of the cap would otherwise produce.

The tall cap was the trademark headwear of the Saka Tigraxauda. Xaud is the precursor word for present day 'hood' in English, and 'khud' (meaning helmet) in Persian. However, other Saka groups also wore a tall cap, such as the Saka Haumvarga mobilised by Xerxe for the Greek expedition (481-480 BC). They all wore tall stiff caps rising to a point. In the reliefs at Persepolis (Apadana, East Stairway), the Skudra also wore a cap that came up to a protrusion on the top, albeit in the shape of a modest knob. In the art of Gandhara in the Indian subcontinent, the Saka men appear with their characteristic pointed cap.

The Rise and Fall of the Saka in India

The Great Wall of China could not stop the movements of the nomadic tribes. At least three overlapping independent migrations during the second and first centuries BC led the Saka into the Indian subcontinent (Dani 1999).

The Saka ultimately established a kingdom in northwest India, based in Taxila, with two branches (known as Satraps). The Northern branch ruled the eastern region from Mathura. With its base in Ujjain, the Western branch extended its sway up to the Godavari River in the southern region of Dakshinapatha (Deccan).

The Saka established their homeland in India on the pattern of their homeland in eastern Iran called Seistan/Sagastan. These were called Sakastana (sarvasa sakastana pujas), as mentioned in the Mathura Lion Capital Inscriptions as well as in the Chandravalli inscriptions of the Kadamba King Mayurasarman. The Periplus (78 AD) and the *Geography* of Ptolemy (140 AD) informs us that the Indian Sakastana comprised of Patalence (Sindh), Abiria (South Sindh), and Saurashtra (modern Gujarat), and that this entire territory was occupied by the Saka. In fact, the Roman period Tabula Peutingeriana and the Ptolemy world map prominently shows "Scythia" around the mouth of the Indus River.

The Satavahana (300 BC–200 AD) dynasty in the north western part of Deccan, centred on modern day Nasik in Maharashtra, attempted to arrest the growing power of these foreign rulers. However, the Saka succeeded in chasing them out to the eastern coast of the Andhra region. Altogether, 27 independent Saka rulers—known as Western Satrapa or the Kshaharata—ruled western Deccan for a period of 350 years, with Ujjain as their capital. Rudrasimha is the last known Western Saka Satrap in 395 AD. By the middle of fifth century, the major Saka principalities were an integral part of the growing Gupta Empire in India (Majumdar 1977, p. 239).

The Survival of the Saka in Mahisaka

After the decline of the Satavahana, another family belonging to the Saka group emerged in the Deccan, under the leadership of its chief Mana. The new Saka leader declared his independence and laid the foundation of a dynasty that continued to rule from the middle of the third century to 433 AD in the Deccan. The new king was connected with the Saka dynasty of Nahapana.

Apparently, after the overthrow of Nahapana by the Satavahana ruler Gautamiputra Satakarni, the Saka moved to the south under the leadership of Man, where they rehabilitated themselves and established the principality of Mahisaka. This consisted of the southern part of the present day state of Andhra and the adjoining Kannada district of Mysore. The references to this country occurring in the *Puranas* and the epics suggest that it was situated in the Deccan. The *Ramayana* mentions Mahisaka as one of the countries of South India to which Sugriva directed the monkeys in search of Sita. Other references to this country in the Mahabharata and the *Puranas* also indicate its situation in this region (Dhulia District Gazetteer, Maharashtra).

The Saka Migration

After political dislocation in the western Deccan, the migration of Saka people to different parts of India and beyond was quite natural. The Saka were present in the kingdom of Funan (present day Cambodia and Southern Vietnam) in the first centuries of the Christian era. The Saka connections in the early centuries of the Christian era might have continued without being documented for the posterity. In the beginning of the seventh century, a new rallying point emerged with the presence of a Saka from southern India in the city of Ishanapura (Sambor Prei Kuk) in Central Cambodia.

As revealed by an inscription of Sambor Prei Kuk, the Saka Durgasvami, the son-in-law of the early seventh century Cambodian king Ishanavarman, was a native of Southern India (Dakshinapatha-janmā). The Saka had been assimilated in Indian society for more than five hundred years before Durgasvami would have left for Ishanapura. In reality, he was no more only an Indianised Saka—he was an Indian Saka. With all his learning in Vedic lore, he was an erudite Brahmana. The inscription which he left at Ishanapura is now so mutilated that an express mention of his Brahmin affiliation no longer figures there. But the Sakabrahmana are expressly mentioned and were raised to the status of a god-head in the Angkor period. This could be convincingly interpreted as a direct legacy of Ishanapura from where the first documented evidence is available. It has been suggested that Durgasvami, or one of his kinsmen, was deified at least by the ninth century in ancient Cambodia (Sahai, 2007, pp. 71-72).

The Sakabrahmana

By the middle of the fifth century, in the reign of the Gupta Emperor Skandagupta, the Saka seems to have lost all political power, but they were assimilated in Indian society. The *Manusmriti* (X, 43-44) mentions Saka along with a number of foreign ethnic groups in India, whom the commentator Kulluka considers as degraded warriors (Kshatriyas). So does the Anusasanaparva of the *Mahabharata*. In his *Mahabhasya* (II. 4.10) Patanjali regards the Saka and Yavana as pure Sudra. The *Puranas*, particularly the *Samba Purana* and the *Bhavishya Purana* mention a group of the Sun-worshipping Maga Brahman who were brought from Iran to India. The alien Saka rulers brought a particular type of sun worship of Iranian origin and, with them, came a particular set of priests who became famous as the Sakadvipi Brahmins, hailing from the island of Saka (Sahai 2007, 69-73). While in Indian sources they are generally called Maga Brahman, Saakadvipi or Saakaladvipi Brahman, in the inscriptions of Angkor they are called Sakabrahamana. In Indian sources, Saakadvipa is interpreted as the island where the Saaka tree grows.

A divinity called vrah kamraten an Sakabrahmana was being worshipped at Prasat Kok Chak, in northwest of Angkor Thom (K 521) between the reign of Jayavarman III (869 AD) and Suryavarman I (1001). This last king made donations, assuring the continuity of the worship of Sakabrahmana at least through the eleventh century. The Sakabrahmana appears as a god of the category of the Lord of the Universe (kamrateng jagat) in an inscription of 1041 AD in the temple of Prasta Khna in the province of Preah Vihear (K 606) in the Angkorean Empire of mainland Southeast Asia. Two other inscriptions (K 365 and K 136) of the Angkorean period also mention the Sakabrahmana.

The same divinity is twice mentioned as a god (kamrateng jagat) at the Bayon (Angkor). The first time the god appears in the outer gallery of the Bayon in an obscure context of a royal march, an unspecified battle, and the construction of a fortification (durga). This reference connects the Saka with the art of fort building (thve durgga). It is interesting to note that the Sakabrahmana at Ishanapura has a name which literally means 'the master of fort' (Durgasvami). The second time the Sakabrahmana is mentioned is in an inscription in tower no 63 (K 293-2) of Bayon, along with important territorial gods of the Angkor empire.

In the Angkor period, a number of temples and images were dedicated to the Sakabrahmana. As most of the images established at the Bayon are the replicas of the local gods of the empire, it is legitimate to ask whether the Sakabrahmana at Bayon represented the god of some locality. Whether Sakabrahmana is a generic name for a particular god worshipped at different places, or a particular historical Sakabrahmana such as Durgasvami of the time of Ishanavarman, is not very clear. That the Saka Durgasvami of Ishanapura was deified to perpetuate the memory of the magically endowed alien Brahmins of India seems to be quite a plausible hypothesis which needs further exploration in the complex diffusion of the Saka culture.

The Saka Era

The Saka era was the most popular for dating text and inscriptions especially in Deccan and South India. There are, however, differing traditions about the origin of this era. The earliest tradition traced it to the coronation of a Saka king. The later tradition traces its commencement to commemorate the termination of the Saka rule in India. Yet another tradition associates this era with the Satavahana. This is a glaring example of reworking the past memory to suit the mood of the changing times.

In India, a number of inscriptions refer to this era by its actual name: the current Saka year 322 in an inscription of the Bhoja-Mayura king Suketuvarman, the year 380 of the Saka in an inscription of the Vakataka king Devasena; Saka year 465 in the Badami Rock Inscription of Vallabheshvara (Pulakeshin I). An inscription of the Chalukya king Mangaleshvara, expressly dated Saka year 500, clearly states that this era marks the crowning of a Saka king (saka-nripati-rajya-abhiseka-samvatsara). Other inscriptions of the Chalukya of Badami also relate the era to the same event. It is not possible to ascertain when the use of term Saka era began in ancient Cambodia. Sanskrit inscriptions found from Funan (second–sixth century AD) are not dated. So it is not possible to ascertain whether the Saka era was used in the time of Funan, when the contacts with the Saka were already established.

An inscription of Si Thep in Thailand (K 978) mentions King Bhavavarman whom Cœdès considers as the first king of this name. The expression, 'the year (samvatsara) of the Saka king (sakapati)' survives in the text; but the actual figures of the date are lost.

Interestingly the first Khmer language inscription dated in the Saka era, found from Angkor Borei (K 557 and K 600) in present-day southern Cambodia, mentions the Saka year 533 (611 AD). The inscription does not mention any ruling king. But it may belong to the reign of Ishanavarman, if the king started to rule as early as 610 AD. The Thma Kre inscription (K 926), dated the Saka year 546, falls in the reign of King Ishanavarman, though his name is not mentioned. The place is also known for the inscription of his father, Mahendravarman, who has not used the Saka era or any other dating system for his inscriptions.

Some inscriptions from Sambor Prei Kuk are dated in the Saka era. K 604 at the temple F, dated in the Saka year (sakabda) 549 (627 AD), mentions King Ishanavarman as the ruling king. An inscription from Srei Krop Leak also mentions the same king. Recalling the event of the time of his predecessor King Bhavavarman I, the text mentions the Saka time (saka=avadhi) 520 (598 AD). The stele of Wat Chakret (K 60) found from the neighbourhood of the sacred mountain of Ba Phnom notes the Saka year (sakabde) 548 (626 AD) and the ruling king Ishanavarman. The Wat Prei Vier inscription, dated Shaka year 586 (664 AD) uses the expression 'sakapatisamayabde' or the era of the Saka king.

Barth pertinently observes the following:

> It would be remarked with what fidelity the formula used to designate the Saka era have preserved the memory of the veritable origin of this era instituted by a conqueror of foreign race, the memory of which was rather soon altered in Indian literature. The same fact is noticed in the inscriptions of ancient India.[2]

The inscriptions of Champa also use the expression sakapatisamaye or sakaraje to denote a Saka as the founder of the era (Bergaigne 1893, pp. 223, 235).

Unfortunately, there is no unanimity among scholars about the founder of the Saka era. The continued reckoning in ascending numerals in Kushan and Saka inscriptions bear no specific name for the era. The inscriptions in India and Southeast Asia which name the era as the Saka era were written much later—when the Saka and the Kushan had almost disappeared as political powers. It is also to be noted that the Saka did not call themselves as Saka in their own inscriptions. A number of contradictory theories have been put forward to identify the founder of the Saka era.

The Kushan origin of the theory of the Saka era has a number of critics, who question the validity of attributing an era of a Saka king to the Kushans. However, the most popular view is the one originally propounded by James Fergusson, attributing the foundation of this era to the Kushan emperor, Kanishka I, beginning with the first year of his reign. However, there is no unanimity about the dates of Kanishka I. Most Indian historians favour 78 AD as the first year of the Saka era. Most European scholars are inclined to place this event in 128 AD or 144 AD.

The French scholars who edited and translated the inscriptions of ancient Cambodia have accepted the view that the Saka era began in 78 AD. Instead of changing this stand, it is useful to imagine a margin of fifty to seventy years for dating the events in the history of the Khmer civilisation, taking into account all the differing views about the beginning of this era.

The year of the era uniformly begins on the first day of the bright half of the month of Chaitra, and its month ends on the fifteenth day of the dark half in South India and on the full moon day in North India. Its expired years are mostly used in inscriptions and literature; the current year is rarely referred to.

The Saka and Kushan kings began counting their regnal years. Kanishka I and his successors counted from the year 1 to 98. It is supposed that the Saka of Western India (Gujarat and Malawa) used the Kushan regnal year for dating their inscriptions and coins, up to the year 337. It is argued that since they were the provincial governors of the Kushan, they were obliged to use the reckoning of their overlord. It was a continued counting of years during the rule of the Saka and Kushan rulers without using any specific name for the era. As noted above, the name Saka era was popularised by the later Indian dynasties (such as the Maurya, Bhoja, Vakataka, Vishnukundin, Chalukyas, etc.) ruling over Dakshinapatha, the region north of the Narmada River, from the fifth century onward. The migration of the Kanarese dynasties (like the Ganga and the Sena) to Bengal and Bihar resulted in the spread of this era to eastern India. It may, however, be pointed out that the Vimkrama era, not the Saka era, is popular in North India. The Saka era is confined to astronomical-astrological works as well as the almanacs in northern India where it is generally not used in the inscriptions. With effect from 22 March 1957, the Government of India adopted and reintroduced the Saka era along with Christian era for the entire country, introducing certain changes in the traditional Saka calendar (Shastri 1996).

The foregoing analysis suggests that the Saka era was introduced from the Dakshinapatha region of India in the early seventh century post-Funan period. Since no document of Funan from the second to sixth century bears any date, it is impossible to imagine that the people of Funan used the Saka era, in spite of their known links with the Saka. There was no question of the introduction of the Saka era in the early centuries of Christian era because this regnal year counting was given the name of Saka era in Dakshinapatha not before the fourth century AD. The presence of the Saka Durgasvami in Ishanapura in the beginning of the seventh century must have given impetus to the greater use of this era in the inscriptions issued by King Ishanavarman and his successors.

NOTES

1. Please see, http://www.heritageinstitute.com/zorastrianism/saka.
2. Auguste Barth, *Inscriptions Sanscrites du Cambodge*, Paris: Imprimerie Nationale, 1885, 63.

REFERENCES

Bailey, H.W., *The Ancient Kingdom of Khotan*, British Institute of Persian Studies 8, 1970, pp. 65–72.

Barth, Auguste, *Inscriptions Sanscrites du Cambodge*. Paris: Imprimerie Nationale, 1885.

Bergaigne, Abel Bergaigne, *Inscriptions Sanscrites du Cambodge et de Champa*. Paris: Imprimerie Nationale 1893.

Dani, Ahmad Hasan (ed.), *History of Civilization of Central Asia: The Development of Sedentary and Nomadic Civilizations 700 BC to AD 250*, Delhi: Motilala Banrasadiass, 1999.

Dhulia District Gazetteer, Maharashtra

Kuz'mina, Elena Efimovna, *The Origins of Indo-Iranians*, Leiden: Brill, 2007.

Majumdar, R.C., *Ancient India*, Delhi: Motilal Banarsidass, 1977.

Mallory, J.P., 'Bronze Age Languages of Tarim Basin', *Expedition*, 52(3), 2010.

Mirfendereski, Guive, 'The Saka Nomenclature, a Persian appraisal', in 'The Circle of Ancient Iranian Studies', at http://www.cais-soas.com/CAIS/Anthropology/Scythian/saka_nomenclature.

Sahai, Sachchidanand, *The Bayon of Angkor Thom*, Bangkok: White Lotus Press, 2007.

Shastri, Ajay Mitra, 'Saka Era', *Indian Journal of History of Science* 31(1), 1996.

WAY FORWARD: TOWARDS 25TH ANNIVERSARY OF ASEAN-INDIA RELATIONS

Chaired by

Gopinath Pillai

26

Strengthening ASEAN-India Strategic Partnership

*Nguyen Thai Yen Huong**

Entering the 21st century, particularly in the context of the global economic and financial crisis, the world is moving towards a multi-polar and multi-layered setting, embedding increasingly important roles for India and the ASEAN community in the evolving architecture of the Asia-Pacific region. India and ASEAN's interests are aligned more closely than ever before, especially after ASEAN has become a full-fledged community since the end of 2015, and India itself has made remarkable achievements in national developments as well as grown in international significance. It is time now to build a stronger ASEAN-Indian strategic partnership in the 21st century, heading towards the 25th Anniversary of ASEAN-India relations.

India's Look East Policy: ASEAN Perceptions

India's Look East Policy (LEP) is the cornerstone of India's foreign policy towards ASEAN after the Cold War. India's LEP has undergone two phases. The first phase started with the aim of enhancing economic relations, and reached towards greater strategic, political, and institutional linkages with ASEAN. The second phase was more extended and comprehensive, with the adoption of "extended neighbourhood" theory which included not only ASEAN but also Northeast Asia (China, Japan and South Korea), apart from Australia and New Zealand. India's Look East Policy developed into a dynamic

* Professor Nguyen Thai Yen Huong is Vice-President, Diplomatic Academy of Vietnam. The views expressed herein are those of the author and do not necessarily reflect the views of the Government of Vietnam. Please do not quote without permission from the author.

and action oriented Act East Policy in November 2014. Through the Act East Policy, India has intensified its outreach to India's key partners, such as Japan, Vietnam, Australia, and ASEAN. The shift towards the Act East Policy can be seen as a manifestation of Prime Minister Modi government's stronger commitment to engage with Southeast Asia.[1]

The Look East Policy Phase I (1990-2002)

During his visit to the Institute of Southeast Asian Studies in Singapore in 1994, Indian Prime Minister P.V. Narasimha Rao made a speech which reflected the essence of the idea behind India's Look East Policy. In his speech, Rao mentioned close, long-term, historic and cultural relations between India and Southeast Asia. He also calmed down fears and suspicions amongst some Asia-Pacific countries about Indian Navy presence and Indian performance in the region. On this occasion, he also introduced India's economic reforms and explained the Indian Government's attempts in implementing these reforms.

The speech showed four major aspects of India's Look East Policy: (i) expanding Indian influence over the sea, space, and the external area surrounding India's territory; (ii) increasing the mutual understanding and cultural exchanges between India and Southeast Asia; (iii) utilising the enormous resources in India's development process; (iv) promoting cooperation and exchange between India and the region in economic-political fields, such as human rights, labour standards, the management of resources, environmental protection, and to take advantage of liberalisation in information.

Thus, Phase I of India's Look East Policy focused on strengthening relations between India and ASEAN countries in trade, investment, politics, and security. Moreover, this first phase provided the foundations for India to join other regional security, economic, and political organisations, such as APEC, WTO, and ARF. India's aim was to use economic diplomacy as a pillar of its foreign policy. Southeast Asia was considered as "springboard" for India to enter into the regional market.[2]

The Look East Policy Phase II (2003–2014)

In October 2003, Indian Prime Minister Vajpayee attended the 2nd ASEAN-India Summit in Indonesia, and also made a visit to Thailand. These trips marked India's LEP's achievements after its inception nearly a decade earlier under Prime Minister Narasimha Rao; they also marked a new phase in the India Look East Policy.

Earlier, in September 2003, India's External Affairs Minister, Yashwant Sinha, made a speech at Harvard University in which he mentioned India's new initiative regarding Asia:

> In the past, India's engagement with much of Asia, including Southeast and East Asia, was built on an idealistic conception of Asian brotherhood, based on shared experiences of colonialism and of cultural ties. The rhythm of the region today is determined, however, as much by trade, investment and production as by history and culture. That is what motivates our decade-old 'Look East' policy. Already, this region accounts for 45 per cent of our external trade.[3]

In his speech, Sinha pointed out the differences between the two phases of LEP:

> The first phase of India's Look East policy was ASEAN-centered and focused primarily on trade and investment linkages. The new phase of this policy is characterised by an expanded definition of 'East', extending from Australia to East Asia, with ASEAN at its core. The new phase also marked a shift from trade to wider economic and security issues, including joint efforts to protect the sea-lanes and coordinate counter-terrorism activities.[4]

Sinha also highlighted a number of points to illustrate the second phase of the LEP: firstly, geographic scope of the LEP was broader, spreading from Southeast Asia to East Asia and the South Pacific. The LEP phase II was marked by the concept of extension in Look East Policy, "stretching from Australia to China and East Asia, with ASEAN at center";[5] secondly, there was a change of focus from different single issues in the first phase of LEP to one on comprehensive issues in the second phase. In the early 1990s, there were only lower level joint exercises and the military visits between India and ASEAN countries. Things have now changed. Comprehensive defence cooperation agreements have been signed between the two sides. India has also built up bilateral agreements which have allowed naval ships go to the ports in Southeast Asia regularly. India has expanded defence exchanges with Japan, South Korea, and China. Never before has India deployed its multilateral defence policy as strongly in Asia.

Thirdly, there has been an increase in transportation and infrastructure cooperation between India and ASEAN. For example, India actively built the transportation corridor which linked India with Southeast Asia. Also included are trilateral projects on building motorway routes connecting India with Myanmar and Thailand as well as building a railroad linking New Delhi to Hanoi.

Fourthly, the second phase of LEP does not aim to deal with the "China threat." As mentioned by the Indian Prime Minister Vajpayee (in his visit to China in June 2003), the second phase of LEP focused on the resolution of issues in Indian bilateral relations with other countries, and then took advantage in LEP phase II to create opportunities for economic cooperation and bilateral trade.

Recently, under Prime Minister Narendra Modi, India's Look East Policy has gathered greater momentum. It was upgraded to the Act East Policy at the India-ASEAN Summit in November 2014. India's objective in the Act East Policy is to improve strategic relations with major powers by taking them to a higher level, and to create conditions for India to emerge as a "global power"—that is, reinforcing the recognition of India as a regional power.[6]

Indeed, Prime Minister Modi's recent movements have shown some major changes in the Act East Policy. The first is that Prime Minister Modi's government has broadened the agenda for economic development, including connectivity. Prior to the 2014 election, Prime Minister Modi strengthened Gujarat's existing economic links with China, Japan, and Singapore in order to deepen India's engagement with the Asia region. During his visit to Japan in August 2014, Prime Minister Abe promised to mobilise nearly US$ 35 billion dollars of aid and investment into India in the next five years. Also, during his visit to India in September 2014, the Chinese President Xi Jinping, set an investment target of about US$ 20 billion in the coming years. Both Japan and China have ambitions to build trans-border transport corridors between India and East Asia. Connectivity over land and sea is also a major priority for Prime Minister Modi's government in its engagement with ASEAN. As the business and economic environment improved under his government, more investments are likely to come from across East Asia, including Korea, Australia, and the South East Asian nations.[7]

Secondly, Prime Minister Modi has also significantly expanded the geographic scope of India's Act East policy. He has become the first Indian Prime Minister in 28 years to visit Australia which has emerged as a major partner for India. Prime Minister Modi also became the first Indian Prime Minister in 33 years to travel to Fiji in November 2014.

Thirdly, Prime Minister Modi's government has put special emphasis on promoting India's soft power in the region. This is being done through a vigorous engagement with the Indian diaspora and a strong commitment to build on shared civilisational bonds. India's new government considers enhancing cultural and spiritual links as an important part of connectivity with Asia.[8]

Fourthly, India also fully engages with the emerging political players in East Asia. Prime Minister Modi has reaffirmed the centrality of ASEAN in building a stable and prosperous order in East Asia and the Asia-Pacific. On the territorial disputes in the South China Sea, Prime Minister Modi has stated that India shares a deep interest in the freedom of navigation in sea and air. He has underlined the importance of all parties abiding by the principles of the United Nations Convention on the Law of the Seas. This is a new aspect in Prime Minister Modi's policy. He has emphasised the importance of maritime security and the need to expand India's defence partnerships with Asia. In the last few months, India has deepened defence ties with the USA, Japan, Australia, and Vietnam.

Thus, for over two decades, India's Look East policy has shaped the way India deals with its neighbours in the Asia-Pacific region, leading to substantially deep economic, politic, institutional, security, cultural, and sub-regional relations. India's Look East Policy was initiated in the early 1990s, with the aim of increasing its economic ties with Southeast Asia. Since then, the objectives of Look East have broadened to all fields, and to the entire Asia-Pacific. Given the swiftly changing security dynamics in the region, Prime Minister Narendra Modi has rechristened the Look East as the Act East policy, thus underlining the importance of strengthening deeper ties with partners such as Japan, Vietnam, South Korea, and Australia. India's interest in Southeast Asia is being driven by mutual understanding and mutual interest in many fields, especially in the economic and security spheres.

Review: India-ASEAN Relations

Under the impact of the India's Act East Policy, India-ASEAN relations have improved rapidly and flourished in many fields.

Political Cooperation

ASEAN-India political cooperation is constantly being tightened and expanded, creating a foundation for cooperation in other fields. The first milestone marking warmth in India-ASEAN relations was in 1992 when India became a sectoral dialogue partner. Then, India became a full dialogue partner of ASEAN in December 1995, and a member of the ASEAN Regional Forum in 1996. These dialogues established and promoted India's activities in other regional mechanisms such as in the ASEAN Regional Forum (ARF), the East Asia Summit (EAS), the Mekong-Ganga Cooperation, and the Bengal Initiative for Multi-Sectoral Technical and Economic Cooperation (BIMSTEC). The relationship further elevated with the convening of the ASEAN-India Summit in 2002 in Phnom Penh, Cambodia. Since then, the ASEAN-India Summit has been held annually. In 2004, the two sides signed a "Partnership for peace, progress and shared prosperity". At the ASEAN-India Commemorative Summit held on 20 December 2012 in New Delhi, the ASEAN-India Partnership was elevated to a Strategic Partnership. This was considered an important breakthrough which laid the foundations for bringing about the comprehensive development of the relationship between India and ASEAN.

Political cooperation between India and ASEAN was also demonstrated through the visits of Indian government officials to the ASEAN member countries, and vice versa. In 2014–2015 particularly, the Indian Prime Minister and his Minister for External Affairs, Sushma Swaraj, paid visits to most ASEAN member countries, including Myanmar, Singapore, and Vietnam. During these visits, India always affirmed its support to the peace, stability, and development of ASEAN, and clearly demonstrated the role of Southeast Asia in India's strategic development in particular, in the region, and the world in general.

Economic Cooperation

India's Look East Policy focused on strengthening Indian economic relations with ASEAN countries. Since then, India-ASEAN economic cooperation has obtained great achievements. The two sides have established various mechanisms to promote economic, trade, and investment cooperation. The establishment of the ASEAN-India Free Trade Area (FTA) is the most important economic framework which also covers other fields of cooperation, such as goods, investment, services, connectivity, infrastructure, tourism, as well as the agriculture and forestry sector. The ASEAN-India Trade in Goods Agreements (TIG), the ASEAN-India Trade in Services and Investment Agreements (2012), The India–Myanmar–Thailand Trilateral Highway Project; India's Inter-Ministerial Group on Connectivity are also important agreements which have been signed.

Trade and investment ties between the two sides has been strengthened and accelerated. In 2014, total trade amounted to US$ 77 billion, a significant increase over the US$ 44 billion seen during 2009–10. Over the past decade, bilateral trade has increased at an average annual rate of a blistering 23 per cent.[9] The key factors underlying the growth in trade and investment has been India's Act East policy as well as the establishment of the ASEAN Economic Community at the end of 2015. The ASEAN-India Trade in Goods Agreement (2010), combined with Prime Minister Modi's new FDI policy opened up a range of investment opportunities into India, particularly in the services sector. Moreover, economic cooperation between India and ASEAN has also brought benefits to other fields, including connectivity, infrastructure, tourism, agriculture, and forestry.

Defence Cooperation

In the field of defence and security cooperation, India and ASEAN have shared mutual interests and understanding with regard to regional security challenges, including traditional and non-traditional security issues such as terrorism, piracy, transnational crimes, climate change, maritime security, cyber security, water security, etc. India-ASEAN defence cooperation includes exchanges of high-level visits, strategic dialogue, port calls, training exchanges, joint exercises, and the provision of defence equipment. At the bilateral level, India has strengthened its military and defence links with some ASEAN countries, including Singapore, Philippines, Indonesia, and Vietnam. At the multilateral level, India has become a member of the ASEAN Defence Ministers' Meeting Plus (ADMM+) and the ASEAN Regional Forum (ARF).

The basic objective of the ADMM+ framework is to bring a cooperative security mechanism in the areas of humanitarian assistance, disaster relief, maritime security, counter-terrorism, and peace-keeping operations. Joint exercises between India and ASEAN members are organised regularly, which has made the ASEAN-India defence cooperation key factor in Prime Minister Modi's Act East policy. Moreover, on the anti-terrorism battlefront, the two sides signed the Declaration on Cooperation against Terrorism in 2003. On the border issue, both India and ASEAN agreed to maintain stability in border areas to create favourable conditions for the economic development of both sides. Furthermore, India also provides ASEAN military equipment, experts, and military training.

ASEAN and India also have shared mutual interests in maritime security in the South China Sea and the Indian Ocean. Thus, both ASEAN and India support maritime safety and security, freedom of navigation, and settling territorial disputes through peaceful means on the basis of international law, including UNCLOS 1982. ASEAN urged India's support for the full implementation of the Declaration of the Conduct (DOC), and early finalisation of the Code of Conduct (COC).

Socio-Cultural Cooperation

India and ASEAN have worked together to promote human resources development and educational exchanges, science and technology cooperation, information technology, SMEs development, tourism, and other cultural activities. Moreover, India has contributed to narrowing the developmental gaps in ASEAN by supporting the capacity building programs in the CLMV countries, especially in the creation of Entrepreneurship Development Centres (EDC) as well as Centres for English Language Training (CELT) in Cambodia, Lao PDR, Myanmar and Vietnam.[10]

In conclusion, there is no doubt that India's Look East Policy is being implemented in the right direction, and has contributed greatly to promoting India-ASEAN relations in many fields. Economic cooperation is always the bright side, which contributes to other fields such as politics, military-defence, and socio-culture. However, beyond those achievements, some limitations also exist in India-ASEAN cooperation, such as the economic development gap, and differences in political regimes, culture, as well as sensitive security issues. These have prevented ASEAN-India relations from developing their full potential. Thus, forging a strong India-ASEAN relationship requires not only addressing future challenges, but also seizing new opportunities as well as proactively initiating new ideas for future cooperation.

The Way Forward

As we head towards the 25th Anniversary of India-ASEAN relations in 2017, it is time now to consider how the ASEAN-India relationship could be improved, and elevated to a higher level strategic partnership which goes beyond the plan of action in 2016–2020 periods. Firstly, in globalised and inter-connected world, the top priority in ASEAN–India relations is to ensure an open, inclusive, sustainable, and transparent regional architecture for peace and stability in Asia. Both India and ASEAN should seek to build up strategic trust, uphold international law, and consolidate existing and emerging regional arrangements. India remains ASEAN's indispensable partner in this goal.

Secondly, in this interconnected world, it is imperative to enhance the global dimension of cooperation in response to common challenges. India and ASEAN need to cooperate in addressing global issues, including climate change, natural disasters, epidemics, food-water-energy security, maritime safety and security, terrorism, transnational crimes, money laundering, drug trafficking, and cyber security.

Thirdly, ASEAN and India should forge two-way economic and trade linkages. ASEAN and India should redouble efforts to promote India-ASEAN economic relations in the framework of FTAs, RCEP, and ASEAN Economic Community (AEC). Regarding the promotion of economic cooperation between the two sides, the India-ASEAN Business Council could have annual meetings, or its thematic sub-group can meet more frequently with the inclusion of small and medium entrepreneurs (SMEs). India and ASEAN should work together to outline the difficulties and opportunities for SMEs when entering into regional economic integration, and jointly work out ways to grasp the opportunities as well as overcome difficulties for mutual benefit.

Fourthly, connectivity should be developed in all dimensions of ASEAN-India's strategic partnership. The infrastructure developments along the India, Myanmar, and Thailand borders, Mekong-Ganga Cooperation (MGC), the Bay of Bengal Initiative for Multi-sectoral Technical and Economic Cooperation (BIMSTEC), and the ASEAN-India Highway Network are the major connectivity projects between India and ASEAN. Both India and

ASEAN should encourage people-to-people exchanges among academics, scholars and journalists, policymakers, and business leaders. In addition, India and ASEAN need to pay more attention to mass media cooperation. To implement these initiatives, financial and technical resources are needed. Thus, it is necessary to expand both the ASEAN-India Cooperation Fund and the ASEAN Development Fund.[11]

Fifthly, India-ASEAN's defence and security cooperation should deepen through such mechanisms as ADMM+1, between ASEAN and other power partners. These mechanisms would create more favourable conditions for India and ASEAN cooperation in security and defence related issues. Moreover, India and ASEAN can cooperate and coordinate to improve the ARF's operation, move the ARF agenda forward, and enhance practical cooperation in confidence-building and preventive diplomacy—particularly in the context of many emerging regional security mechanisms in the region (ADMM+, EAS) competing with ARF.

As a coordinator of ASEAN-India relations in the 2016–2018 period, Vietnam is ready to provide broader gateways for India's stronger engagement in South East Asia, especially through India's Look East and now Act East Policy. Vietnam could actively give new initiatives to strengthen and enhance India-ASEAN relations in priority areas, especially in economic, security-related, and socio-cultural areas.

In the field of economic cooperation, ASEAN—particularly Vietnam—is becoming a hub for India's attempts in promoting strategic partnerships, comprehensive partnerships, and FTAs with all the leading economic partners in the region. Thus, Vietnam will continue to support India's economic engagement in the region and create favourable conditions for Indian enterprises to come to the ASEAN market. In the security arena, Vietnam supports India joining the ADMM+1 mechanism, and to play a bigger role in ARF. As a coordinator, Vietnam will increase and enhance ASEAN-India cooperation in joint defence research, designing, developing and manufacturing military equipment, including the transfer of technology regarding weapon and defence equipment.

In the field of socio-cultural cooperation, India being an IT power could help ASEAN in establishing an e-network for tele-medicine and tele-education in Cambodia, Laos, Myanmar, and Vietnam. Moreover, tourism is the strength of both India and ASEAN countries, including Vietnam. In 2016, ASEAN chairman Laos, might promote tourism as its priority field. Thus, both India and Vietnam could increase tourism trips along the Mekong River, the Bay of Bengal region, and the Malacca Strait. Moreover, direct air links from Delhi (or at least a major Indian city) to Jakarta, Manila, and the capitals of CLMV countries as well as to commercial centres, like Ho Chi Minh City in Vietnam, are desirable. Last but not least, the Delhi Dialogue should be maintained on the lines of a Strategic Dialogue that focuses on specific projects and action plans, like the Transport Transit Agreement, border trade, or other specific issues.

In conclusion, the robust cultural and civilisational connections between ASEAN and India in the past as well as the common interests both parties share today provide significant potential for the development of a strong strategic partnership for tomorrow. However, an agenda for future relations cannot be forged by common interests alone. It will require bold decisions, innovative policies, and smart politics on the part of ASEAN and Indian leaders in order to get over potential obstacles as well as push through initiatives that provide opportunities for enhancing relations. Only when both parties are determined to build a strong ASEAN-India strategic partnership, can here be an outcome that is beneficial not only to India and ASEAN, but to the entire Asia-Pacific as well.

NOTES

1. Prime Minister Modi articulated the 'Act East' strategy in his remarks at the ASEAN-India summit at Myanmar, in November 2014. He emphasized a more action-oriented strategy for engaging Southeast Asia. See, http://thediplomat.com/2014/11/modi-unveils-indias-act-east-policy-to-asean-in-myanmar/
2. P.V.N. Rao, *India and the Asia-Pacific: Forging a New Relationship*, Institute of Southeast Asian Studies, Singapore: 1994, p. 6.
3. Speech by External Affairs Minister, Yashwant Sinha, at Harvard University on 29/9/2003, at http://mea.gov.in/Speeches-Statements.htm?dtl/4744/Speech+by+External+Affairs+Minister+Shri+Yashwant+Sinha+at+Harvard+University
4. Speech by External Affairs Minister, Yashwant Sinha, at Harvard University on 29/9/2003, at http://mea.gov.in/Speeches-Statements.htm?dtl/4744/Speech+by+External+ Affairs+Minister+Shri+Yashwant+Sinha+at+Harvard+University
5. Speech by External Affairs Minister, Yashwant Sinha at Harvard University on 29/9/2003, at http://mea.gov.in/Speeches-Statements.htm?dtl/4744/Speech+by+External+ Affairs + Minister+Shri+Yashwant+Sinha+at+Harvard+University
6. East Sea Studies, "India's foreign policy was leverage to a new level", at http://nghiencuubiendong.vn/nghien-cuu-khu-vuc-khac/4486-nm-2014-chinh-sach-doi-ngoai-cua-an-do

7. C. Raja Mohan, 'From Looking East to Acting East', January 2015, at http://www.mea.gov.in/in-focus-article.htm?24714/From+Looking+East+to+Acting+East
8. Ibid.
9. 'The future of ASEAN-India trade looks bright', at http://www.aseanbriefing.com/news/2015/08/10/the-future-of-asean-india-trade-looks-bright.html
10. Vannarith Chheang, 'ASEAN-India Forging new Partnership', at http://www.diplomatist.com/dipom04y2014/article023.html
11. Vannarith Chheang, 'ASEAN-India going beyond Delhi Dialogue VI', at http://www.diplomatist.com/dipom04y2014/article023.html

REFERENCES

"ASEAN-India Dialogue Relations", ASEAN web, March 2010, at http://www.asean.org/asean/external-relations/india

"ASEAN-India Joint Declaration on Cooperation to Combat International Terrorism", ASEAN web, 2003

"Act East: India's ASEAN Journey", Ministry of External Affairs, Government of India; 10 November 2014, at http://mea.gov.in/in-focus-article.htm?

Palit, Amitendu, "India-Southeast Asia Relations: Enhancing Mutual Benefits", May 2015, at http://www.brookings.in/wp-content/uploads/2015/06/India-Southeast-Asia-Relations-Amitendu.pdf

Panda, Ankit, "ASEAN-India and East Asia Summits: India's Opportunity to 'Act East'", at http://thediplomat.com/2015/11/asean-india-and-east-asia-summits-indias-opportunity-to-act-east/

Sundaram, A., "Look East Policy", *International Journal of Advancements in Research and Technology*, Volume 2, Issue 5, May 2013, at http://www.ijoart.org/docs/Look-East-Policy.pdf

Raja Mohan, C., "From Looking East to Acting East", January 2015, at http://www.mea.gov.in/in-focus-article.htm?24714/From+Looking+East+to+Acting+East,

Zhang, Dong, "India Looks East: Strategic and Impacts", AUSAID working paper, September 2006

Danielle Rajendram, "India's new Asia –Pacific strategy: Modi acts East", December 2014, at http://www.lowyinstitute.org/files/indias-new-asia-pacific-strategy-modi-acts-east.pdf

"India's foreign policy was accelerated to a new level", East Sea Studies, at http://nghiencuubiendong.vn/nghien-cuu-khu-vuc-khac/4486-nm-2014-chinh-sach-doi-ngoai-cua-an-do

Saikia, Hemanta, "Look East Policy: Southeast Asian Economic integration of India", *Economics Journal* [17 (2), 1–11, http://www.journal.eco.ku.ac.th/upload/document/thai/20110914 121014.pdf

"India-ASEAN relations expanding East", *Security Risks Monitors*, 27 August 2014, at www.security-risks.com/security-issues-south-asia/other-security-issue/india-asean-relations-expanding-east-3351.html

Jyoti, "India's Look East Policy: In Its Second Phase", *Global Journal of Pharmaceutical Sciences and Education*, Vol 2, Number 1 (2013), pp. 1–14, at http://www.ripublication.com/gjpse/gjpsv1n1_01.pdf

"Plan of Action to Implement the ASEAN-India Partnership for Peace, Progress and Shared Prosperity", (2016–2020), at http://www.asean.org/wp-content/uploads/images/2015/August/POA_India/ASEAN-India%20POA%20-%20FINAL.pdf

Parameswaran, Prashanth, "Strengthening ASEAN-India Relations in the 21st century", *Project 2049 Institute*, May 27, 2010, at https://project2049.net/documents/strengthening_asean_india_ relations_ 21st_century_parameswaran.pdf

Parameswaran, Prashanth, "Modi Unveils India's 'Act East Policy' to ASEAN in Myanmar", 2014, http://thediplomat.com/2014/11/modi-unveils-indias-act-east-policy-to-asean-in-myanmar/

Rao, P.V.N., *India and the Asia-Pacific: Forging a New Relationship*, Institute of Southeast Asian

Studies, Singapore, 1994, p. 6.

Banlaoi, Rommel C., "Challenges in India-ASEAN Security Cooperation", Delhi Dialogue V, 20 February 2013, at http://www.slideshare.net/RommelBanlaoi/challenges-in-india-asean-security-relations-banlaoi-speech

Muni, S.D. and See Chak Mun, "ASEAN-India Relations: Future Directions", ISAS Special Reports, 25 May 2012, at ISAS_Special_Report_05__-Asean-India_Relations_-_Future_ Directions_New_25052012172612.pdf

Speech by External Affairs Minister, Shri Yashwant Sinha, at Harvard University on 29 September 2003, at http://mea.gov.in/Speeches-Statements.htm?dtl/4744/Speech+by+External+Affairs+Minister+Shri+Yashwant+Sinha+at+Harvard+University

"The future of ASEAN-India trade looks bright", at http://www.aseanbriefing.com/news/2015/08/10/the-future-of-asean-india-trade-looks-bright.html

Chheang, Vannarith, "ASEAN-India going beyond Delhi Dialogue VI", at http://www.diplomatist.com/dipom04y2014/article023.html

Chheang, Vannarith, "ASEAN-India forging new partnership", at http://www.diplomatist.com/articles/article001.html

Shekhar, Vibhanshu, "India-ASEAN Relations enter a New Discourse", Indian Council of World Affairs, 2 January 2013, at http://www.icwa.in/pdfs/vpindiaasean.pdf

"India in the aim becoming a superpower", *Vietnam News Agency*, 2004, p. 20.

27

India and the ASEAN

R. Ravindran

In the last decade, India has taken many steps to improve relations with ASEAN and has committed to undertaking many more projects in ASEAN. Details of these are available in the Plan of Action of India for ASEAN from 2015–2020 as well as in ASEAN's Plan for the ASEAN community up to 2025.

Three key points are important. First, what is India's role in ASEAN? It is somewhat perturbing to hear some analysts speaking and writing about the ASEAN region wherein a great game is being played out. Other analysts have even called upon one of the super powers to not interfere in an issue that the ASEAN is confronted with. I beg to differ. In my view, ASEAN remains strong. It has always faced problems and challenges from day one—that is, from 1967 till the present day. It has gone through many crises which have been sorted out, and I am sure that the current crisis that ASEAN is facing among some member States will also sort itself out in a matter of time.

The key issue is that although there are competing interests trying to exert their influence in, for instance, the issue of South China Sea, the critical factor is that the key players—the stakeholders in the ASEAN region as well as in the greater Asia Pacific region—must stay involved in the region. Just because one super power is flexing its muscle and another emerging power decides to also flex its muscle does not mean the other stakeholders should stay out of the region. Everybody has a role in the ASEAN region; everybody has a stake in ensuring that the regional architecture—the security architecture in particular—that is evolving ensures that there is a place and a role for everybody, even for India. India historically has been a maritime nation. It has had historical trading relations right up to Japan and China. Its trading links with Asia spans many centuries. Historically and culturally, it has a significant presence and linkage in Asia.

Two issues remain significant. One is that the centrality of ASEAN should be maintained in the regional architecture in the Asia Pacific. Secondly, all disputes must be resolved in a peaceful manner and in accordance with international law. On these, all ASEAN countries are in agreement. Recently there appears to be some disagreement within ASEAN in what should be reflected in the joint ASEAN communiqué. This disagreement within ASEAN reflects a wider power play. The message that needs to be conveyed to Indian thinkers and policymakers is that under no eventuality should India concede its space in the ASEAN region—indeed it should be guarded zealously. This is very important since the moment India concedes its space, someone else will claim it and make it their domain, their sphere of influence. In fact, one sometimes wonders why the Americans actually left their space in Asia initially, and now they say they are now 'rebalancing' towards Asia. One has to ask: did the Americans ever leave South East Asia in the first place? They continue to be the biggest investor in South East Asia, and have a sizeable military presence in the Asia Pacific and even in South East Asia. Thus, just because an issue has arisen, and competing stakeholders want to exert their influence, does not mean that other stakeholders need to step aside and be mere spectators watching the scenario unfolding. India should stay committed and not concede its space.

It is significant that in his lecture in Singapore, Prime Minister Modi specifically mentioned that India will continue to ensure that the sea lanes in the South China Sea continue to remain open and safe for the use of all who need them for maritime trade.[1] Thus, it is imperative that India stays engaged with ASEAN. ASEAN needs India; ASEAN needs all strong stakeholders to remain committed because only with the participation and support of all the stakeholders can ASEAN bring about peace and prosperity for the ASEAN region as well as for the Asia-Pacific region as a whole.

The second issue is in the area of economics. With the slowdown of the global economy as well as the Chinese economy, ASEAN countries are trying to identify new avenues of economic growth. A big importer from ASEAN, China is transitioning its economy by moving from manufacturing towards services and more domestic consumption. On the other hand, India is moving from a more consumption based economy towards a manufacturing and services based one. All this has a great impact on ASEAN. ASEAN is trying to find its next economic trajectory for growth. One route some of the ASEAN countries are trying to take is supporting the TPP with the USA so that US investments continue to stay in some of these South East Asian countries; at the same time, they are also encouraging India, China, and the other partners of ASEAN to get into RCEP.

Thus, it is in India's interest to ensure that the RCEP gets wrapped up soon. The RCEP will effectively replace the ASEAN Free Trade Agreement with the six ASEAN partners in the long run. It is critical for India that, in order to stay engaged with ASEAN, it signs on to RCEP. It must also ensure that it is quickly implemented because many dynamic changes in the global economic patterns are emerging. Nobody seems sure where the next big growth sector is going to be. In India, everybody is talking about the industrial revolution where manufacturing is the solution for India's growth. However, I am not so sure because the way the global economy is moving nobody knows where exactly the next growth wing is going to be. This is critical. Economic cooperation is very essential. One must work together on the many opportunities that have been identified by the Indian government as also by the ASEAN countries. There is a lot of scope. If we focus on many of the projects which have already been identified and both regions are working on, India can ride on each other's strengths, and be a beneficiary.

The third issue is India's Make in India policy. India has embarked on this path because it wants to grow its manufacturing sector. However, when India emphasises its Make in India policy there is concern among ASEAN countries about whether India will take away FDI investments which could have gone to ASEAN. Thus, while India talks about its Make in India policy, it should also ensure that growth flows into neighbouring countries of the ASEAN. This becomes important because being a very big economy, India has to carry along neighbouring countries and ensure that they also prosper along with itself. Indian policymakers need to take into account the following: how can India create a supply chain? How can it make value chains which are linked together with the production centres in ASEAN? And, how can India carry the development of ASEAN together with everyone so that all the countries in the two regions prosper together?

There are various other issues also. One suggestion is with reference to connectivity between India's North East and Myanmar (in ASEAN). There has always been a call for land connectivity. One of the speediest ways connecting—which was also mentioned by one of the Chief Ministers—is air connectivity. It is somewhat puzzling that sometimes it is India that calls upon ASEAN carriers to start air connectivity. Why do Indian carriers not start air connectivity with ASEAN countries themselves? It is surprising that even today there is no direct air connectivity between India and Indonesia, Philippines, etc. Thus, this certainly seems to be an area in which India can move ahead and do more.

Another suggestion is that while ASEAN is made of ten countries, India can do more at the bilateral level. More bilateral projects—especially economic projects—can be undertaken with countries such as the Philippines and Indonesia. These are two very big countries; but the linkages with India are weak. If the linkages between these two countries are enhanced generally, the engagement of India with ASEAN, and particularly with these countries, will definitely benefit ASEAN and India.

NOTES

1. Prime Minister Narendra Modi delivered the 37th Singapore Lecture at ISEAS on 23 November 2015.

28

The Way Forward: Some Pointers for ASEAN-India Relations

Rajiv Bhatia

India's links with Southeast Asia began and flourished long before 2002, or even 1967. Yet, there is little doubt that the launch of the sectoral dialogue partnership in 1992 was a significant milestone and, therefore, its 25th anniversary should be celebrated with enthusiasm. It is also apt to underline that, with the formation of ASEAN Community, and the upgradation of LEP to AEP, ASEAN-India relations have entered 'a new paradigm'. Where do we stand now in our shared journey? Several points are pertinent here.

First, unfortunately, our trade seems to have stagnated. Between 2011-12 and 2014-15, its value has fluctuated between US$ 74 billion and US$ 79 billion. We have been unable to attain our target of US$ 100 billion by 2015. Our two-way flow of investment also needs speedier expansion. All this calls for deep introspection. Business leaders now need to deliver on the optimal use of existing FTAs, co-manufacturing, and other measures. Governments need to quickly complete the review of ASEAN-India FTA in Goods as well as conclude RCEP negotiations by December 2016. This will be a critical benchmark.

Second, as dispassionate scholars, we need to undertake a simple exercise on the vital question of connectivity. We need to distinguish between ambitious proposals and plans on the one hand, and actual progress of projects on the ground, on the other. Without forgetting the past burden of under-performance, let us prepare a realistic inventory of what must be completed and made fully operational in the next five years, ending in December 2020. And, let us then deploy our combined resources to achieve this goal.

Third, CLMV countries will remain a prime object of India's focus in the coming years. With Laos as the ASEAN Chair, Vietnam as a member of TPP, and Myanmar standing on the verge of a major transformation, India will do well to enhance the quotient of resilience and dynamism in its policy approach. We should not be content with what we have been doing; we have to attempt to scale new heights.

Fourth, the future health of ASEAN-India relations will be moulded partially by the strength and diversity of the new bonds we are able to create between our northeastern and eastern neighbours—Myanmar, Thailand, and also Bangladesh. In this creative exercise, voices from the 'Third Space'—that is, from institutions and scholars, especially young scholars, from our northeastern states—should be heard with greater attention and respect. Holding a major pre-Delhi Dialogue IX activity in a state capital in the Northeast would no doubt help further this goal. The Asian Confluence and ICWA succeeded in doing this splendidly at Shillong in 2014 and 2015.

Finally, some concerns over a few aspects of the strategic dimension of our relations as well as the evolving regional scene need to be addressed. Our pledges and planning for shared prosperity are dependent on the maintenance of peace, security, and stability in the region. There is a pressing need to safeguard and promote the culture of peaceful dialogue and negotiation while resolving inter-state differences and disputes. The arsenal of destroyers, fighter jets, and surface-to-air missiles should have no place in this development-oriented narrative. We must unite to avoid the grim possibilities resulting from their use in which our peoples will only suffer.

29

Look East to Act East: Shaping the ASEAN-India Partnership in the Third Decade

*Prabir De**

Introduction

Two and half decades have passed since India undertook the Look East Policy (LEP) as an effort to strengthen economic and strategic relations with Southeast and East Asian countries. The impetus in regional integration received through LEP has gained new momentum through the recently unveiled Act East Policy (AEP). India's proactive role in building a common market with an ambitious but realistic connectivity programme have increased India's footprint in Southeast and East Asia considerably. ASEAN has been the key focus to India's Look East-Act East Policy.

While ASEAN and India are celebrating the third decade of partnership, the relationship of both partners is not a mere recent product. They have indeed had a long experience of interactions. It has been an association made up of exchanges and peaceful interactive influences. India became a sectoral partner of ASEAN in 1992, a dialogue partner in 1996, and a summit-level partner at Phnom Penh in 2002. The ASEAN-India strategic partnership—the elevated relationship that began at the 2012 Commemorative Summit—gives greater hope for delivering stronger bilateral relations. ASEAN and India will be

* Professor, Research and Information System for Developing Countries (RIS), and Coordinator, ASEAN-India Centre (AIC), New Delhi. E-mail: prabirde@hotmail.com. An earlier version of this paper was presented by the author at the academic session of Delhi Dialogue VIII, held at New Delhi in March 2016. The author is grateful to Durairaj Kumarsamy for research assistance. The views expressed are personal. The usual disclaimers apply.

celebrating 25 years of their dialogue relations, 15 years of summit level relations, and 5 years of a strategic partnership in 2017.

ASEAN has embraced the ASEAN Economic Community (AEC) on 1st January 2016, albeit on a smaller scale. In parallel, ASEAN has undertaken a series of initiatives to achieve the AEC 2025 milestones. AEC comprises four pillars: a single market and production base; a highly competitive economic region; a region of equitable economic development; and a region fully integrated into the global economy. Each has strong implications for India and other dialogue partners of ASEAN.

India and ASEAN countries are striving for greater regional integration. The relationship is set to deepen in the coming days as ASEAN and India step up their collaboration across a range of economic and strategic issues. For example, ASEAN and India (along with other countries) have been working towards establishing a Comprehensive Free Trade Area through a Regional Comprehensive Economic Partnership (RCEP) Agreement. India's deeper cooperation with ASEAN, and vice versa, would positively influence the future course of regional integration in the Asia-Pacific.[1]

ASEAN-India economic integration has made substantial progress in relative terms in lowering trade costs, economic integration seems to advance further (AIC-RIS, 2015). However, both of them have been facing several challenges that cover a number of areas and which call for a concerted effort by ASEAN member states and India. Some serious challenges at present are the declining trade between ASEAN and India; these include the incomplete physical connectivity projects; a near stagnation of bilateral FDI flows, to mention a few.

This essay discusses the current economic engagement between ASEAN and India, analyses the challenges faced by both of them, and presents an action plan for shaping the strategic partnership between ASEAN and India.

Why is Trade between ASEAN and India Declining?

The world is in the throes of uncertainty. A gloomy outlook is enveloping the world's economies. Weak global demand has started reducing Asia's exports. Global trade growth remained below 3 per cent in 2015[2]. Exports of Asian open economies having strong links in global value chains have been slowing faster. The effects of a slowing Chinese economy are rippling across Asia, and there is rising tide of protectionism across the world. At the same time, bilateral trade between ASEAN and India declined to US$ 66 billion in 2015, compared to US$ 75 in 2014. Figure 1 captures a sharp decline in India's export to, and import from ASEAN, since 2014.

Why is trade between ASEAN and India been declining? There are three primary reasons for this decline.

First, the fall in commodity prices of major petroleum products, such as diesel, have affected the dollar earnings from exports of refined petroleum products, like diesel and petrol. This has resulted in falling Indian exports to ASEAN.

Second, ASEAN's market size has been shrinking in recent years due to structural changes in China's import demand. As a spiralling effect, ASEAN is importing less from India.

Third, China's shift of import demand from labour/resource intensive to capital intensive goods has made India perplexed. India is yet to transform to meet the new import demand in ASEAN and China.

Given India's narrow base of merchandise exports, its export basket is no longer as price elastic as it once was. This is also because of close substitutes

Figure 1: Trends in India's Trade with ASEAN

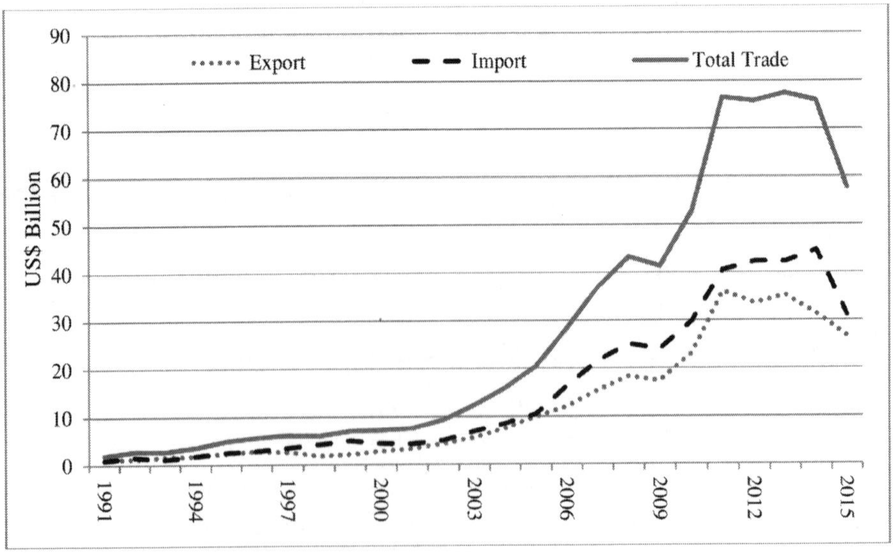

Source: Author based on DOTS, IMF.

of products supplied by other countries. At the same time, India's merchandise exports are facing declining price competitiveness due to inadequate transport infrastructure and trade facilitation measures. Indian exporters to ASEAN are unable to improve the export margin due to high trade costs due to poor infrastructure, non-tariff measures (NTMs), etc. Exports incentives are too negligible to compensate for the additional cost incurred on account of poor trade infrastructure. Moreover, India's major exports have been facing prohibitive NTMs in ASEAN. In some ASEAN countries, where tariffs are lower, India's exports are subject to heavy NTMs. Therefore, one can easily guess why the utilisation of ASEAN-India FTA has been low.

Current Engagements between ASEAN and India

India shares both land and maritime boundaries with ASEAN. Civilisational and cultural links between India and the Southeast Asia date back thousands of years. Probably no other country has such strong links with the Southeast Asia region as much as India by way of religion, language, culture and civilisation. People in Southeast Asia, by nature, seem to enjoy and treasure the feelings of this closeness. India is perceived as a benevolent power by Southeast Asian countries.

The India-ASEAN relationship has entered into the third decade. India became a sectoral partner of ASEAN in 1992, a dialogue partner in 1996, and a summit-level partner at Phnom Penh in 2002. The relation between ASEAN and India has been elevated to Strategic Partnership level since 2012. As a Strategic Partner of ASEAN, India is also actively associated with various ASEAN-led fora dealing with defence and strategic issues. These include the East Asia Summit (EAS), the ASEAN Regional Forum, ADDM+ (ASEAN Defence Ministers Meeting Plus), and the Expanded ASEAN Maritime Forum. India's engagement with ASEAN has been expanded rapidly. Today, India has over 26 annual dialogue mechanisms with the ASEAN including a Summit and seven Ministerial level meetings in key sectors. Table 1 presents selected engagements between ASEAN and India.

Out of US$ 65 billion in 2015–16 bilateral trade, India's export to and import from ASEAN were US$ 25.2 billion and US$ 39.8 billion, respectively. Despite geographical proximity and cultural affinity, trade and investment between ASEAN and India are substantially lower than the potential. The Free Trade Agreement (FTA) in goods, implemented in 2010, and the services trade and investment agreement in 2015 between ASEAN and India represent an important effort to enhancing regional integration. India is also member of the RCEP Agreement, which is presently being negotiated among ASEAN+6 countries. Till June 2016, a total 13 rounds of negotiations were held for RCEP Agreement.

At the sectoral level, ASEAN is India's fourth largest trade partner, next to EU, USA and China. ASEAN-India FTA has become a comprehensive trade agreement with the implementation of ASEAN-India services and investment agreement in 2015. As argued before, rising trade deficit and low utilisation of ASEAN-India FTA have been the major concerns. It is hoped that services trade agreement may facilitate India's exports to ASEAN, thereby narrowing the trade deficits.

Table 1: Present Scenario of ASEAN-India Engagements

ASEAN-India FTA	• Completed with the entering into force of the Services and Investment agreement in 2015	• Bilateral trade: US$ 65 billion in 2015–16 (India's export to ASEAN US$ 25.2 billion, India's import from ASEAN US$ 39.8 billion) • Emerging value chain, but slowly • Rising trade deficit is a matter of concern • Low utilisation of FTA
RCEP	• Being negotiated	• 13th round of RCEP was held in Auckland, New Zealand in June, 2016
Trade facilitation (e.g. Customs cooperation)	• Unilateral initiatives • WTO TFA	• ASEAN single window under implementation and India's SWIFT working already
ASEAN-India maritime transport agreement	• Being negotiated	• Target date of signing of agreement - 2017
ASEAN-India airtransport agreement	• Proposed	• High imbalance between carriers; major ASEAN airlines (e.g. SQ or TG) utilise 100% slots
Land transport	• Trilateral highway & extension to CLV • MIEC • Kaladan MMTTP	• Ongoing but slow pace • Must build strong backward linkages in India's NER
Digital network	• Optical fibre network between India and ASEAN	• Ongoing but slow pace

Source: Author.

Another important aspect of ASEAN-India trade is regional value chains. India is yet to witness the value chains with ASEAN in large way. These value chains are emerging, but slowly. For example, mobile phone, automobiles, computers, etc. are being manufactured in India, with parts and components sourced from ASEAN countries, China and Taiwan.[3]

Trade facilitation, particularly in customs cooperation, is an area where member countries of ASEAN and India have taken unilateral initiatives and are committed to initiating trade facilitation measures through the WTO Trade Facilitation Agreement (TFA). Most ASEAN countries, including India, are signatories of WTO TFA and have ratified the TFA. ASEAN Single Window is under implementation, whereas India's SWIFT has started working since 1 April 2016.[4] Both platforms should support the exchange of certificates of origin and advance cargo information. Nevertheless, inter-operability between the two single windows in customs will make trade faster and paperless.

ASEAN and India also share maritime borders. Barring shipping links between India and Singapore or those between India and Malaysia, maritime connectivity between ASEAN and India is not yet fully developed.[5] The ASEAN-India maritime transport agreement, which is presently being negotiated, is likely to be signed in 2017. The ASEAN-India air transport agreement has also been proposed. There has been high imbalance between carriers in ASEAN and India serving each other's regions. While major ASEAN airlines (e.g. SQ or TG) have already utilised slots, airlines from India, particularly Air India, are yet to make any substantial entry into ASEAN. The 'Make-in-India' syndrome has been moving fast, and therefore connectivity over the Bay of Bengal is important. Since air cargo is growing faster than sea cargo, ASEAN and India need more airports.

Overland physical and digital networks between ASEAN and India are the pillars of ASEAN-India integration.[6] In case of land transportation, work on Trilateral Highway (TH) has been going on with the replacement of 69 old bridges between Tamu and Kalewa, and the construction of a road between Kalewa and Yargi in Myanmar. The Trilateral Highway is likely to be completed by 2020. India has also proposed the extension of a Trilateral Highway to Lao PDR, Vietnam and Cambodia. Besides, port and inland water transportation components of the Kaladan multimodal transit transport project are almost ready. The Myanmar Port Authority (MPA) is likely to take over the re-developed Sittwe port. The connecting road inside Myanmar and India as part of Kaladan project is also getting ready. The Detailed Project Report

(DPR) for the construction of a road between Rih and Tidim (82 km) has been completed.

India is planning to set up the Sittwe Economic Zone (SEZ). This economic zone is proposed to be located at Ponnar Kyun, 18 km upstream of Sittwe port in Myanmnar. The Myanmar government has identified about 1833 acres of land at Ponnar Kyun for the economic zone. Agro and fisheries are likely to have a good development potential in the region. This economic zone may accommodate industrial projects which will cater to the local and larger Indian and Southeast Asian markets.

The Mekong-India Economic Corridor (MIEC) is another important connectivity project that aims to connect South Asia (India) with Southeast Asia (Vietnam), cutting across Thailand and Cambodia. Mainly a Japanese initiative, this corridor aims to strengthen the connectivity between South and Southeast Asia.[7] The emphasis of the corridor is on expanding the manufacturing base and trade with the rest of the world, particularly with India. The corridor will enable economies of ASEAN and India to integrate further, and collectively emerge as a globally competitive economic bloc.

India is also setting up a fibre optic network between India and ASEAN countries. While the physical work of laying the network is not yet started, the tele-medicine or tele-education part of the project has been ongoing, and has received high welcome in ASEAN.

ASEAN and India are not doing much on cooperation in the energy sector. India and ASEAN have to connect their energy grids. In view of India's SDG commitments, more sustainable energy projects, particularly solar energy, are good for both the regions. Several ASEAN countries are part of the International Solar Alliance project. India may consider reviving the India-Myanmar-Bangladesh gas pipeline project.

India's regional connectivity with Southeast Asia has been evolving on two pillars: northeast India for multimodal and intermodal operations, and southern India for multimodal operation. At present, several connectivity projects have been ongoing. Once connectivity projects start attracting investment, engage in the development of the region, and improve the quality of life of the local people through generations of employment and the reduction of poverty, these projects will then become a truly public good, and subsequently turn to be economic corridors.

The Way Forward

It is often claimed that the regional integration process in Southeast Asia has been driven by market forces, with little support from formal institutional arrangements. However, the situation began to change when the ASEAN Free Trade Area (AFTA) was launched in 1993. The integration has gained momentum with the implementation of various FTAs with the dialogue partners including the ASEAN-India FTA, which came into effect in 2010. Furthermore, ASEAN has taken a further step forward, transforming itself from a mere free trade area into the ASEAN Economic Community (AEC), which could enhance the free movement of goods, services, investment, capital, and skilled labour, and could contribute to the formation of single market as well as a single production base. ASEAN has embraced the AEC on 1st January 2016, albeit on a smaller scale. In parallel, ASEAN has undertaken a series of initiatives to achieve the AEC 2025 milestones. AEC comprises four pillars: a single market and production base; a highly competitive economic region; a region of equitable economic development; and a region fully integrated into the global economy. Each has strong implications for India and other dialogue partners of ASEAN (Mikic, 2016).

ASEAN-India FTA represents an important first step towards fostering closer economic ties among the member countries of this agreement. However, the potential for a constructive political relation between India and ASEAN remains largely untapped. There is urgent need to take the political relations to the next level as India is serious about its engagement with the Asia-Pacific. ASEAN is undoubtedly a first-choice partner.

Unless the high external protection levels are dismantled across the board, regional tariff liberalisation at the ASEAN-India level (or for that matter within RCEP) could lead to substantial trade diversion. This has been happening in the ASEAN-India region, where firms are taking shelter of such protections and getting into less efficient production process (Sally, 2013). On the issue of how to make ASEAN-India FTA itself as effective as possible, the sensitive goods lists should be minimised. Liberal rules of origin need to be negotiated between the two partners. Trade facilitation by means of the harmonisation of standards and customs procedures and cooperation in transport infrastructure is very important. MRAs have to be signed in services trade sectors. It would be logical to undertake a review of the ASEAN-India FTA, and monitor problems and obstacles relevant to both tariff and non-tariff measures (NTMs) in order to promote and increase the FTA utilisation. These reforms and liberalisation will contribute to strengthening the integration process even if all bilateral FTAs are subsumed into RCEP. However, success would depend on how strongly ASEAN and India are getting integrated with the world economy (AIC-RIS, 2015).

Automobile, pharmaceutical, machinery, electronics are the sectors which can be promoted to develop relational model with the lead firms, thereby strengthening the production networks between ASEAN and India. To facilitate the production networks, free flow of investment and movement of skilled labourers across the region are a must.

Implementation matters; the mere signing of the FTA is not enough. In implementing FTAs, we need to keep in mind that regional integration can only be successful if it unleashes new competition that lowers prices, introduces new technology, and gains productivity. Both ASEAN and India have been facing several challenges, which are quite obvious. It is also quite usual that FTA may give rise to negative effects, including rise in poverty and inequality, when variations exist in economic and social sectors. These effects should be identified, and appropriate measures should be taken to address them. Coordinated efforts are necessary to realise sustainable growth and development in India and Southeast Asia. Good coordination among countries, national line ministries, regional sector institutions, and other stakeholders is essential. Besides, harmonising political, legal, and regulatory regimes between India and ASEAN is needed.

Conclusion

Regional integration, if done correctly, can work. The time is ripe for India to establish a strong economic partnership with ASEAN. While this will reinforce India's security, it would also gradually remove the economic isolation of India's North East Region (NER).

Under the Act East Policy, investment potential may considerably go up in NER, when we consider its geographical proximity to Southeast and East Asian markets. However, in order to reap benefits, NER has to improve its 'backend' infrastructure, which would not only help the region to raise its competitiveness but also narrow the development gaps. India's connectivity with ASEAN, although at present at an initial stage of development, may appear as a great facilitator of pan-Asian integration in coming years.

Until recently, political cooperation was the weak link in the relationship between ASEAN and India. Twenty five years after the establishment of the ASEAN-India dialogue relations, ASEAN-India cooperation needs a new impulsion—or, more precisely, a real, substantive beginning to go beyond the wishful thinking level.

ASEAN-India relations have achieved much over the last 25 years. However, its success has given rise to new challenges. It will continue to play a central role in promoting economic integration and inclusive development over the next 25 years.

NOTES

1. Prabir De, and Suthiphand Chirathivat, *Celebrating the Third Decade and Beyond: New Challenges to ASEAN-India Economic Partnership*, New Delhi: Knowledge World, 2016.
2. Refer, World Trade Statistical Review 2016, WTO.
3. Biswajit Nag, 'India-ASEAN Production Networks: What is There for Indian SMEs?', in De and Chirathivat, *Celebrating the Third Decade and Beyond: New Challenges to ASEAN-India Economic Partnership*, Knowledge World, New Delhi, 2016.
4. The ASEAN Single Window currently supports the exchange of the intra-ASEAN certificate of origin (ATIGA Form D) and ASEAN Customs Declaration Document (ACDD) on a pilot basis among seven Member States, and will be expanded to exchange other types of data.
5. AIC, *ASEAN-India Maritime Connectivity Report*, ASEAN-India Centre (AIC), New Delhi, 2014.
6. J. François, P. Rana, and G. Wignaraja, *Pan-Asian Integration: Linking East and South Asia*, London: Palgrave Macmillan, 2009; Kimura, F. and S. Umezaki, *ASEAN–India Connectivity: The Comprehensive Asia Development Plan (CAPD) Phase 2*, Jakart: Economic Research Institute of ASEAN and East Asia (ERIA), 2011; RIS, *ASEAN-India Connectivity Report: India Country Study*, New Delhi: Research and Information System for Developing Countries (RIS), 2012; De, P., 'India's Emerging Connectivity with Southeast Asia: Progress and Prospects', Working Paper, Asian Development Bank Institute (ADBI), Tokyo, 2014.
7. B. Bhattacharyay, R. Nag and M. Kawai, *Infrastructure for Asian Connectivity*, Edward Elgar, Cheltenham, 2012.

REFERENCES

AIC-RIS, *ASEAN-India Development and Cooperation Report 2015*, ASEAN-India Centre (AIC), Research and Information System for Developing Countries (RIS), New Delhi: Routledge, 2015

AIC, *ASEAN-India Maritime Connectivity Report*, ASEAN-India Centre (AIC), New Delhi, 2014

Bhattacharyay B., R. Nag and M. Kawai, *Infrastructure for Asian Connectivity*, Edward Elgar, Cheltenham, 2012

De, Prabir and Suthiphand Chirathivat, *Celebrating the Third Decade and Beyond: New Challenges to ASEAN-India Economic Partnership*, New Delhi: Knowledge World, 2016

De, P., "India's Emerging Connectivity with Southeast Asia: Progress and Prospects", Working Paper, Asian Development Bank Institute (ADBI), Tokyo, 2014

François, J., P. Rana, and G. Wignaraja, *Pan-Asian Integration: Linking East and South Asia*, London: Palgrave Macmillan, 2009

Kimura, F. and S. Umezaki, *ASEAN–India Connectivity: The Comprehensive Asia Development Plan (CAPD) Phase 2*, Jakart: Economic Research Institute of ASEAN and East Asia (ERIA), 2011

Mikic, Mia, "Trade Implications of the ASEAN+ Agreements for Other Asian Countries", in Mia Mikic and Bruno Jetin (eds.) *ASEAN Economic Community: A Model for Asia-wide Regional Integration?* New York: Palgrave Macmillan, 2016

Nag, Biswajit, "India-ASEAN Production Networks: What is There for Indian SMEs?" in De and Chirathivat, *Celebrating the Third Decade and Beyond: New Challenges to ASEAN-India Economic Partnership*, Knowledge World, New Delhi, 2016

Plummer, Michael, Peter J. Morgan, and Ganeshan Wignaraja, *Connecting Asia: Infrastructure for Integrating South and Southeast Asia*, Cheltenham: Edward Elgar, 2015

RIS, *ASEAN-India Connectivity Report: India Country Study*, New Delhi: Research and Information System for Developing Countries (RIS), 2012

Sally, Razeen, "ASEAN FTAs: State of Play and Outlook for ASEAN's Regional and Global Integration", in Sanchita Basu Das, Jayant Menon, Rodolfo C Severino, Okmar Lal Shrestha (eds.) *The ASEAN Economic Community: A Work in Progress*, Singapore: Institute of Southeast Asian Studies (ISEAS), and Manila: Asian Development Bank (ADB), 2013

30

Cambodia-India Relations: Achievements and the Way Forward

Yang Peou

Cambodia-India relations, as they exist today are, in many ways, a history of age old ties which go back 2,000 years. Historically, India-Cambodia relations are a product of Hindu and Buddhist religious and cultural influences emanating out of India in the 4th–6th century AD, and spreading to various parts of South-East Asia. Though Cambodia, like most of its neighbours, is a Buddhist nation, there is a strong influence of Hindu rituals, idolatry, and mythology. The all pervading influence of Hinduism, Buddhism, and Indian architecture are clearly visible in the magnificent structures of Angkor Wat, Angkor Thom, Bayon, Ta Phrom, and other religious and historical sites in Cambodia.

The political relations between India and Cambodia can be described as very warm and cordial. In the 1950s, India was associated with the International Control Commission on Indo-China. After the collapse of the Khmer Rouge regime, India recognised the new government and opened its Embassy in Phnom Penh in 1981, when much of the world shunned Cambodia. This fact along with India's association with the Paris Peace Accords and their finalisation in 1991, is fondly remembered by the Cambodian leadership. India also committed military and non-military personnel for the conduct of the UNTAC-sponsored elections in 1993. India was one of the original contributors to UN de-mining operations in Cambodia. The Government of India agreed to preserve the Angkor Wat temple when the Government of Cambodia appealed for help, between 1986 and 1993. The

Indian Government has supported Cambodia in many other different fields as well.

Cambodia and India have had very good relations with each other for more than one thousand years. Cambodia and India have very similar cultures and traditions, and many Cambodians are followers of Buddhism which originated in India. Presently, many Cambodian Buddhist followers around the world travel to India to pay homage to Buddhist sites in India. Indeed, India and Cambodia should be even closer to each other since Cambodia is the only country that has sculptures and temples that look very similar to Indian temples. Cambodia should be as close to India as it was during the great Angkor period. The spirit of Cambodia and India should be together.

Regarding the ASEAN community, Cambodia has been a strong proponent of enhancing relations between India and ASEAN, and it has played a pivotal role in achieving the goal of an ASEAN-India Summit which was held for the first time in Phnom Penh in 2002. Cambodia also supported India within the ASEAN for participation in the first East Asia Summit meeting held in December 2005, in Kuala Lumpur. There are many other activities and places in which Cambodia supported India in the ASEAN community as well as on the international stage. The royal government of Cambodia and the Cambodian people will always support India for the freedom and development of both countries.

It is very important for the ASEAN community to have India as its development partner since India has the second largest population in the world, behind China. Moreover, India is the biggest democracy in the world. India is a country that loves peace, harmony, and freedom for the world—a good example is when India gave shelter to the Dalai Lama of Tibet, and allowed Tibetans to live peacefully in India. India has never declared war on any country; it only protects its territory and its freedom when rivals fight with it or commit to do bad things to India. Thus, it is imperative for the ASEAN community to have India as a development partner for trade. Furthermore, in terms of population, India has the potential for economic cooperation in our region as well as in the world.

I would like to suggest strengthening cooperation between Cambodia and India in three areas.

i) improve cultural cooperation between Cambodian and India, within the already existing mechanism of the Cambodian-India Centre at the Royal Academy of Cambodia

ii) to strengthen cooperation on ICT

iii) to promote investment in the health care sector

Finally, I would like to thank Institute for Defence Studies and Analyses of India for inviting me to share experience as well as to learn from Indian and ASEAN's scholars in order to strengthen relations between Cambodia and India as well as to strengthen the relationship of the ASEAN community with India for the prosperity of the two countries, and of the ASEAN community and India.

31

Building Linkages, Creating Connections: The Nalanda Way

Gopa Sabharwal

It is indeed wonderful for Nalanda University to once again find a place in the Delhi Dialogue—a forum that one would expect would confine itself to discussing the established paths of diplomacy and economic exchange. For the Delhi Dialogue, and indeed the ASEAN, to recognise and include perspectives beyond the established confines of international discourse is to acknowledge that linkages between nations and regions span myriad forms, beyond the control of formal diplomatic and bureaucratic controls, and that all of these 'other linkages' contribute in significant ways to a greater understanding of disparate cultures and peoples as well as contribute to developing civilisational dialogues.

The sub regions of Asia have been interlinked since about the first century CE,[1] and the connections have historically taken the form of conflict, conquest, trade, religion and education as well as trading routes—both maritime and land based. It has been shown that some overland paths and maritime routes that connected the coastal regions of ancient India and China existed even prior to this date, since "significant numbers of trade goods, including beads and glass, reached present-day Malaysia, Cambodia, Vietnam, and Thailand during the last two centuries BCE".[2] These interchanges were not confined to goods and services but also extended to ideas, knowledge, the development of networks, technologies, among others. Nor were the exchanges and interactions always peaceful—there were many that were violent which is to be expected, given the political and mercantile interests that dominated such activity.

It also needs to be noted that these inter-regional linkages were not confined to regions we now describe as Asia. They extended to regions beyond the southern and eastern part of the Indian subcontinent, all the way into parts of Africa and Europe. Different levels of networks of interaction existed in different places—from smaller exclusive sub-regional networks to wider cross-continental networks.[3]

These linkages, which existed from pre-modern times were, over time, confronted with newer capitalist networks which resulted from the historical processes of colonialism and imperialism, the subsequent emergence of anti-imperialistic movements, and the demands for the creation of unified political nation states. The idea of Asia as we know it today was articulated by many intellectuals of the time, with varying degree of success; no one vision really took dominant shape. This process has been described in detail by Prasenjit Duara[4] in a much cited article with the words *Asia Redux*[5] in the title.

Duara is of the view that Asian inter-connections in the current post globalisation era which are marked by large population movements across national boundaries, and the emergence of what is called "the knowledge economy or knowledge based service and production in the global economy".[6] He also says,

> To be sure today's cultural identities are shaped by circulations of culture, knowledge, technology, goods, services and finance that are dizzying in their velocity while also becoming deeply commodified or consumerist. Nonetheless, the older Asian models of cultural circulation without state domination of identity presents us with a historical resource to explore new possibilities.[7]

A similar thought was probably the starting point for considering the establishment, in 2010, of a Nalanda University for our times. The idea of such a university draws upon the oldest and most well known names in religious, pedagogical, and knowledge linkages in the Asian region. The purpose was to establish anew—this time by design and legislation—an international Nalanda university which could once again be

> an icon of the Asian renaissance in the 21st century, and should draw students and scholars from everywhere, as it once did. It should be a centre of civilisational dialogue and inter-faith understanding, as it once was. It should again make available for the common betterment of all human beings knowledge already existing in the world.[8]

These words, articulated by George Yeo, former Foreign Minister of Singapore and a person of multifaceted intellect, who also became the second Chancellor of the University, are evocative of much of the founding discourse of the new Nalanda University, established formally in 2010 by the Indian Parliament through a stand-alone legislation. In fact, it was George Yeo who put forth a Nalanda proposal to Government of India, because "of his faith in a future that can draw upon Asia's pre-colonial past and produce something new and outstanding from which the contemporary world...can benefit".[9]

Another mention of rebuilding Nalanda was made by former Indian President, APJ Abdul Kalam, on a trip to Patna—an idea that found ready acceptance by Chief Minister Nitish Kumar. It was decided that the project would be the creation of the central Government of India—an idea that was accepted by the Bihar Government which worked with great agility to keep their part of the commitment, including identifying and acquiring almost 500 acres of land in Rajgir, a short distance from the site of historical Nalanda. The Government of India, on its part, put in place a Nalanda Mentor Group (NMG) comprising leading academics and others, including George Yeo, under the Chairmanship of Professor Amartya Sen, another polymath who holds Chairs both in Economics and Philosophy at Harvard, and is trained in Sanskrit. The Mentor Group together amounted to a few centuries of University experience between them.[10]

The NMG's task was to envision the basic structure of the new secular university which would have international status, and be free of the restrictions that govern Indian universities in general, as befits a world-class university. This stand-alone one-of-a-kind post graduate research university has been assured autonomy in governance and to set its own curriculum and schools. The NMG took passionate ownership of the mission, and provided leadership and guidance including in the selection of institutional leadership. They took over as the first Governing Board of the University, once it formally came into being.

While this ideational work was progressing, and realising that Nalanda could be a good meeting ground for Asian countries to come together, the Government of India shared the idea with the East Asia Summit (EAS), a grouping that is arranged with ASEAN as its core. The EAS participating countries welcomed the idea, and supported the university. Based on that acceptance, the Government of India drafted the Nalanda University Act 2010.

The establishment of a university like Nalanda by the Government of India marks a significant step in the higher education domain where universities have traditionally been established to serve national needs. To establish an international "world class" university— which will be at the cutting edge of knowledge production in its chosen areas—is a sign that the Government of India is ready to walk the path of establishing new institutions with more autonomy and freedom to set their vision, and achieve excellence.

The countries in the south Asian and South East Asian region have been chosen as integral partners of the project, and it is hoped that, as the university establishes itself, there will be greater participation from all around the world but especially from various regions of Asia. Nalanda is not Asia focused only in name—it is envisaged as a university where Asia and Asian perspectives figure both in the curriculum and in the other activities which the university undertakes.

Today, the university is up and running in Rajgir (Nalanda District, Bihar) at a distance of about 12 kilometres from the site of the original Nalanda, and is in the process of achieving its stated goals. Bricks and mortar do not make a university. It is ideas that lie at the core of any university. Ideas are invisible, and we can see them only in their working. Ideas include both those that dominate the philosophy of the institution at large as well as those that pertain to the focus areas of each of the Schools. At the broadest level, the central idea that guides the University is drawn from Buddhist philosophy: man living in harmony with man; man living in harmony with nature; and man living as part of nature. This idea—which is now called the Nalanda way—has been incorporated into the University logo, and serves as a guideline for a lot of what the university stands for and the engagements it is developing.

This idea also played a part in the roll out plan for the various Schools at the University which began functioning since September 2014 when Nalanda opened its doors to students once again. These are the Schools of Historical Studies, Ecology and Environment Studies, and the newest one, the School of Buddhist studies, Philosophy and Comparative Religion (launched August 2016). The order in which the Schools have been established is determined by the rationale that the university will begin with academic programmes that can immediately impact the surroundings while also serving to establish the central rules of learning at Nalanda.

The University has evolved a curriculum that engages with the context of its location in various ways—that is, in terms of actualising parts of the curriculum, doing projects in surrounding hills and villages, and also by building links with the community. Nalanda is a non-metropolitan university being situated in a rural farming area in Rajgir; indeed, the university regards this locale as its unique strength. The university is committed to the idea of experiential learning—that is, learning by doing and applying knowledge. Young scholars are being encouraged to go out, and not only apply what they learn to real life situations outside the classrooms but to also respect the fact that knowledge does not always come in easy packets of printed material. Much of it is enshrined in the daily practices of the farming and other communities as well as in the local flora and fauna.

Secondly, the Asian interconnections perspective is something that informs the curriculum in all schools. A university that seeks to be the focal point for Asia needs to have Asia in the classrooms, both in terms of ideas and student body. The university has students and faculty representing 19 countries, and is teaching classical languages such as Sanskrit and Pali as also Korean and Tibetan. As the university grows, this list will also grow. The library too has a multilingual collection as well as some library collections gifted by leading scholars and collectors from India, Australia, and Singapore which are very impressive.

The third feature of the teaching and research at Nalanda is that it is interdisciplinary. As a new university, Nalanda had the choice of breaking down silos of exclusivity that have emerged in all established universities—making it very difficult for students and faculty to reach out and seek connections in their work. Nalanda has been able to build a culture of inter-disciplinarity on campus, with all students being exposed to ideas in each of the three Schools. Courses between Schools are also cross-posted so that students may benefit from the faculty and their expertise across Schools.

None of this would be possible without the recruitment of qualified and creative faculty who are willing to support the spirit if Nalanda, and to help the university become what it aims to be. Faculty recruitment is global, and the university has succeeded in hiring some very talented people from around the world, all of whom have made a commitment to come and live in Rajgir.

The university also has impressive academic partnerships with international organisations and institutions. There is a partnership with the Nalanda Sriwijaya Centre at the ISEAS-Yusof Ishak Institute in Singapore; an MoU with Peking University; and linkages with the School of Forestry at Yale, the School of Agriculture at the University of Illinois at Urbana Champaign, the Borlaug Institute of South Asia, among others. The university has also signed a Memorandum of Understanding (MoU) with the Bihar Heritage Development Society, the Ministry of Art, Culture and Youth, Government of Bihar for the Rajgir Archaeological Survey Project (RASP). The project aims to do an archaeological survey of Rajgir to better understand the archaeological landscape of this historical city through available antiquarian remains. RASP will examine the multi-phased and multi-layered development of Rajgir as an urban, political, and religious centre.

All universities require funds; and while Government of India is paying for all of the revenue and capital expenditure of the University, endowments are coming in both from other governments and from individuals. Singapore has a group that is donating a library for Nalanda. Their idea is to design, build, and deliver the library for new Nalanda, with a cap of 10 million Singapore dollars. Other endowments—one private and one from the Government of Australia—pay for a professorial chair each in the School of Historical Studies and the School of Ecology and Environment studies, respectively. As the university stabilises and grows, we expect these endowments to grow further.

The most visible parts of any university are the buildings, and this aspect of the university has not been neglected. Following a global design competition, the university chose architects who will build probably the largest ground-up net-zero campus that has been attempted anywhere in the world. Net zero means striving to be a Net Zero Energy, Net Zero Emissions, Net Zero Water, and Net Zero Waste campus. With the physical infrastructure being built following the development of the core curriculum, the attempt is also for the infrastructure to be guided by the pedagogical and research needs of the faculty and the students. By phrasing a net zero energy vision for the university, we have attempted to tie up the historical legacy inherited by Nalanda University with one of the most urgent contemporary issues that needs to be addressed: environmental sustainability. The learning from Nalanda University campus will demonstrate the feasibility of implementing and operating NZEBs in India, and create awareness amongst the building industry.

It is hoped that, in the next 25 years, Nalanda will become the space where the new Asian renaissance will take place. It will take some time for Nalanda to be able to match the excellence of old Nalanda, and to recover a lot of valuable old insights, linkages, etc. The university is committed to building a Common Archival Resource Centre on the Mekong Ganga Deltaic region by preserving archival records in various media and formats. The university hopes to become the hub where Asia, once again, meets intellectually and rediscovers linkages as well as respond to the needs of the world once again. This cultural resource will help that process in an important way.

Nalanda is slowly but surely developing into an international community. By August 2016, almost 19 countries were represented on campus, including the USA, Italy, Poland, France, Germany, Japan, Laos, Bhutan, Myanmar, Sri Lanka, Peru, Brazil, etc. With a community of 150 faculty and students, the university has steadily grown in numbers. The presence of international faculty and students on campus as also Indian students representing many states, leads to everyone encountering India via the university. In a recent article, David Lowe has examined the Australian experiences of international students, in the Colombo Plan and the New Colombo Plan.[11] He terms this daily experience as everyday or 'vernacular' internationalism—played out as a phenomenon of international students visiting, travelling, and otherwise encountering different groups of Australians. Nalanda university campus is providing this space for all members of its community to act as cultural carriers, cultural resources, and as links to their cultures, both on and off campus.

To build a strong edifice, one needs strong foundations—and deep foundations are not visible above the ground. Having put down its foundations, Nalanda is firmly on its path of visible growth to achieve its targets: the pursuit of excellence; the promotion of internationalism; and the building of alliances and networks with other institutions of excellence.

NOTES

1. Tansen Sen, 'The Intricacies of Pre-modern Asian Connections', *The Journal of Asian Studies*, Vol. 69, No. 4, November 2010, Association for Asian Studies, pp. 991–999.
2. Ibid. p. 992.
3. Ibid. p. 998.
4. Prasenjit Duara, 'Asia Redux: Conceptualizing a Region for Our Times', in *The Journal of Asian Studies* 69(04), November 2010, pp. 963–983.
5. Ibid.
6. Ibid.

7. Ibid.
8. George Yeo, 'Nalanda and the Asian Renaissance', *Straits Times*, Singapore, 14 April 2011.
9. Amartya Sen, Foreword: in Asad-ul Iqbal Latif and Lee Huay Leng, Eds, George Yeo on Bonsai, Banyan and the Tao, World Scientific Publishing, p. xii.
10. Other members of the Mentor Group were: Professor Wang Gung Wu; Professor Wang Bang Wei; Professor Sugata Bose; Professor Lord Meghnad Desai; Professor Tansen Sen; Professor Prapod Assavavirulhakarn; Ikuo Hirayama and later Susumu Nakanishi, N.K. Singh, and Secretary (East) Ministry of External Affairs, New Delhi.
11. David Lowe, "Australia's Colombo plans, old and new: international students as foreign relations", *International Journal of Cultural Policy*, Vol. 21, No. 4, 2015, pp. 448–462.

32

Outcome Document

The academic session held at IDSA was inaugurated with the Welcome Remarks by Mr Jayant Prasad, Director General of the IDSA, followed by the Keynote Address by Mr Anil Wadhwa, Secretary (East) Ministry of External Affairs, Government of India. The academic session focused on four themes: ASEAN and the Security of the Asia-Pacific; ASEAN-India and the Ocean Economy Dynamics; Reinvigorating the Civilisational Links; and Way Forward: Towards 25th Anniversary of ASEAN-India Relations.

The Academic Session made the following recommendations:

1. In the discussion on 'ASEAN and the Security of the Asia-Pacific', the need for regional security architecture that is open, transparent and equal was emphasised. ASEAN which straddles not just the Asia Pacific but provides the link to the Indo-Pacific, is central to the whole process. India shares land and maritime boundaries with most of the ASEAN countries which makes for an interlinked security. East Asia is the new theatre of the Great Game, where the US and China are principal players; peace and stability depends on how the two can coexist and accommodate their core interests. Between the two major actors there is only one emerging power, i.e. India and India's approach to Southeast Asia becomes fundamental for the region's stability. Others felt that ASEAN which straddles not just the Asia Pacific but provides the link to the Indo-Pacific, is central to the whole process. Striking a note of caution one speaker said centrality of ASEAN had to be earned and Members needed to be resilient. Increased trade flow increased the possibility of disputes over sovereignty and ownership. Hence the importance of dispute settlement. ASEAN should remain

impartial towards its member states and should not be neutral as regards violations of international laws.

2. The technological revolution has transformed the 'ocean economy' or 'blue economy' unfolding an era of new opportunities (to harness the oceanic resources, which could serve as an economic accelerator to achieve the Sustainable Development Goals)—and new challenges (arising from the competition for those resources). China's 'One Belt One Road' and the development of road and port infrastructure enables it to bypass the Suez Canal and the Malacca Strait, and provides Chinese goods a competitive edge. The question that remains is: how should other countries respond to this? A strategy for blue economy requires policy development, implementation and audit, market regulation in a transparent manner, development of organisational and managerial skills, besides integration with global academic and research networks and mass communication of shared vision. India (having vital maritime interests in the South China Sea), in pursuance of its Act East Policy, increased manifold its engagement with the extended neighbourhood, in particular the resident nations of the SCS. Blue economy is a vital new paradigm for ASEAN-India cooperation. That engagement is not just a government to government initiative: it has components of private institutional involvement as well. India has collaborative programs with ASEAN States like the Philippines and Vietnam on areas ranging from food security, promotion of sustainable marine development and management, to creating wealth generating opportunities based on inclusive oceans based economic growth. In this Indian and ASEAN business and industrial sectors could complement government initiatives in effectively managing both fisheries and non-living sea resources.
3. In the discussion in the sub session on Reinvigorating the Cultural Links between ASEAN and India, panelists deliberated on the challenges of protecting and preserving the shared cultural heritage with a view to reinvigorate these linkages to facilitate greater ASEAN-India cooperation in the present. India's elements of Statecraft, diffusion of knowledge and secular-composite culture's contemporary relevance for Southeast Asia was emphasised. Challenges to cooperation included regional complexity, lack of institutional

framework, the growth of terrorism (which should be viewed as a 'Cultural War') It was noted that the discourse on culture was perceived as an element of State's 'soft power' to communicate its identity to others. (Instances of adverse utilisation of culture were cited as well). Media can play a significant role in promoting 'culture as usable history' just as promoting study of languages would serve as an effective means of facilitating culture dialogue between India and ASEAN countries. States needed to create an enabling environment to facilitate the free exchange of ideas and culture between ASEAN and India.

4. The concluding session on Way Forward highlighted the prospects for both ASEAN-India cooperation and the outlook for the next Delhi Dialogue (DD IX) in the strategic, economic, social and cultural arenas. As ASEAN-India were bound by a strong strategic partnership in the 21st century there is a need to define the role of India in ASEAN. ADMM+ and other mechanisms should be used to enhance cooperation. India's maritime interests require that it should not concede space. ASEAN needs all stakeholders to remain committed given the need to promote a stable and peaceful strategic regional environment.

A suggestion was made to redouble the efforts for economic cooperation (with the objective of growth and development) and speedily implement RCEP. Trade (including the deficit) and connectivity challenges needed to be looked into. Dispute settlement mechanisms need to be strengthened. Deeper integration in the service sector needs to be promoted with increased people to people contacts and easier travel for skilled people as well as tourists. The need for involving young scholars from Northeast Indian States was emphasised. Besides, ASEAN countries are an integral part of the project for building the Nalanda University in eastern India.

Index